Environmental economics
DW Pearce

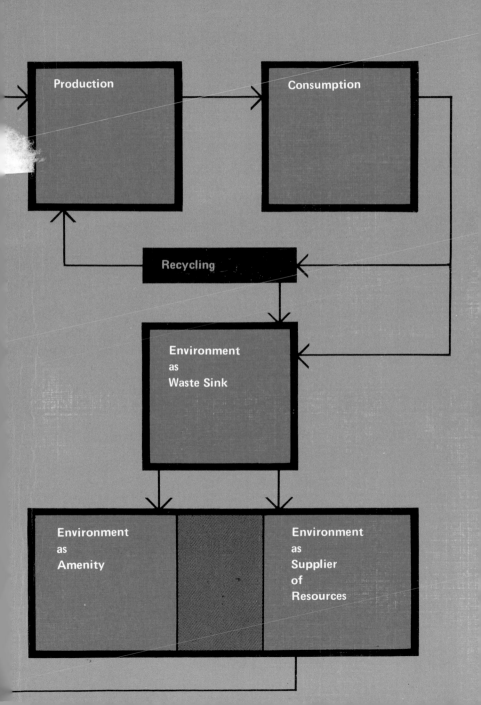

Environmental economics

Modern economics
Series editor: David W Pearce

Environmental economics

DW Pearce

Professor of Political Economy,
University of Aberdeen

Longman

LONDON and NEW YORK

Longman Group Limited London

*Associated companies, branches and representatives
throughout the world*

*Published in the United States of America
by Longman Inc., New York*

© D. W. Pearce 1976

First published 1976

Second impression 1977

Library of Congress Cataloging in Publication Data

Pearce, David William.
    Environmental economics.

    (Modern economics)
    Bibliography: p.
    Includes index.
    1. Environmental policy. 2. Pollution — Economic
aspects. 3. Conservation of natural resources —
Economic aspects. I. Title.
    HC79.E5P38 1976   301.31   75-44207
    ISBN 0 582 44622 8
    ISBN 0 582 44623 6 pbk.

Set in IBM Journal 10 on 12pt
and printed in Great Britain by
Whitstable Litho Ltd, Kent

Contents

Preface

The "balance" of this book may well strike many readers as odd. I have not, for example, sought to write in detail about the growth *versus* environment debate, but I have tried to indicate, at some length, the practical problems of estimating damage costs and control costs. Arguments which I have presented in journal article form, about the ecological impact of pollution and its implications for economic approaches to environment, are developed at the expense of, say, more detailed work on input—output analysis. In some cases the bias is due to the fact that some new books deal with the issues far more clearly than I could. On the growth debate, for example, the reader is referred to Richard Lecomber's valuable volume *Economic Growth versus Environmental Quality* (Macmillan, 1975). In other cases the bias reflects either what I consider to be important (as with the ecological effects of pollutants) or what I feel have been neglected issues in other texts on environment (measurement problems for damage costs are an example here). As a result, the book is mildly idiosyncratic. Nonetheless, I hope it appeals for its general coverage and for the occasional personal argument.

DWP

Acknowledgements

I am, as always, deeply indebted to my friends and colleagues at Southampton University, where this book was conceived and largely written, for their comments and arguments over the years on matters environmental. Particular thanks are owed to Michael Common and Christopher Nash who know that much of what I write is owed to them. My thanks too to my good friends Jean-Philippe Barde and Ariel Alexandre of OECD Environment Directorate in Paris, with whom I have worked on various issues over the past four years. I have learnt much from them. Paul Baker, Wendy Doe, Peter Smith, Sheeagh Weereratne and Gillian Wyatt acted as student guinea pigs both in terms of having had various parts of the book tried out on them and in terms of having been the first "ecocrats" on the combined Economics and Ecology course at Southampton University. I am grateful to them for the characteristically unreserved expression of their views over the last year.

Others who have written in this field will recognize their own inputs to the book: there are too many debts for them to be acknowledged here. I can only hope that I have interpreted my selection of the now voluminous literature correctly.

Finally, a special debt is owed to my wife, Sue, who maintains a sustained and healthy indifference to all the writings of economists. This book will undoubtedly be no exception. I have more than a sneaking suspicion that we all have something to learn in this respect. Nonetheless, the book would not have been written without her tolerance and forbearance.

I haven't the slightest doubt that errors and obscurities remain. These are my responsibility alone.

D. W. Pearce,
October 1974

*For Daniel. And in memory of someone
who would have loved you dearly.*

1

Welfare economics

1.1 Environmental economics and welfare economics

In approaching the subject matter of environmental economics it is important to understand that, with some exceptions, economists have regarded environmental degradation as a particular instance of "market failure". What this means is that the "environment" tends not to be used in an optimal fashion: the best use is not made of its functions. From man's point of view, these functions consist of supplying "natural goods" such as beautiful landscape, supplying natural resources which are used to create economic goods, and supplying a "sink" into which the inevitable by-products of economic activity can be discarded. As we shall see, those who find the "economic viewpoint" limited often point to a further, vital, function of the environment: it acts as an integrated and, in many respects, highly sensitive system providing the means whereby all life-forms are sustained. To the extent that the economic viewpoint ignores this function — if, indeed, it does ignore it — environmental economics cannot make a claim to be a complete science of environment. Part of the theme of this book concerns an assessment of this claim against environmental economics. In general, it will be argued that the claim has much substance and we shall investigate what this implies for a modified environmental economics.

But if we concentrate on the first three functions of environment, it is not difficult to see that environmental economics will appear to fit neatly into the established framework of welfare economics. As far as natural resource provision is concerned, resources are extracted from the environment and are marketed for intermediate or final consumption. Most, though not all, natural resources have market prices. Solar energy is an example of a natural resource that is not (at the moment) marketed. In addition, its price if it were marketed would be zero unless it became necessary to construct facilities for redirecting or storing such energy (as would be the case if we chose to use such energy for domestic or industrial heating). "Market failure" in this context will refer to any divergence between the market prices of resources and those prices that would have to exist if an optimal state of affairs is to be secured. When it comes to the environment as supplier of final goods and as supplier of waste receiving facilities, these functions are generally not marketed at all. But their "shadow" price — the price that would exist if these functions were marketed in an optimal way — is clearly positive because using the environment in this way precludes its use for another purpose. If we permit watercourses to be used as dumps for municipal or industrial effluent, we preclude using that watercourse for fishing, bathing and recreation, although some amount of these activities may occur simultaneously. If prices were charged for using these functions of the environment we would expect a different pattern of uses, and a different total usage, compared to a situation in which prices are not charged. Here then is a basic source of market failure, although it may seem slightly odd to call it that since markets do not in fact exist at all, in that many environmental services are being treated *as if* they were free because they are owned by everyone — there are no individually ascribed property rights.

Viewed in this way, the functions and services of the environment become instances of goods which either have prices which may or may not be optimal, or have no prices because they are not marketed. In the latter case the actual zero price is clearly non-optimal. This immediately enables us to treat environmental problems as problems of non-optimal pricing, and hence as something that conforms precisely with the subject matter of welfare economics. Welfare economics tries to assess what an optimal configuration of an economy would look like in terms of prices and quantities of outputs and inputs. If we are to understand why economists have come to say the things they do about environmental issues, we must understand the rudiments of welfare economics. This latter task is the subject matter of the rest of this chapter. Readers who are familiar with neoclassical welfare theorems are advised to omit the rest of this chapter and start at Chapter 2, although section 1.4 should be read.

1.2 Consumer's surplus

The first concept we shall need is that of *consumer's surplus*. As we shall see, consumer's surplus (CS) purports to be a measure of the actual gain or loss in welfare experienced by an individual whose situation is altered by some economic event, say a price change or a quantity change. If such a measure is valid, it may be possible to go further and add up all such gains and subtract all losses for any economic change. The result would be an aggregate social measure which could indicate the net social worth of that economic change.

In a seminal paper, Hicks (1943) developed a classification of different measures of CS. Figure 1.1 shows the indifference map of the individual consumer. Two indifference curves, i_1 and i_2, are shown, together with the consumer's budget lines B_1 which reflects relative prices in an initial situation, and B_2 which shows the result of an assumed lowering of the price of good X_1. The hypothetical budget lines B_3 and B_4 are drawn parallel to B_1 and B_2 respectively. The initial equilibrium is at X, the new equilibrium at Y. What we require is a measure of how much better off the consumer is at Y than at X. Hicks proposed four possible measures. First, the distance CV_p measures the *compensating variation* in income. Once the consumer reaches Y, he could be taxed by an equal amount to CV_p and this would put him on budget line B_4 and would enable him to enjoy his initial level of welfare i_1 at point W. Notice that the consumer, if taxed in this way, ends up buying a different combination of goods at W than he did at X: he is free to vary the quantities he purchases. If, for any reason, he cannot do this, he would be contrained to buy the amount of X_1 in the combination shown at point Y. In this situation, the amount CV_q would measure the welfare gain of moving from X to Y, for once at Y the consumer can be

Fig. 1.1

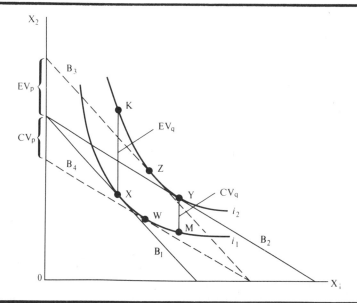

taxed by an amount CV_q and be returned to his original welfare level i_1 while still consuming the amount of X_1 he consumed at point Y. So far, then, we have two measures of the consumer's gain in moving from X to Y. These measures relate to sums of money which, when paid or received, leave the consumer in his *initial* welfare position.

We can correspondingly develop measures which relate to sums of money which would leave the consumer in his *subsequent* welfare position. Thus, if the consumer begins at X we can ask what sum of money he would need to make him as well off as he is at Y — i.e. the sum of money needed to forego the price fall. If he is unconstrained as to the quantities he purchases, this sum will be measured by EV_p since such a sum would put him at Z which is on i_2. If he is constrained to buy the amount of X_1 at X the relevant measure will be EV_q — i.e. the distance XK. EV_p and EV_q are the *equivalent variations* in income.

We can summarize the four measures shown in Fig. 1.1.

(i) CV_p = the maximum sum of money the consumer should be willing to pay in order to secure the price fall shown by the move from B_1 to B_2.

(ii) CV_q = the maximum sum the consumer should be willing to pay to secure the price fall, assuming he is constrained to buy the quantity of X_1 at point Y.

(iii) EV_p = the minimum sum of money the consumer will require in order to forego the benefit of the price fall.

(iv) EV_q = the minimum sum of money the consumer will require in order to forego the benefit of the price fall assuming he is constrained to buy the quantity of X_1 at X.

Since, in general, consumers are not constrained as to the quantities they can buy, the relevant measures will be CV_p and EV_p. The preceding analysis relates to a *potential benefit*: the price fall implicit in the move from X to Y. Hence we can say that the compensating variation measures (maximum) willingness to pay for benefits, and the equivalent variation measures (minimum) required compensation to forego a benefit. If, in Fig. 1.1 we began at Y and considered the price implicit in going from Y to X, similar analysis would show that the CV equivalent to the price rise would equal our preceding measure of EV, and the EV equivalent to the price rise would equal our preceding measure of CV (the reader should be able to check this himself). We can think of a price rise as a *potential loss* for the consumer. Hence, for potential losses, CV will measure the sum of money required by the consumer to compensate him for tolerating position X compared to position Y, and will be equal to EV_p in Fig. 1.1. The equivalent variation for the price rise will be the sum of money the consumer is prepared to pay to avoid the move from Y to X, and will be equal to CV_p in Fig. 1.1.

We can summarize these relationships as follows:

CV (potential gain) = EV (potential loss)
CV (potential loss) = EV (potential gain)

Figure 1.2 shows the relationship between CV, EV and the demand curve for commodity X_1. The price change from P_1 to P_2 in the lower half of the diagram corresponds to the price change implicit in the move from B_1 to B_2 in the upper half of the diagram. It can be shown (for detailed proof, see Winch (1971), pp. 141–2) that

CV_p = area P_1P_2DB
EV_p = area P_1P_2EC

Fig. 1.2

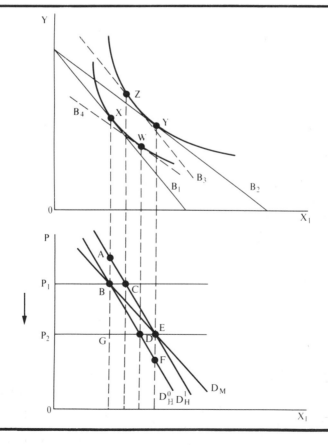

It will be noted that the CV measure corresponds to a demand curve drawn with respect to points X and W in the upper part of Fig. 1.2. Such a demand curve shows only the substitution effect of the price change from B_1 to B_2, so that demand curve D_H^0 is a compensated demand curve (often called a Hicksian demand curve). Similarly, demand curve D_H^1, which gives us the EV measure, relates to points Z and Y which again show the substitution effect but this time with respect to the income position relating to point Y.

We have one other candidate for a measure of the welfare change of the price fall: area P_1P_2EB which, in this case, appears as a sort of average of the other two measures. Referring back to the upper part of the diagram we see that the move from B to E corresponds directly to the move from X to Y. In other words, the demand curve through B and E contains both the income and substitution effects. It is in fact the conventional Marshallian demand curve, uncompensated for income effects. Thus, area P_1P_2EB will be a direct measure of "Marshallian" consumer surplus. Figure 1.2 shows that

$$EV_p > M > CV_p$$

where M is Marshallian consumer surplus.

In practice there are arguments for the use of each of the three measures noted above. CV_p is widely preferred, but we note that it requires us to estimate a compensated demand curve. This can, and is, done for many practical studies, but often it is only measure M that can be obtained. Others have argued for the use of EV_p if it can be found. If income effects are insignificant, the debate about which measure of CS to use will not matter since the three demand curves shown in Fig. 1.2 will then coincide. In the event that income effects *are* important, it will matter which measure we choose. Our task in this book is merely to draw the reader's attention to the existence of the debate. For a recent contribution see Foster and Neuberger (1974).

1.3 Compensation tests

The problem with adding up surpluses in the manner suggested in the previous section is that policy measures almost necessarily make some people better off and some worse off. Since no goods are free, any policy measure will involve benefits to some and costs to others, even if the costs accrue in the form of higher taxes only. Consequently, a rule which approved of policies which made everyone better off (increased their consumer surpluses) and no-one worse off would be an unexceptionable but fruitless rule. For reference purposes we should note that such situations, in which a policy makes at least some people better off and no-one worse off, are called *Pareto Improvements*. Obviously, however, we require a modification of this rule to allow for the fact that there are always losers.

The modification proposed by neoclassical welfare economics is the *compensation test*. Essentially, it is very simple. If we add up the consumer's surpluses of those who gain and add up the lost consumers' surpluses of those who lose, we shall have one of three situations:

(*a*) The sum of gainers' CS exceeds the sum of losers' CS;
(*b*) The sum of gainers' CS is less than the sum of losers' CS;
(*c*) The two sums are equal.

If (*a*) occurs, we could argue that the gainers could transfer money to the losers in such a way as to make the losers no worse off than they were before. The amount transferred would be less than the gainers have gained so that they would still have something left over. Hence the gainers still gain (but not so much compared to their gains if they did not pay the compensation) and the losers stay at the same utility level as before. The transfer enables us to determine that such a situation would be a Pareto improvement in the sense defined above. Similar reasoning would show that situation (*b*) would be a Pareto deterioration, and situation (*c*) would imply a policy which offered neither improvement nor worsening of the present situation.

The idea that policies can be judged in terms of the feasibility of compensation originates with articles by Kaldor (1939) and Hicks (1939). Hence, a policy is said to meet the *Kaldor–Hicks* test if the sum of gainers' consumers' surplus exceeds the sum of the losers' consumers' surplus. The test is not met if the situation is as in (*b*) or (*c*) above, and the policy would be judged not worthwhile. A complication with the criterion, however, is that it is not suggested that compensation *should* be paid. It is argued that it is only necessary for compensation to be payable in principle. That is, a policy will be judged worthwhile if case (*a*) above is met, but no compensation is paid, so that the losers remain losers and the gainers actually secure their initial gains. Obviously, a rule which does not require payment of compensation will be a much stronger rule since universal transfers of the kind that would be required would involve complexity of organization that no economy is likely to manage.

Consider a policy which entails a price fall benefiting some people and a price rise which gives rise to losses for others. We can say that CV_p will reflect the maximum compensation which the gainers would be willing to pay. Similarly, the compensating variation of the price rise will measure the minimum that the losers would accept.

The Kaldor–Hicks test would *not* be met — that is, the policy would not be worth undertaking — if

$$\sum_B CV < \sum_L CV$$

where the subscripts B and L remind us that there are two groups, beneficiaries and losers. Now consider the possibility of the losers paying the beneficiaries to forego the change. Since the (potential) beneficiaries are now to go without a benefit they will require some equivalent compensation — measured by their EV's. Equally, the maximum sum that the potential losers will be willing to pay is their EV. Clearly, the potential losers will succeed in preventing the change if

$$\sum_B EV < \sum_L EV$$

but the will *fail* to prevent the change if

$$\sum_B EV > \sum_L EV$$

Consequently, a contradiction could arise if gainers' CV's were less than losers' CV's, *and* if gainers' EV's were greater than losers' EV's. We wish to know if

$$\sum_B CV < \sum_L CV \qquad [1]$$

$$\sum_B EV > \sum_L EV \qquad [2]$$

can both be true. In addition, we have to remember that

$$\sum_B EV > \sum_B CV \qquad [3]$$

$$\sum_L CV > \sum_L EV \qquad [4]$$

If inequalities [1] − [4] can be satisfied simultaneously we shall have shown that (*a*) a policy is not worth undertaking on the Kaldor–Hicks test, but (*b*), if undertaken, could not be repealed by using the test. In short, the test would not justify the policy, but nor would it justify the repeal of the policy if it were undertaken, which would be odd.

Some arbitrary numbers will demonstrate that propositions [1] − [4] can be simultaneously satisfied. Let $CV_L = 6$, $CV_B = 2$, $EV_B = 4$ and $EV_L = 3$. Then, on substitution in [1] − [4] all equations are seen to be satisfied. The possibility of this "paradox" was first noted by Scitovsky (1941). The paradox may also arise for the case where the policy move is justified by the Kaldor–Hicks test, but the move back is also justified. This happens when either $EV_B < CV_B$ (the opposite of condition [3] above) or $EV_L > CV_L$ (negating condition [4]), or both. This can only arise if one of the goods has a negative income effect — i.e. is an inferior good.

1.4 Pareto optimality and distributive justice

Using the results of the section on compensation tests we can now define Pareto optimality and Pareto improvements. Essentially, if we can avoid the Scitovsky paradox, the summation of positive and negative consumer's surpluses, as measured by CV_p, EV_p or M (see section 1.2) will tell us whether a policy is, potentially anyway, worthwhile undertaking. Thus, an excess of positive surpluses over negative surpluses will indicate that the policy will bring about a (potential) Pareto improvement. It is best to avoid calling such a situation an actual Pareto improvement because, as we saw, if compensation to losers is not actually paid out of the benefits of gainers, the strict requirements for a Pareto improvement are not met. Equally, an excess of negative CS's over positive CS's will indicate a (potential) Pareto deterioration. A Pareto optimum will exist when it is impossible to increase some people's surpluses without decreasing others.

Now, we must be clear that there is little point in developing this theoretical normative framework unless it has some claim to practical relevance. Two points need to be stressed in this respect. First, the potential Pareto improvement rule is actually embodied in the technique of *cost—benefit analysis* (CBA). Indeed, as it is widely practised, CBA is nothing other than neoclassical welfare economics and rests for its measurement technique on consumer surplus theory, and for its aggregate decision rules on the Kaldor—Hicks compensation tests. It cannot be assumed that all applications of CBA keep to these rules — unfortunately, many studies use the terminology of CBA without actually having much in common with the original requirements of the technique — but the fact that CBA is widespread means that an investigation of its philosophical and theoretical basis is worthwhile. Second, just because CBA *is* practised and just because it does tend to embody the welfare economics outlined in the preceding sections, does *not* mean that this is the *only* way of carrying out a cost—benefit study. The reason for this is that CBA of the kind so far discussed embodies certain value judgements. If we alter those judgements, we shall have a different kind of CBA. Further, since there can be nothing sacred about choosing one set of value judgements rather than another set, we must always be morally free to change value judgements. The value judgements underlying the view of CBA so far discussed are essentially: (*a*) that individuals' preferences shall count, and; (*b*) that these preferences shall be weighted by market power. Proposition (*a*) should be obvious from the fact that we require the consumer to indicate his willingness to pay or his compensation requirement. Proposition (*a*) is in fact nothing other than the widely accepted view that "consumers are sovereign". Just because it is widely accepted does not mean that we have to abide by it — we may have sound moral reasons for overriding consumers' preferences. As we shall see, some pollution problems are not amenable to sensible prescriptive study if we intend to rely totally on consumers' responses. Proposition (*b*) is less obvious, but if we consider that willingness to pay will show up in actual sums of money it should be obvious that those sums will vary according to individuals' *ability* to pay. Allowing our decision rule to be influenced in this way is as much a value judgement as is deciding that our rule should be more "fair", perhaps with the gains and losses of the poor being given more weight than the gains and losses of the rich. There can be no final ethical argument to settle what we should do. Accordingly, the most sensible thing to do is to indicate how our cost—benefit result will change if we alter the value judgements underlying it. This kind of study could be called "value sensitivity analysis" (Nash, Pearce and Stanley, 1975).

In this way we may have several decision rules and not just the one rule about the net summation of consumer's surpluses. We can, however, always begin with the rule developed in section 1.3: i.e. that for a policy to be judged worthwhile we require

$$\sum_{B} CV > \sum_{L} CV \tag{1}$$

We can now introduce two types of "weighting" for distributive justice. First, we could argue that poor people have a higher marginal utility of income than rich people. If we could measure these marginal utilities relative to some base group we would have a formula like the following:

$$\sum_{i=1}^{i=n} u_i CV_i > \sum_{j=1}^{j=m} u_j CV_j \tag{2}$$

where $i = 1 \ldots n$ refers to various groups of beneficiaries, and $j = 1 \ldots m$ refers to various groups of losers. The u_i and u_j are then the marginal utility of income measures of the ith and jth groups relative to some base group. Rule [2] would give us an evaluation in terms of absolute utility, and, of course, its value is heavily dependent on how valid it is to measure marginal utilities of income, an issue which is, at the very least, debatable. Nonetheless, it is the principle that is important here.

More than this, however, we can now argue about who "deserves" utility. That is, we can modify rule [2] to allow for differences in deservingness among groups. If we did this, we would have a rule as follows:

$$\sum_{i=1}^{j=n} e_i u_i CV_i > \sum_{j=1}^{j=m} e_j u_j CV_j \qquad [3]$$

where e_i and e_j now refer to the relative deserts of the ith and jth groups.

How we derive the "e" weights is another matter: various proposals are surveyed in Dasgupta and Pearce (1972), in Pearce (1971) and an empirical application of the "e" weighting and marginal utility of income weighting procedure is given in Pearce and Wise (1972). If it is felt that marginal utility of income weighting is illicit, we might have another rule [4] which would simply have the CV's weighted by the "e" weights.

Once we allow for the possibility of weighting as in the rules above, we effectively abandon Pareto optimality as an objective. While many economists find this tantamount to sacrilege, we have tried to show that there is nothing sacred at all about Pareto rules. Having demonstrated this we have a problem of procedure. As noted at the beginning of the chapter, environmental economics has, to date, largely been regarded as an application of neoclassical (Paretian) welfare economics. In surveying the subject matter, then, we have either to remind the reader continually that it need not be treated this way, or we have to look at the results obtained and leave it to the reader to recall that these results can be modified along the lines of the decision rules that have just been introduced. To avoid repetition, we shall adopt the second course.

1.5 Rules for Pareto optimality

If we now revert to an analysis of Paretian welfare economics we can investigate what requirements must be met for Pareto optimality to exist. This section details these requirements in terms of rates of substitution and rates of transformation. Section 1.6 translates these equivalences in terms of prices.

We can illustrate the idea of a Pareto optimum by looking at an economy in which we assume there are only two people, A and B. Figure 1.3 shows A's indifference map in the normal way. But we have superimposed B's indifference map on the diagram as well. This is done by turning B's map upside down and beginning at point "O". The resulting *box* diagram is then easily interpreted.

The size of the "box" is set by the available quantities of X_1 and X_2 in our simple economy. We shall return to the issue of how these amounts are determined: for the moment we take them as given. So far then we have (*a*) some given amounts of two goods (*b*) utility functions for individuals A and B.

Suppose we allocate goods so as to achieve point X. Then A will have

Fig. 1.3

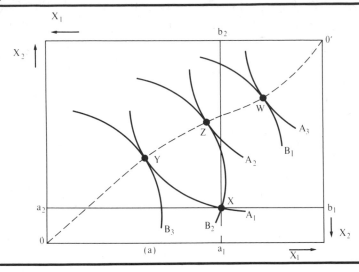

(a)

Oa$_1$ of X$_1$, and Oa$_2$ of X$_2$. B must then have the rest — i.e. O'b$_1$ of X$_2$, and O'b$_2$ of X$_1$. The question we need to answer is whether this allocation at X is optimal. It is easy to see that it is not. Suppose we reallocate goods so as to move along the section XZ of B$_2$ — one of B's indifference curves. By definition B is indifferent between X and Z. Hence he is no worse off by such a move. But A's utility increases because we take him off indifference curve A$_1$ and move him to A$_2$. The move from X to Z must therefore be a Pareto improvement. Similarly, a move from X to Y would be an improvement. If the exercise is repeated, it will be seen that a move from *any* point *off* the line through YZW to a point *on* that line will be a Pareto improvement. But a move from, say, Y to Z is one we cannot evaluate on the simple rule advanced so far, for it involves an improvement for A but a deterioration in utility for B. The line YZW is the *contract curve*: it shows all the combinations of goods that will give rise to a Pareto optimum. But, as we have seen, there are many optima, each corresponding to a different combination of abilities to buy the goods in question — i.e. to differing distributions of income. If we persist in the view that we should not make judgements about the desirable distribution of income, it is obvious that we shall have nothing to say about which point on the contract curve is best. If, on the other hand, we do permit such judgements, we shall be able to pinpoint an *optimum optimorum* — i.e. the most desirable point on the contract curve.

If we look at the optima in Fig. 1.3 we see that they all occur where indifference curves are tangential to each other. Such a tangency means that the marginal rates of substitution of A and B between the two goods must be equal. That is, we can write that an optimum requires

$$MRS^A_{X_1, X_2} = MRS^B_{X_1, X_2}$$

and this equation can be generalized for any number of individuals. Note too that this equation relates back to our measures of consumer's surplus. The move from X to Z, for example, was a move which enabled A's surplus to increase and B's to stay the same.

We now need to consider what determines the size of the box in Fig. 1.3 and its particular dimensions. In fact, we can illustrate this fairly easily by the use of a similar box diagram. In Fig. 1.4 the axes are now capital (K) and labour (L) and instead of two consumers we consider two products 1 and 2, with the production function of good 1 being "viewed" from origin O, and good 2 from origin O'. The production isoquants are shown as Q_{11}, Q_{12}, Q_{13} for good 1 and Q_{21}, Q_{22}, Q_{23} for good 2. Consideration of a point such as X will show that it is inefficient in the sense that we can move to Z and increase the output of good 1 without decreasing the output of good 2. Unless good 1 is undesirable, this results in an increase in utility. Hence Z must be preferred to X. If the analysis is repeated it will be found that *any* point *off* the locus OYZWO' is inefficient in this sense.

Fig. 1.4

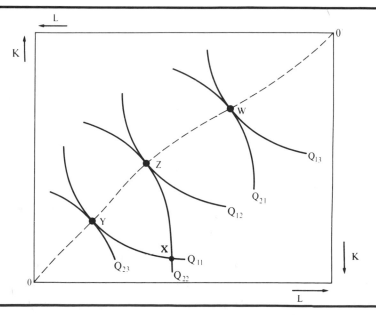

Now, the efficiency locus in Fig. 1.3 shows different combinations of inputs, but it also shows us the different combinations of outputs which are efficient. We can therefore plot these output combinations in Fig. 1.5 as a transformation *curve*. Note that, since production isoquants in Fig. 1.4 are tangential on the efficiency locus, we have

$$MRTS^1_{K, L} = MRTS^2_{K, L}$$

i.e. marginal rates of technical substitution are equal, along the transformation curve in Fig. 1.5. Points inside the frontier correspond to points off the efficiency locus in Fig. 1.4.[1]*

Fig. 1.5

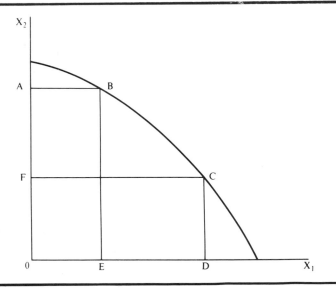

We can integrate the consumer box (Fig. 1.3) with the transformation curve in Fig. 1.5. Quite simply, the consumer box must fit inside the frontier. Two examples are given in Fig. 1.5 — a particular box might be OABE or it might be OFCD. Figure 1.6 takes one of these and shows the indifference maps inside the consumer box which, in turn, is inside the frontier. We have not yet said how a particular box is to be selected. To this we must now turn.

Figure 1.7 again shows the transformation curve. But this time we shall fix the amounts of X_1 and X_2 that A possesses. Suppose he has a combination such that he is at point A. What is left is therefore available for B.

* Superior figures refer to the "Notes" at the end of chapters.

Fig. 1.6

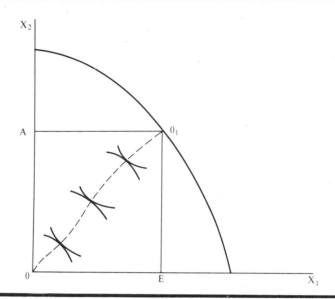

Consequently, we can think of point A as the origin of consumer B's indifference map. Placing his indifference map on the diagram shows that B will aim to reach point K since this maximizes his utility. If he was at Z for example, he could improve his utility level by moving to K without in anyway affecting A. Such a move would, by definition, be a Pareto improvement. We could switch consumers, making A the origin for A's indifference map and the same conclusion would follow. But we already know that the marginal rates of substitution must be equal for there to be a Pareto optimum. Figure 1.7 suggests that each individual's marginal rate of substitution should also be equal to the marginal rate of product transformation shown by the slope of the transformation curve. In short, we shall not reach a Pareto optimum unless we meet the following total condition:

$$MRS^A_{X_1, X_2} = MRS^B_{X_1, X_2} = MRT_{X_1, X_2}$$

1.6 Pareto optimality and prices
From the equation for overall Pareto optimality we can derive some interesting results. MRT_{X_1, X_2} can be written as

$$\frac{dX_1}{dX_2}$$

Fig. 1.7

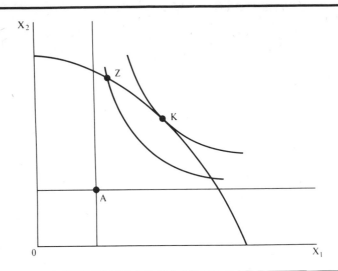

since it is the slope of the transformation curve. But dX_1 is the change in the output of X_1 and must be equal to

$$dX_1 = -[dL \cdot MP_L(X_1) + dK \cdot MP_K(X_1)]$$

where MP refers to marginal product.

Similarly,

$$dX_2 = -[dL \cdot MP_L(X_2) + dK \cdot MP_K(X_2)]$$

so that

$$MRT_{X_1, X_2} = \frac{dX_1}{dX_2} = \frac{-MP_L(X_1)}{MP_L(X_2)} = \frac{-MP_K(X_1)}{MP_K(X_2)}$$

Now, for any firm we know that

$$MC = \frac{W}{MP_L} = \frac{R}{MP_K}$$

where MC is marginal cost, W is the price of labour, and R the price of capital (rate of interest). Hence

$$MP_L = \frac{W}{MC} = \frac{R}{MC}$$

We also know that, for any consumer in equilibrium,

$$MRS_{X_1, X_2} = \frac{MU_{X_2}}{MU_{X_1}} = \frac{P_{X_2}}{P_{X_1}}$$

Where MRS refers to the marginal rate of substitution, and MU to marginal utility.
Hence,

$$\frac{P^A_{X_2}}{P^A_{X_1}} = \frac{P^B_{X_2}}{P^B_{X_1}} = \frac{W_1 \cdot MC_{X_2}}{W_2 \cdot MC_{X_1}}$$

which tells us that the ratio of prices faced by each consumer, A and B, must be equal to the ratio of wage rates in the two industries multiplied by the ratio of marginal costs, for there to be Pareto optimality.

Now, under perfect competition, price discrimination cannot be practised so that

$$P^A_{X_1} = P^B_{X_1}$$

and

$$W_1 = W_2$$

Substituting back gives

$$\frac{P_{X_2}}{P_{X_1}} = \frac{MC_{X_2}}{MC_{X_1}}$$

Now we consider the supply of labour. In balancing the claims of leisure and work on his time the consumer will meet the following condition

$$MRS_{D, X} = MRT_{D, X}$$

Where D is leisure and X is a good bought by the consumer. But the $MRT_{D, X}$ must be the output which would be produced if leisuretime was used as work, so that

$$\frac{dX}{dD} = MPL(X)$$

Also, $MRS_{D, X}$ must equal a ratio of prices. But the price of leisure is the wage foregone, W. Hence

$$MRS_{D, X} = \frac{W}{P_X}$$

Hence we have

$$MRS_{D, X} = MRT_{D, X} = \frac{W}{P_X} = MPL(X) = \frac{W}{MC_X}$$

But this last equation will hold true only if

$$P_X = MC_X$$

We establish, then, that a Pareto optimum will exist if prices everywhere are set equal to marginal cost. But under perfect competition prices are equal to marginal cost since this condition maximizes profits for firms. Hence, on the heroic assumption that our analysis has not omitted major qualifications, we establish that perfect competition maximizes welfare in the sense that it secures a Pareto optimum. We shall see in later chapters that this equivalence is of fundamental importance.

1.7 The problem of "second best"

There are in fact many serious modifications to be made to the conclusion of the previous section. We know that factor and product markets are not perfect, that economies of scale exist, that marginal private cost does not reflect the true cost of production to society (because of things like pollution) and so on. This section considers one problem.

Suppose we have an economy in which some products are not priced equal to marginal cost, and that we have no way of altering this situation. We shall not be able to secure a Pareto optimum in the sense of setting price equal to marginal cost everywhere — a "first best" is not available to us. It is tempting to think that we shall do the best we can — that is, secure a "second best" — if we aim to set as many prices as possible equal to marginal cost. In fact, however, it can be demonstrated that observance of the "first best" rules by those firms that can be subjected to direction will not even secure a "second best". The most explicit formulation of this "theorem of the second best" is due to Lipsey and Lancaster (1956).

The Lipsey—Lancaster conclusions can be stated as:

(*a*) If at least one of the Paretian first-best conditions is not met, second-best optima can only be achieved by departing from *all* other Paretian first-best conditions.

(*b*) While it is tempting to think that it will improve things to minimize the number of "failures" to observe first-best conditions, provided at least one first-best condition remains unmet we *cannot* say whether welfare will be improved or not by such a procedure.

In Fig. 1.8 we suppose there are two firms X and Y, each producing goods 1 and 2, quantities of which are denoted by X_1 and X_2. TT′ is the transformation function *for each firm*, assumed identical. The economy's transformation curve is therefore STST′.

Fig. 1.8

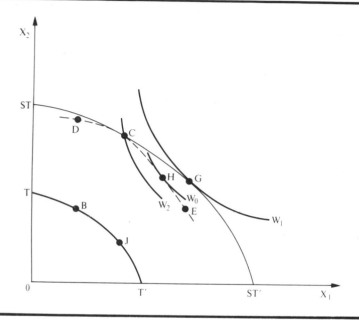

Now suppose firm X is constrained to produce at B on TT′, whereas Y can produce anywhere on his transformation curve. To construct the constrained ST function, suppose Y also produces at B on his TT′. Then point C denotes one point on the constrained ST function. Now suppose Y produces at T, and X is of course still constrained to produce at B. Social output is now the combination of X_1 and X_2 given at B, *plus* OT of X_2, giving point D as a point on the constrained function. If Y selects T′ as his production point, similar analysis will give E as the constrained point.

Thus, whereas STST′ is the unconstrained ST function, the ST function when X is constrained to produce at B is given by DCE. We now introduce a social welfare function W_0, W_1, W_2 showing society's preferences for X_1 and X_2. We see that point G is the *unconstrained* social optimum. At G, rates of product transformation are equal for both firms and are also equal to rates of social substitution. We have a Pareto optimum. But in the constrained case, X produces at B. If firm Y is made to produce at B as well, social welfare is not maximized ($W_2 < W_0$). The second-best solution is in fact at H. But H corresponds to a situation where X is producing at B, and Y is producing at a point like J: i.e. rates of product transformation are not equalized across firms.

This result is clearly of importance, for, as we shall see, much of the substance of pollution economics rests on the idea that product prices can and should be adjusted to reflect the social costs of pollution. As we shall see, the general requirement will be that prices be set equal to marginal product cost plus the marginal cost of externally imposed damage. But, the second-best theorem suggests that such adjustments will not meet the objective of a Pareto improvement if prices elsewhere diverge from this rule.

1.8 Public goods and bads

The preceding rules for securing a Pareto optimum also require modification in the presence of *public goods*. Public goods can be contrasted with *private goods*: the latter are *excludable* — there exists some mechanism whereby the good can be priced or rationed so as to prevent other people from enjoying the benefits of the good. Second, private goods are *rival* — consumption of the good by one person precludes its simultaneous consumption by another person. But a public good has exactly the opposite features — it is *non-rival* in the sense that its provision to individual A entails its provision to individual B, whether he wants it or not. The most obvious example is national defence. In addition, it is *non-excludable* in that we cannot prevent individual B securing the benefits (if they exist) of the good. If such a good exists then, it follows that each individual consumes the same amount of it. Its provision to one person entails its provision to everyone else.

To underline this distinction, we can write the amount available of a *private* good (x_{PR}) as the sum of the amounts consumed by the individuals (A, B, etc.) in the community. We have

$$x_{PR} = x_{PR}^A + x_{PR}^B + x_{PR}^C + \cdots + x_{PR}^N$$

Whereas for the public good (x_{PU}) we shall have to write

$$x_{PU} = x_{PU}^A = x_{PU}^B = x_{PU}^C = \cdots = x_{PU}^N$$

We can now see how the existence of public goods affects the marginal equivalences established in section 1.5. We can deal with the marginal rate of transformation (MRT) straight away. A public good has to be produced just like any other good, so that the equivalence between MRTS's is not affected. We can therefore think of a transformation function between public and private goods just like the transformation function between two private goods.

If we increase the amount of a public good by some small amount Δx the extra utility to any one consumer, i, will be

$$\frac{dU^i}{dx} \cdot \Delta x$$

But in increasing the supply of x to consumer i we have, *ex hypothesi*, increased it for all others. The total "social" increase in utility (SU) must therefore be

$$\Delta SU = \frac{dU^i}{dx} \cdot \Delta x + \frac{dU^j}{dx} \cdot \Delta x + \frac{dU^k}{dx} \cdot \Delta x + \text{etc.}$$

$$= \Delta x \left[\frac{dU^i}{dx} + \frac{dU^j}{dx} + \frac{dU^k}{dx} + \right]$$

$$= \Delta x \sum_i^m \frac{dU}{dx}$$

where m is the number of consumers involved. Now the marginal rate of substitution, $MRS_{PU, PR}$ for any one individual (i) is in fact

$$MRS^i_{PU, PR} = \frac{MU^i_{PU}}{MU^i_{PR}}$$

Hence,

$$\Delta x \cdot \frac{\Delta SU_{PU}}{\Delta SU_{PR}} = \sum_i^m \left[\frac{dU_{PU}}{dx} \bigg/ \frac{dU_{PR}}{dx} \right] = \sum_i^m MRS_{PU, PR}$$

That is, the social rate of marginal substitution between the public and private good is equal to the *sum* of the individual marginal rates of substitution (Samuelson, 1954). It is this sum that must be equated with the MRT to obtain a Pareto optimum in an economy containing public and private goods. In other words, the condition for optimality becomes:

$$MRS^A_{PU, PR} + MRS^B_{PU, PR} + MRS^C_{PU, PR} \text{ etc.} = MRT_{PU, PR}$$

Note that this differs from the condition for an economy containing private goods alone in that it requires the sum of the MRS's to equal MRT, whereas the private-goods-only economy required the MRS's to be equal to each other and also equal to the MRT.

Figure 1.9 shows the implications of this equivalence. MC_{PU} is the marginal cost of providing the public good, assumed to rise as more is provided.[2] To avoid complicating the diagram we have shown marginal *evaluation* curves. These curves show the consumer's valuation of a commodity in terms of the commodity he foregoes in order to have one more unit of the good in question. In other words, it is measured by the slope of the individual's indifference curve. Now MV_1 is the marginal valuation curve for individual 1, and MV_2 is that for individual 2. Since MV measures MRS we can relate the diagram directly to the condition for optimality derived above. For we require the *summation* of MV's to be equal to MRT, where MRT in this case is shown in terms of marginal cost — i.e. as MC_{PU}/MC_{PR}. But instead of deriving an aggregate marginal valuation curve by summing the MV's horizontally (which is what we would do if the MV's were being summed to derive the market demand curve for private goods) we must sum them *vertically*. We must do this because each unit of the public good is consumed by each consumer. The individual marginal valuation curves allow for the fact that consumers will value these units differently, but the fact remains that each unit of the good — e.g. OX_{PU}^1 in Fig. 1.9 — is consumed by each individual. It follows that the optimal provision of the public good is at Z, with quantity X_{PU}^*

Fig. 1.9

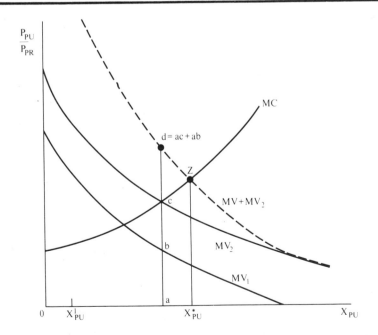

Section 1.6 argued that, under certain highly restrictive conditions, a perfectly competitive economy would automatically secure Pareto optimality. In the presence of public goods — which, notice, do not derive from institutional features but are as "natural" as private goods — this theorem no longer holds. The demonstration of this is simple, given our condition for optimality with public goods. On the production side we require

$$MRT_{PU, PR} = \frac{MC_{PU}}{MC_{PR}} = \frac{P_{PU}}{P_{PR}}$$

For each consumer to be in equilibrium we require

$$\frac{MU^A_{PU}}{MU^A_{PR}} = \frac{P_{PU}}{P_{PR}}$$

and

$$\frac{MU^B_{PU}}{MU^B_{PR}} = \frac{P_{PU}}{P_{PR}}$$

But because we have public goods the overall result of these equations for individual optimization is

$$\frac{MU^A_{PU}}{MU^A_{PR}} + \frac{MU^B_{PU}}{MU^B_{PR}} = \frac{2 \cdot P_{PU}}{P_{PR}} > MRT_{PU, PR}$$

That is, the optimal amount of the public good is greater than the amount actually provided by producers (consumers' valuations exceed producers' willingness to supply). The public good will be under supplied in an economy which relies on the price mechanism to allocate goods.

We need to note a further point. The very characteristics of public goods make it difficult to find out exactly what valuation people place on them. This arises for the simple reason that, if the good is provided to one person, the other person will secure the benefits as well, regardless of whether he has paid for it or not. That is, there is a clear incentive for individuals to understate their preferences for public goods. Those who do not reveal their preferences for the public good (even though they really want it) on the grounds that they think they will benefit from its supply to others, are often called "free riders". How important this non-revelation of preferences is, is difficult to assess. Certainly, environmental goods and investments often have "publicness" as an attribute. Consider pollution abatement: if improved abatement equipment is installed in factories emitting air pollutants, everyone in the pollution catchment area benefits regardless of whether they have indicated their willingness to pay for the abatement programme. Equally, of course, pollution itself is a "public bad" the opposite of a "public good". The extent to which individuals can adjust to "bads" of this kind will depend on the geographical distribution of the bad. If air pollution is localized, one reaction on the part of a pollution sensitive individual could be to move location. Indeed, some of the most sophisticated models of pollution evaluation rest on this reaction, as we shall see. But if pollution is "global" — as many recent writers have stressed — no such reaction is possible. There is no escape. We shall have occasion to refer back to these problems later in the book.

1.9 Externality

Perhaps the most widely relevant feature of environmental goods and environmental degradation is the "spillover" effect noted with public goods. Another way of talking about these effects is to say that public goods exhibit *external benefits* and public bads exhibit *external costs*. We might expect externality to be a wider phenomenon than publicness, however, because interdependence of this kind tends to be a basic feature of any economy. Indeed, Chapter 3 shows a formalization of this statement in terms of a "materials balance" model of an economy.

This externality aspect may arise because of the inputs used, or because the act of consumption itself is a nuisance. In the former case we can think of pollution due to the use of chemicals as inputs; in the latter case we can think of offensive behaviour, lighting bonfires, unsightly landscape, and so on.

The essence of an externality then, is that it involves: (*a*) an interdependence between two or more economic agents; and (*b*) a failure to price that interdependence. The interdependence could be between consumers, between producers, or between producers and consumers. It is also the case that the existence of externalities will mean that Pareto optimality cannot be achieved, unless the price mechanism contains some automatic adjustment procedures whereby externalities are "corrected". The first proposition can be demonstrated as follows. Suppose we have two firms producing, respectively, outputs X_1 and X_2. Then we could write

$$\frac{dX_1}{dL_1} = MP_{L,\,1} \tag{1}$$

$$\frac{dX_2}{dL_2} = MP_{L,\,2} \tag{2}$$

where dX simply refers to the change in output, dL to the change in the input labour (we assume one variable input for convenience) and $MP_{L,1}$ means the marginal product of labour in producing X_1. This much is self-evident since all we have done is define marginal products. Now suppose that the output of X_2 is affected by the level of production in firm 1: the production function in firm 2 will involve the dependence of output not just on the labour input in firm 2 but also on the output of firm 1. This establishes that there is an interdependence. We shall further assume that it is "untraded" — no price is paid for this interdependence. Hence we have an externality.

With this interdependence we shall need to redefine marginal product. Equations [1] and [2] above stand as definitions of *private* marginal product. But they do not express *social* marginal product. If the externality is negative — firm 1 imposes costs on firm 2 and does not compensate firm 2 — we shall have to write

$$SMP_{L,1} = \frac{dX_1}{dL_1} - \frac{dX_2}{dL_1} \qquad [3]$$

$$SMP_{L,2} = \frac{dX_2}{dL_2} \qquad [4]$$

Equation [3] is the important one. For from private marginal product we have subtracted an expression dX_2/dL_1: this is the change in the output of X_2 due to a change in the input labour in producing good 1. (Notice that we have expressed it in terms of output changes with respect to labour inputs — this allows for the fact that output of good 2 varies with the output of good 1 which in turn varies with the input of labour to good 1.)

Now, if we have perfect competition and firms are profit maximizers, we shall have

$$W \frac{dX_1}{dL_1} = MC_1 = P_1$$

and

$$W \frac{dX_2}{dL_2} = MC_2 = P_2$$

which in turn, under perfect competition, implies

$$\frac{dX_1}{dL_1} = \frac{dX_2}{dL_2}$$

That is, the self-interested behaviour of firms under perfect competition will lead to the equality of (real) marginal products. But it is *private* marginal products that are equated, not social marginal products. For if it was the latter we would require, in our example,

$$\frac{dX_1}{dL_1} - \frac{dX_2}{dL_1} = \frac{dX_L}{dL_1}$$

In other words, Pareto optimality would require the equivalence of social marginal products. But our competitive state secures only the equivalence of private marginal products. Hence externalities entail non-optimality. If the externality is negative, the output of the "offending" activity will be too large. If the externality is positive, the output will be too small.

We can finally illustrate external effects by looking at the familiar diagram for the firm's equilibrium under perfect competition. In Fig. 1.10 the curve PMC measures private marginal cost. The curve SMC measures social marginal cost and is shown lying above PMC because a negative externality is assumed to exist (social marginal product is less than private marginal product: hence social marginal cost is above private marginal cost). The optimal output is seen to be X_S and not X_P which is the private profit maximizing solution

Fig. 1.10

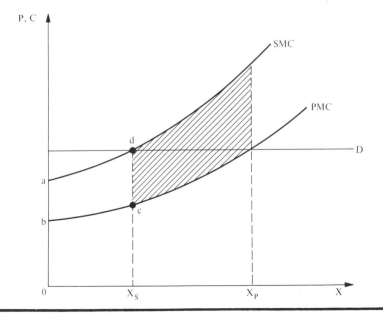

In fact the amount of externality that is undesirable is shown by the shaded area in the diagram. This is sometimes called the "Pareto-relevant" externality. Notice that at X_S some external loss remains, and we could measure this by the area abcd. In this way we can derive the following general propositions:

1. A negative externality implies that the output of the "offending" activity is too large. Vice versa for a positive externality.
2. A negative externality should not be removed altogether. Instead, the aim should be to secure the *optimal amount of externality*.

1.10 Unmarketed goods

As we noted earlier, one feature of many environmental goods and bads is that they have no market, at least not in the normal sense. Pure air is not bought and sold on the market, nor, in general, are fine views, wildlife and wilderness, although we often pay to see them. It is often suggested that commodities (and "discommodities") that lie outside the sphere of the market cannot be valued in monetary terms. Economists tend to react critically to such a view. They argue that simply because property rights happen not to exist for many items it does not mean that we cannot find individuals' preferences for those commodities. That is, they tend to see the actual configuration of property rights as an historically determined thing, rather than something which arises because of the nature of the universe. If we parcelled out the oceans outside of current territorial waters, for example, we might expect completely different behaviour on the part of shipping lines, fishermen, whalers, and so on, than we have now. We can see such changes in operation when countries try to extend their territorial waters. The economist's second argument is that the totality of resources is scarce in relation to the demands made upon those resources. Indeed, it is odd that non-economists often hail the discovery of the finitude of the earth's resources as if it is something entirely new to our knowledge, when in fact it has always been the fundamental feature of economic science. Nonetheless, many economists often behave as if they have forgotten this fundamental point. Given this scarcity, resources must be allocated according to relative valuations, although, as we have seen, we are all entitled to argue about how those valuations are achieved. Environmental goods are no exception. They too have a "price" even if that price is not observed in the market. The problem with environmental goods, on this view, is that their actual price appears to be zero simply because there is no market, when in fact their "true" price is positive. Perhaps what non-economists mean when they object to the idea of all things having prices is that they themselves would want to put much higher prices on environmental goods than cost—benefit studies suggest are the prices. We shall have occasion to consider this conflict of views again.

1.11 Future generations

The welfare economics so far discussed has all been derived in a "static" framework. We have not attempted to assess how resources should be allocated over time. In particular, we shall want to know how future generations' welfare can be taken account of in any social decision rule, bearing in mind that decisions have to be made by any given generation at a point in time.

If current generations care about future generations they will incorporate this factor in their currently expressed preferences. We would expect this form of caring to be quite marked, at least because parents care for the welfare of their children. Correspondingly, the children will have children for whose welfare they care, and so on. This establishes a chain of linkages between generations, so that the welfare (W) of generation depends not just on the welfare-generating goods (M_t) consumed during the time period t, but also on the welfare of the next generation (W_{t+1}). Thus we would have:

$$W_t = W_t(M_t, W_{t+1}),$$
$$W_{t+1} = W_{t+1}(M_{t+1}, W_{t+2}),$$

and so on.

This form of caring, then, should show up in current decision-taking by individuals. Suppose for example that we are considering a pollution abatement scheme, and it has a flow of benefits over time of

$$-C_0 + B_1 + B_2 + B_3 + B_4 + \cdots + B_N$$

Where B refers to benefits, C to costs (assumed to occur in the initial period), and the subscripts to time periods. Then, a current generation at time 0, that cares little for future generations can be thought of as weighting the early costs and benefits more than the later ones. Where w_i refer to the weight attached to the ith period, we would have

$$-w_0 C_0 + w_1 B_1 + w_2 B_2 + w_3 B_3 + w_4 B_4 + \cdots + w_N B_N$$

and we can take it that $w_0 > w_1 > w_2 > w_3 > w_4 > \cdots > w_n$. Similarly, a society that cares a great deal about future generations will have a weighting system which makes $w_N > w_4 > w_3$ and so on.

If we take the case of a current generation that weights early benefits and costs more than later ones, a case which appears to fit actual conditions, and considering only three periods, we have

$$-w_0 C_0 + w_1 B_1 + w_2 B_2$$

Letting $w_0 = 1$, we know that $w_1 < 1$ and $w_2 < w_1$. If the *rate* at which current generations "downgrade" the future is constant, we could let $w_1 = 1/1 + r$ and w_2 would then equal $(1/1 + r) \cdot (1/1 + r)$. We would have

$$-C_0 + \frac{B_1}{(1 + r)} + \frac{B_2}{(1 + r)^2}$$

as the flow of costs and benefits *as the current generation sees them*. We can easily convert this to a decision rule: no investment in pollution abatement should take place unless the benefits, as the current generation sees them, outweigh the costs as the current generation sees them. This rule would of course be nothing more than the cost−benefit rule already derived in the static framework earlier in the chapter. That is, for the investment to be worthwhile, we would require

$$\frac{B_1}{(1 + r)} + \frac{B_2}{(1 + r)^2} > C_0$$

More generally, if costs and benefits are both distributed over time, our rule is

$$\sum_{t = 0}^{t = N} \frac{B_t}{(1 + r)^t} > \sum_{t = 0}^{t = N} \frac{C_t}{(1 + r)^t}$$

And this is in fact the basic decision rule of cost−benefit analysis. The crucial new element in this rule compared to those obtained for the static framework is the item "r" which we saw reflects the current generation's intertemporal weighting of the flow of benefits and costs. r is in fact the *social rate of discount* − it measures the rate at which current generations downgrade, or "discount", the future. How r is derived in practice, and how it should be derived, are issues that generally lie outside the scope of this text. For surveys of the literature see Pearce (1971) and Dasgupta and Pearce (1972). But what is important to note is that a *low* discount rate will tend to favour future generations, and a *high* rate will tend to work to their disadvantage, at least as far as the normal ranges of capital investment programmes are concerned. As we shall see in Chapter 7, a low discount rate applied to natural resource exploitation rates will tend to favour rapid exploitation, and high rates will discourage exploitation and will favour the leaving of resources in the ground. Arguably, the latter is better for future generations (they have more natural resources left) than the former. The issue is discussed more fully in Chapter 7.

One other problem with discounting is that it might leave future generations with immense social costs to be borne *ad infinitum* in return for comparatively insignificant gains to current generations. Nash (1973) gives the example of a project that yields net benefits over the next 50 years but which yields £1,000,000 per annum of social costs thereafter *for ever*. The present value (the discounted value) of social costs of this magnitude from year 51 to year infinity, using r = 10 per cent, is £85,000, so that if the present value of benefits from year 0 to year 50 is only £85,000 such an investment would be sanctioned by the cost—benefit rule. If our earlier argument, that current generations necessarily take account of future generations' requirements in their decisions, is correct, then such a conclusion should not surprise us. But it is more than questionable as to whether any such mechanism operates in that it requires current generations to gauge what future generations will want, and to gauge what the effects of current decisions will be on future generations' welfare. Further, as Nash argues, projects with very long-term effects should be treated differently to projects with short-term effects.

"Just because the rate of interest used in evaluating next year's benefits happens to be 10%, so that they are assigned a weight of 0.909 in terms of present consumption, this is no reason why effects a century distant should also be assessed at 10% per annum, and hence assigned a weight of only 0.00007." (Nash, 1973, p. 615.)

What this implies, then, is a careful scrutiny of investments so that projects with likely long-term consequences are considered separately to those with fairly well-defined short-term consequences. This in itself raises many problems. We return to a discussion of these in a later chapter.

Notes
1. The production possibility frontier shown assumes non-increasing returns to scale in both products. If there are increasing returns the frontier will be concave.

2. Notice that this is the marginal cost of increasing the physical quantity supplied. The marginal cost of adding one consumer — i.e. of increasing consumption as opposed to availability — is of course zero for a pure public good. Indeed, this equivalence is often used to define public goods.

2

Some ecology

2.1 Economics and ecology

No serious student of environmental economics can afford to ignore the subject matter of "ecology", the widely embracing science which looks at the relationship between living species and their habitats. Unfortunately, "ecology" has come to mean all things to all people. Frequently it is taken to refer to *any* subject matter which reveals some concern for the environment, and the term "ecologist" has all too often been used to refer to individuals who have predicted some dire state of the world to be brought about by any or all of the following: overpopulation, pollution, natural resource depletion, congestion and "human alienation". These ascriptions of the term "ecology" are unfortunate not because those who use them are necessarily wrong in their views, but because they have diverted attention away from the scientific foundations of ecology towards the highly popular and journalistic pronouncements about the future course of mankind. Again, the latter *may* be correct, but it is one of the themes of this book that a more rigorous view is to be obtained by looking at the rudiments of ecology as a science and then asking what the links are between this science and economics. This chapter looks at ecological principles in so far as they relate directly to economic analysis. Some suggested links between economics and ecology are discussed in Chapter 4. There can be no question that further links exist, nor that the treatment given to certain economic–ecological relationships in this chapter and Chapter 4 is slight. Much more research is required into this "interface" between the two disciplines.

Part of the function of investigating the links between economics and ecology is to see what common ground the two disciplines have, and to see what contrasts, incompatibilities and inconsistencies there are in the two approaches. This kind of investigation is much needed not least because economists and non-economists appear to have little in common when it comes to debating environmental issues.

What we might loosely call the "life scientists" do tend to look unfavourably upon economists because of their apparent narrowness of vision. In his *Doomsday Book*, Rattray Taylor (1970) spoke of the "bankruptcy of economics", arguing that economics falsely aims to put a price tag on everything, including natural endowments, and equally falsely attaches normative significance to those prices. Ian McHarg in his highly literate *Design with Nature* (1969) refers to economists as seeing the "world as Commodity", a view which "fails to evaluate and incorporate physical and biological processes". Perhaps, because of the relatively small number of economists working on environmental issues, the crossfire is less frequently returned. But Beckerman (1972) has spoken of the "arrogant" attitudes of scientists in commenting on economics, a subject about which many of them seemed to possess "astronomic ignorance". And Downs (1973), has recently declared that "the essentially conservative and non-objective oriented nature of ecology as a science or mode of thinking makes it ill suited to serve as the basis for developing the central public policies of the modern world". Of course, it is easy to find dozens of examples of ecologists and scientists who do not share their colleagues' misgivings about the environmental future, and there exists too a number of economists who doubt the wisdom of the economic approach. Whereas Beckerman (1972) is in no doubt that "the problem of environmental pollution is a *simple* matter of correcting a *minor* resource allocation problem by means of pollution charges" (our italics), Kapp (1972) speaks of the need to "raise new questions about the adequacy and relevance of the old framework of analysis", and Coddington (1970) has suggested the possibility that "the greatest service economists can render to posterity is to remain silent". These exchanges seem to suggest that, if economics and ecology really are compatible sciences, something has gone wrong with each discipline's understanding of the other's content. If on the other hand, they are incompatible, we need to know which is the right discipline to use when planning resource use and residuals disposal: if ecology really is falsely biased towards conservation policies, ecological policies will unnecessarily reduce material standards of living; if economics is falsely optimistic, use of economic principles to guide planning may entail risks to the quality of life and perhaps even to survival. It matters a great deal, then, to know which is right.

2.2 The nature of ecology
Ecology studies the interdependencies of living things, both between them-

selves as species, and between them and their environments. We must be clear that, as such, ecology is a vast, and immensely complex subject, attempting to integrate, as it does, so many of the life sciences, and the natural sciences. Accordingly, we select only those aspects of ecology that we require to demonstrate some particular connections with economics. It needs to be said also that, just as one would not expect economists to agree totally on their subject matter, so ecologists dispute some of the major tendencies of natural ecological systems. The interested reader is referred to any of the several excellent textbooks on introductory ecology for further detail on the nature of disagreements within ecological science (see especially Colinvaux, 1973; and Krebs, 1972).

A system of living things (or, *biota*) in relationship with their environment is called an *ecosystem*. Ecosystems are not static communities — they change with exogenous factors such as climate, and in light of endogenous factors whereby the occupying species alter their own habitat, often making it unsuitable for their own continued occupation. Consequently, we have to think of ecosystems as constantly changing. One school of thought in ecology suggests, however, that the process of change in ecosystems is an orderly one and that it eventually converges on a particular form of community, called a *climax system*. This idea is due mainly to Clements (1916) and many of his followers still maintain the essential ingredients of his theories. Essentially, the process operates as follows. If a natural area, say some sand dunes, are left alone, particular kinds of vegetation begin to appear. These are the *pioneer plants*. These are eventually succeeded (the dynamic process of plants being replaced by others is in fact called "succession") by other plants, and so on, until forests are formed. Thereafter no successional change is observed, and it is judged that "climax" has been achieved. A climax state is defined then as a state in which successional change does not occur, or at least, such change as does occur is held to be due to only minor "cycles" in the system which iron themselves out so as to restore the self-perpetuating nature of the climax state. More than this, the absence of succession in the climax state entails that the ecosystem is in a state of constant *biomass*. Biomass is a measure of the amount of organic matter in the system. If biomass is increasing, the system has net *productivity*, i.e. organic matter is being added to the system (productivity of ecosystems is explained in more detail in section 2.3). If biomass is decreasing, the system must be "running down", i.e. it has negative net productivity. Biomass is then a *stock* concept and productivity is a flow concept, entirely analogous to the economic concepts of income (flow) and wealth (stock). The climax state, in which biomass is, to all intents and purposes, constant is often referred to as a *steady-state system*. It is important to recognise this terminology since it has been widely used, often indiscriminately, by those who have sought to popularise ecological ideas. We shall confine its use, as seems proper, to the constant biomass state only. As we shall see, prescriptions for "zero economic growth" often have this analogous objective in mind. Indeed, zero economic growth is often referred to as steady state growth by those who advocate it (Daly, 1972).

2.3 Ecosystem productivity

An ecosystem has inputs and outputs just like an economy. The two categories of inputs are *energy inputs* and *materials inputs*. Both of these flow through the ecosystem, but with a crucial difference. Energy, once used, cannot be re-used. The stored-up energy in the food we eat, for example, once eaten, is not available to us again: it is uselessly dissipated to the atmosphere. The flow of energy through ecosystems (and through economies, to press the analogy) is therefore *one-way*. Materials, on the other hand, can be used over and over again, and this is exactly how ecosystems use materials inputs. Nitrogen exists in the atmosphere, of course. Highly specialized bacteria present in ecosystems (for example, in the roots of legumes) are able to "fix" this nitrogen and it is thus converted to nitrogenous compounds essential for the survival of living species. It is worthy of note that very few species are capable of this fixing operation — apart from nitrogen released to the soil from animal waste, the fixation occurs only via blue-green algae, bacteria in roots of plants, and via lichen and other algae on plants. Other plants and animals have no such capability, despite the fact that nitrogen is essential to them. This interdependence is therefore vital, and one can also begin to see how delicate it is too. Once fixed in this way and once used by plants and animals, denitrifying bacteria then release the nitrogen back to the atmosphere. Large quantities are also released into watercourses.

The circular flow of nitrogen through an ecosystem is an example of a *biogeochemical cycle*. Others, equally as vital, occur for sulphur, carbon, and so on. Major economic changes that upset these cycles, perhaps by reducing the crucial populations of bacteria, or plankton, or whatever, must therefore affect the productivity of the ecosystem, its ability to generate a yield of organic matter. Of course, when this happens, it is often possible to "assist" the ecosystem by supplying the materials input "artificially". This is what happens with fertilizers which are effectively a means of supplying deficiencies in nitrogen. Nonetheless, judging the effects of such controls is difficult because of the widespread interdependencies in ecosystems.

The productivity of ecosystems therefore depends directly on energy flow and materials circulation (notice that the latter is the natural "ecological" counterpart of recycling of waste products in the economy). Materials circulation enables systems to supply their own materials requirements without there being any "external" source of materials. Energy flow, on the other hand, being unidirectional, requires a continuous external source. In the case of ecosystems this is met by solar energy. In the case of economies, this source is also available, potentially at least, but it is generally true to say that virtually all energy uses at the moment are met from stocks of "inventoried" solar energy — coal, oil and gas. Given that the principle of non-recyclability of energy applies equally to economies, this usage of fuel stocks can only be sustained as long as those stocks last. This is a further essential distinction between economies and ecosystems.

Some of the solar energy that comes into ecosystems is trapped by plants and converted to glucose through photosynthesis. Some of this glucose is in turn used up by the plants, or *primary producers* as they are called, in the process of *respiration* — the process whereby the primary producer itself grows. Hence, primary producers will have a *gross productivity* rate equal to *net productivity plus respiration*, all measured in energy units. Now, the primary producers (plants) are food for the next category of living forms — the *primary consumers*. The net primary product of the primary producers is (potentially) available as a food supply to this further *trophic level*. Further along the chain, the primary consumers, the herbivores, will be consumed by the next trophic level, the carnivores, and of course the carnivores may in turn be consumed by other carnivores. Humans are often called "top" carnivores, not because there is anything morally supreme about being human and carnivorous, but because humans appear at the top of the *food chain* that began with the primary producers. Equally, we may have aphids feeding on pine trees, spiders on aphids, small birds on spiders, and larger birds on small birds.

Now, as energy is transferred from one trophic level to another, much of it is lost. If food chains are very long, then, we can expect the consumer at the very end of the chain to be consuming a product the energy content of which will be only a minute proportion of the original primary production level. As Odum (1971, p. 40) puts it, "more men can survive on a given square mile if they function as primary rather than secondary consumers". To quote the example given by Odum (1971), if plants as primary producers absorb 1,500 calories of light energy per square metre per day, we can reckon that 15 calories will end up as net primary production (reflecting the enormous respiratory losses of primary producers), 1.5 calories to be reconstituted as primary consumers, and only 0.15 calories as secondary consumers, carnivores.

The relationship between gross productivity and respiration also enables us to define more carefully the difference between seral communities (those in the stage of ecological succession) and climax communities. Essentially, if the ratio of gross primary production to respiration (GPP/R) equals unity, the system is in a steady state. If GPP $\neq$ R the system is in a state of succession. In the early stages of succession it is suggested that GPP/R is high, and converges to unity as climax approaches.

Finally, we need to note that the succession-climax thesis is widely disputed. One reason for doubting its validity is the general absence of observed climaxes. Clements and his followers never suggested that climax communities could not change: climate, for example, would certainly generate change. Nor did they suggest that some change could not occur. But they did tend to believe that in the absence of climatic change, the observed changes in ecosystems were either due to minor cycles that might characterize climax states, or to the fact that what was being observed was a disequilibrium, seral, state. One problem with such an hypothesis is finding what evidence its proponents would accept in order to abandon their view, since all states of the world are consistent with the hypothesis. But there is evidence to suggest that hydrarch succession, the process whereby inland waters are infilled by the detritus of the occupiers of the water community and eventually climax in a forest state, does not fit the facts. Instead, it would appear that "succession" if it can be called that, is disorderly and random. As we shall see, this dispute has some relevance to the links between ecology and economics, although it does not affect the basic arguments we shall be putting forward.

2.4 Ecosystem stability

Any "natural" ecosystem then, is characterized by a process of continual change as habitats are altered either by external factors or by the activities of the species occupying those habitats. The relationship of species to habitat and of species to each other is nonetheless one of harmony. There is evidence to suggest that all species other than man possess some self-regulatory mechanism whereby their populations are internally regulated to meet available food resources. Wynne-Edwards (1962), for example, has proposed a theory whereby the territory of a species is determined by the territory's food productivity and the species' needs for food. Territories may therefore be large in area if food productivity is low relative to the species' needs. Equally, of course, territorial rights ensure non-competition for the food resource and hence ensure the avoidance of an outcome in which the species is threatened with starvation. In fact some form of social status ensures preservation of territorial rights. The outcome is a regulatory mechanism whereby population density, and hence size, is just suited to the food resources available.

Many ecologists believe that successional change in an ecosystem is characterized by a growth in species *diversity*. That is, the more mature an ecosystem is, the nearer it is to a climax state, the more species it is likely to contain. In consequence, the system is also likely to be more complex in so far as more interrelationships must now exist. Since one of the basic relationships between species is that they occupy different stratas in a food chain, species feeding on each other or on the products of each other, the self-regulatory mechanisms also become more complex. While it is a much disputed proposition, it is widely argued that, far from this complexity making the ecosystem more unstable, in a sense to be defined, it makes it more stable. The interrelationships may be more fragile, more delicate, but they nonetheless insure against wide fluctuations both in the size of individual species populations, and in the overall number of species.

The stability of complex systems is crucial to the arguments of many ecologists in their criticism of economic approaches to problems. Basically, what is being said is that modern technology and economic growth induce a tendency towards *monoculture* — the specialization of activity into fairly uniform channels. Thus, factory farming, heavy fertilizer applications in single-crop strain arable farming, and so on, are instances of monoculture. They imply the adoption of unique technologies over a wide range of activity. A diversity of technology, and, for that matter, a diversity of output is not maintained. The idea of monoculture is not confined to farming and technology: it can also be applied to things like urban life. In the absence of conscious attempts to diversify human environments, urban life becomes uniform and the uniformity is widespread. This does not mean that there isn't variety in much city life. The problem is to square urban life with what many biologists believe man to be "genetically programmed" to need. That is, man may be genetically programmed to experience wilderness, the vista of countryside, appreciation of wildlife. Urban life lacks these aspects and, in so far as they are available, their appreciation also becomes uniform in that they are sought only at set times of the year or week according to the regimentation of social institutions. The main point is that what we might call the technology of economic change is fundamentally opposed to the principle of diversity in "natural" ecosystem development. What matters of course is to decide whether this is at all important.

There can be a confusion between the adaptability that ensues after an ecosystem has been "shocked" by pollution, and evolutionary adaptation. The implication sometimes is that evolution is about adaptation to changed environments; man changes environments; hence adaptation to pollution: (*a*) must always be possible; (*b*) must in the long run be sanctioned because evolution is somehow "good". Argument (b) is of course not founded on anything, unless we admit to some Panglossian theology which asserts that everything that happens is for the best. Proposition (a) is of course correct, but it does ignore the fact that evolutionary adaptation includes failure to survive. Unless we adhere to some metaphysic, there is nothing in evolutionary theory to say that man is incapable of altering his own habitat so as not to survive.

More than this, however, there is a difference in time scales, as we have already noted. Successional change in ecosystems is a relatively short-term affair — perhaps ranging over one or several human life-spans. Evolutionary change is a process that takes place over millions of years. Short-term successional change is therefore superimposed on the extremely long-run dynamic path of an evolutionary system. The successional patterns themselves reflect evolutionary change. The important point, as Woodwell (1970) points out is that ". . . as far as our interests in the next decades are concerned pollution operates on the time scale of succession, not of evolution, and we cannot look to evolution to cure this set of problems".

2.5 Pollution and ecosystem stability

Stability implies the ability of the ecosystem to withstand exogenous shocks such as climatic change, and shocks that are man-induced. Pollution is just such a shock to the system because the essence of pollution in the biophysical sense is that it interferes with the relationships which exist between species and which exist because of the need for self-regulation and survival. A monoculture system must therefore be a system less capable of withstanding shocks. This inability will show up in species fluctuations and in a continual reshuffling of the relationships between species and their environment. But because man is equally part of the ecosystem, there are no biological laws which guarantee his perpetuation against this background of self-induced change. Reference to evolution as a process of adaptation to environmental change, as we have already seen, does not offer comfort. Indeed, what evolution does, frequently, is to establish characteristics in a population which make it ideally suited to its environment. If the environment is changed, the species may well disappear because of its high adaptation to specific environments. Man-induced elimination is well-documented and cannot therefore be described as "evolutionary" in the sense that is intended. Consequently, man is as much at risk as any other species. Indeed, he may be more at risk in that his capability for adaptation may be less than that of other species. This is particularly likely to be true if we accept that human understanding of the environment lags behind human induced changes in that environment.

What pollution does in many instances is to accelerate the process of ecological succession, particularly by adding enormous quantities of nutrients to the environment in a short period of time compared to the "natural" rate of accretion. Thus, nutrient build up in, say, a lake may be perfectly "natural" and a precursor of the successional change that the changing habitat will bring. But the problem with pollution is that this accelerated successional change is not matched by any corresponding shift in associated populations. The pollution all too frequently eliminates species, thus reducing diversity, or makes the habitat favourable for one dominant species — algae for example — which ousts other species so as to reduce diversity. Thus what at first sight appears to be merely an acceleration of evolutionary change is in effect a retrogressive step to more simple, and less stable, ecosystems.

Pollution also interferes with the various biogeochemical cycling processes within ecosystems — that is, with the natural processes whereby nitrogen, phosphorus, carbon, oxygen, potassium, etc., are absorbed by living species, returned to the environment and re-absorbed. Bormann and Likens (1970) have suggested that biogeochemical cycling is least efficient — nutrient losses are at their highest level — in early successional communities. Since, as we have seen, pollution has the effect of reducing diversity, it can be seen that pollution may greatly reduce the nutrient efficiency of an ecosystem. As all life forms are critically dependent upon the flows of these nutrients, the instability of the ecosystem is greatly increased.

Lastly, pollutants may well be directly toxic to humans. The effect is to generate mutated genes which, because of the ability of humans to preserve mutated species through medical advances, are transferred to new generations. It seems impossible to predict the effects of mutagenic pollution of this direct kind.

We can extract from this very superficial overview just three points of significance. First, pollution has a physical dimension which shows up in the change that pollution induces in the physical environment and hence in the species composition of the ecosystem. We shall have occasion to contrast this with the economic definition of pollution which, as we have seen, is not defined except with reference to the sufferer's utility function. Second, pollution is not just a product of the *scale* of economic activity. It also has a quality dimension which reflects the current technologies used in producing that level of economic activity.

Third, and most important of all, pollution generates a vicious circle. Pollution reduces system maturity, and reduced maturity lessens the ability of the system to withstand further shocks. *Pollution reduces the capability of the system to withstand further pollution.* On this basis there is every reason to think of pollution as something that exhibits increasing marginal social costs. We shall see that this has a direct counterpart in the economic sphere when we come to look at the acceptability of externality correction policy.

2.6 Ecological policy choices

The preceding analysis suggests two very general directions in which environmental policy might go. If ecological stability really is being reduced to the point where further reductions will generate irreversible changes of considerable consequence, a view which Dubos (1969) for example is quite convinced of, then society, in its global sense, can *either* seek to reduce the "shocks" to such a system by reducing pollution, *or* it can seek to alter the configuration of society in such a way that such shocks, even if continued at the present level, are likely to have less and less impact. The former policy is consistent with not altering the entire structure of society, unless of course the sheer fact of implementing pollution reduction policies brings such a change about, while enabling man to continue treating ecosystems as something to be harnessed for high productivity. We would expect such a policy deliberately to avoid simulating the conditions of climax states. The second policy would attempt to simulate the conditions of climax states, by, for example, implementing zero economic growth and zero population growth. This, hopefully, would increase the stability of the system so that, even if pollution continued on a large scale, perhaps due to technological changes within society, it would have less impact on the structure of the ecosystem.

A third option would be to implement both policies — i.e. attempt to simulate the requirements of a steady-state, and use those requirements as instruments for reducing pollution as well. The second and third options appear to underlie documents such as the Ecologist magazine's, "Blueprint for Survival" (1972). The first option, simply reducing pollution, underlies most prescriptions for environmental improvement.

Lastly, of course, we can implement none of the previous policies and continue to behave as if ecosystems, local and global, can absorb pollution shocks, or, if they cannot, treat their demise as something of lesser importance than the benefits pollution-creating goods bring. If the arguments about ecosystem stability are even partly correct, however, this last option is not one that can be sustained for very long.

3

Materials balance and input-output analysis

3.1 Energy and materials throughput

In Chapter 2 we showed that ecosystems are characterized by the principle of *materials circulation* and *one-way energy flow*. Since economic systems are, ultimately, part of wider ecosystems, we should expect some at least of the governing principles of ecosystems to apply to economic systems. In fact, the materials and energy flow characteristics are equally applicable to economic systems and are of vital importance.

First, consider materials flow. Economists are used to thinking of consumption as the "final act" of the economic system: it is at one and the same time where resources end up (i.e. by being consumed) and what the whole economic system exists to serve because, as Chapter 1 showed, "welfare" or "utility" is thought to derive only from an act of consumption. When compared to the physical attributes of the economic system this picture is seen to be seriously deficient. Boulding (1966), in a now classic essay, was perhaps the first to point to the seriousness of this deficiency. We can think of materials as being some of the natural resources we take out of the natural environment. In Fig. 3.1 we see this source and activity being located at the bottom of the diagram where the environment is depicted (partly) as a resource supplier. These materials now "flow" in the direction of the (lined) arrow to the economic production sector where they are processed to become consumable goods. Of course, some of these resources will be energy resources (the long-dashed lines show their flow). Now, we must remember that the first law of thermodynamics tells us that we cannot create or destroy these resources − not in the sense of annihilating them, that is. So, resources flowing into the production sector must go somewhere. First, some will be embodied in consumable goods and will pass to the consumption sector. Second, some will be made into capital equipment and will stay in the production sector, embodied in physical capital. Whereas in economics we are used to thinking of such capital as being "consumed" at some fairly regular rate (depreciation), in terms of physical flows we can generally expect what is often called "sudden death" depreciation — the capital will wear out and will be replaced. The old capital must of course go somewhere else. It will, in fact, appear as a flow of materials from the production sector to the environment — in the form of unwanted capital, i.e. waste. Last, quite substantial quantities of resources will be discarded as waste during the production process whether it is consumer or capital goods that are being made. Energy resources will also be passed on as consumer goods — usually as energy in directly consumable form — or will be "used up" in the production process. Notice, once again, however that this using-up process does not mean the energy is destroyed: it is merely dissipated to the environment, as waste heat and noise. Some of the materials waste in the production sector will be re-used — i.e. "recycled" — so that we can observe a small loop showing a flow of waste materials from the production sector back to the same sector. Energy cannot be recycled because it must obey the one-way-flow rule, so that no such loop exists for energy.

Apart from recycling and storage in capital, Fig. 3.1 shows that whatever is taken out of the environment in the form of physical resources must reappear, in equal weight, as waste or consumer goods. What recycling and capital embodiment do is to alter the time-phasing of this essential equation: that is, eventually, the materials recycled and embodied must also appear as waste. If we now turn out attention to the consumption sector we can see that this essential equivalence also applies there. For, whatever is passed from the production to the consumption sector must also reappear as waste. Some consumer products will be directly consumed in the physical sense by consumers — e.g. agricultural products — and these will then reappear as human waste, or will be stored in humans as "biological capital". But ultimately, humans are themselves waste. All other consumer goods are either directly consumed and disposed of (e.g. a paper tissue, a piece of coal) or are held for varying periods of time and then disposed of (cars, light bulbs, etc.). Of course, some consumer waste is recycled, and this flow is also shown in Fig. 3.1

The combined materials and energy flows from the production and consumption sectors can now be seen to appear as waste disposed of to the environment. For any given time period, these waste flows may be less than, equal to, or greater than the resource extraction for that period: it all depends on how much "embodiment" of materials is taking place in various forms of capital in that period, and how much "sudden death" depreciation is occurring from past flows. It seems reasonable to suppose,

Fig. 3.1

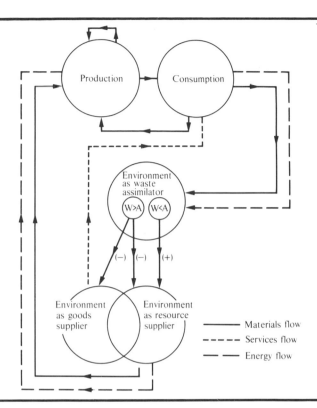

however, that the two flows will be roughly equal for any time period. An essential feature of this extended view of the economic process is that consumption no longer appears as the final act. For whatever is consumed also appears as waste residuals disposed of the environment.

Chapter 2 showed that ecosystems have their own "waste" products which, in a steady-state, are recycled to reappear as nutrients for the ecosystem in such a way as to sustain that system. For non-steady-states the recycling process still operates, but it is likely to generate changes in the structure of the ecosystem. Many of the wastes of the economic system are also degraded by the environment's degrader populations: bacteria in water systems, for example, often deal quickly and efficiently with sewerage. But a crucial new factor enters the picture with respect to such wastes: the environment has a limited *assimilative capacity*. It will not degrade all and any waste. Hence the *quantity* of waste passed on for the environment to degrade becomes important. If this quantity (W) exceeds the environment's assimilative capacity, it will remain as a potentially noxious stock in the environment, eventually preventing the degrader populations themselves from functioning. As far as the environment's other functions are concerned, such a process will: (*a*) prevent the environment being used for amenity or other purposes (stagnant waterways cannot be used for fishing, swimming, or general amenity); and (*b*) will limit the resource supply function (for example by inhibiting the use of such water for domestic or even industrial supply). Instead of a positive materials flow from the "environment as waste assimilator" to the other functions of environment and hence back to the economic system, an excess of waste over assimilative capacity will cause a *negative flow*, as shown in Fig. 3.1. In other words, the size of the resource box is actually reduced by such a process. Equally, of course, there will be a *quality* dimension to waste disposal. If the quality of waste is such as to inhibit the assimilative function of the environment, the same process will ensure: the degrader populations will themselves be prevented from operating and a stock of waste will remain. A small amount of cyanide in an effluent, for example, may be just as important in this respect as a large quantity of sewerage.

Where waste emissions are kept within the bounds of assimilative capacity, we can expect degrader populations to be fairly stable and the wastes will then be properly degraded and recycled as nutrients. We shall see in Chapter 4 that these relationships between waste and assimilative capacity, while simplistic in many respects, permit a useful classification of pollutants which, in turn, will enable us to reconsider the conventional approach to pollution economics.

3.2 Input—output models: some concepts

What section 3.1 described was the *materials balance* view of economic—environmental interaction. This view is implicit in Boulding (1966) but received clear exposition in Ayres and Kneese (1969) and in Kneese, Ayres and D'Arge (1970). These latter works, however, really only deal with materials and energy flows up to the point where these enter the "environment as assimilator" box in Fig. 3.1. What section 3.1 suggested was a way of linking the flows at that point to the biological functions of the environment, and from these back to the economic system.[1]

More formal approaches have been proposed by other writers such as Cumberland (1966, plus later works, mainly unpublished) and Victor (1972). Essentially, the technique used is *input—output analysis*. What input—output analysis does is to relate each industry's demands for each other industry's outputs, and also to relate outputs to final demands by consumers. In this way, the effects of changes in individual industries on each of the other industries can be assessed, as can changes in final demand on each industry. Since the technique is quite general, it is possible to introduce, say, an industrial sector devoted to anti-pollution measures and to assess the effects of such measures on the industrial structure. If prices are put into the model, the effects of such measures on the structure of prices can also be estimated, and so on.

Equally, if we know the relationship between output and wastes, the effects of changes in final demand on waste generation can also be estimated, and further extensions might allow us to estimate the effects of various changes on resource demand. These analyses can become very complex. For a fairly extensive survey the reader is referred to Victor (1972). The remainder of this chapter looks in a fairly simple way at the general principles of input—output as applied to environmental problems.

There are several types of input—output tables. We can illustrate some general principles by looking at an *input—output* table proper. This relates inputs (shown in the first column of Table 3.1(a)), to outputs (shown in the top row of Table 3.1(a)). If we look, for example, at output 1 *one unit* of it requires a certain amount of input 1, a certain amount of input 2, and so on. These required amounts are listed, in the first column of the box in Table 3.1(a) as a_{11}, a_{21}, and so on. The subscript arrangement is easily remembered: the first one refers to *input* and the second to *output*. Hence a_{23} would refer to the amount of input 2 requires to produce *one unit* of output 3. The symbols a_{11}, a_{22}, a_{23}, etc., are called *input coefficients*. The picture given by Table 3.1(a) is static. In the real world we would expect the input coefficients to change with technology and so on. But even the static framework can be useful, as we shall see.

Table 3.1(a)

OUTPUTS

		1	2	3		N
I	1	a_{11}	a_{12}	a_{13}		a_{1N}
N	2	a_{21}	a_{22}	a_{23}		a_{2N}
P	3	a_{31}	a_{32}	a_{33}		a_{3N}
U						
T						
S	N	a_{N1}	a_{N2}	a_{N3}		a_{NN}

Notice that Table 3.1(*a*) tells us nothing about aggregate levels of output. For this we need further information. We "open" the model by introducing a list of *final demands* for the products of each industry. We proceed as follows. If we add the elements in the first *column* in Table 3.1(*a*) we shall have the total cost of inputs, apart from labour and any materials not supplied by other industries, for output 1 per unit of output. If we measure "unit output" as £1 of output, we must have

$$a_{11} + a_{21} + a_{31} + \ldots + a_{N1} < £1$$

If, for example, the left-hand side added up to *more* than £1 output 1 would be costing more to produce than it sells for. Hence the rule — which assumes profit-making — that the sum of the a elements must be less than £1. But, equally, if a unit of output is sold, the revenue must go somewhere. What is missing, of course, in the above irregularity is the *primary input*, say, labour. In this way, we can say that if we add the cost of the primary input per unit output of good 1 to the left-hand side of the inequality we shall have the equation:

$$a_{11} + a_{21} + a_{31} + \cdots + a_{N1} + P_1 = £1$$

We can write this as

$$\sum_{i=1}^{i=n} a_{ij} + P_j = 1$$

Thus the cost of primary input per unit output for any good j must be

$$1 - \sum_{i=1}^{i=n} a_{ij}$$

Now, considering the industry that produces good 1 once more, we denote its output by x_1. This output will need to be equal to the demands by other industries for good 1, plus the final demand of consumers for good 1. In other words

$$x_1 = a_{11}x_1 + a_{12}x_2 + a_{13}x_3 + \cdots + a_{1N}x_N + d_1$$

Thus an expression like $a_{12}x_2$ refers to the demand by industry 2 for good 1 as an input. The expression d_1 is the final demand for good 1. This can be rewritten

$$(1 - a_{11})x_1 - a_{12}x_2 - a_{13}x_3 - \cdots - a_{1N}x_N = d_1 .$$

If we repeat the exercise for good x_2 we shall have

$$-a_{21}x_1 + (1 - a_{22}x_2) - a_{23}x_3 - \cdots - a_{2N}x_N = d_2$$

and so on.

If we now write down the various rows obtained in this way, we shall get a picture as shown in Table 3.1(b).

Table 3.1(b)

$(1 - a_{11})x_1 - a_{12} \cdot x_2 \qquad - a_{13} \cdot x_3 \qquad - \cdots a_{1N}x_N = d_1$

$\qquad - a_{21}\,x_1 + (1 - a_{22}) \cdot x_2 - a_{23}x_3 \qquad - \cdots a_{2N}x_N = d_2$

$\qquad - a_{31}\,x_1 - \qquad a_{32} \cdot x_2 + (1 - a_{33})x_3 \; - \cdots a_{3N}x_N = d_3$

$\qquad - a_N1x_N - a_{N2} \cdot x_2 \qquad - a_{N3} \cdot x_3 \qquad - \cdots + (1 - a_{NN})x_N = d_N$

The reader who is familiar with matrix algebra will know that there is a convenient way of writing Table 3.1(b) down. It will be observed that the expressions $(1 - a_{ij})$ when i = j all occur in a neatly sloping diagonal. This is called the *principal diagonal*. The box-like arrangements of components shown in Tables 3.1(a) and 3.1(b) are known as *matrices*. A matrix that has 1's in the principal diagonal and zero everywhere else is called an identity matrix and is written *I*. A matrix that has the components $-a_{ij}$ is written *A*. Table 3.1(b) is complicated by the appearance of x's as well. In fact, Table 3.1(b) is better written as Table 3.1(c) below.

Table 3.1(c)

$$
\begin{bmatrix}
(1 - a_{11}) - & a_{12} - & a_{13} - \cdots - a_{1N} \\
- a_{21} + (1 - a_{22}) - & a_{23} - \cdots - a_{2N} \\
- a_{31} - & a_{32} + (1 - a_{33}) - \cdots - a_{3N} \\
- a_{N1} - & a_{N2} - & a_{N3} - \cdots + (1 - a_{NN})
\end{bmatrix}
\begin{bmatrix}
x_1 \\ x_2 \\ x_3 \\ x_N
\end{bmatrix}
=
\begin{bmatrix}
d_1 \\ d_2 \\ d_3 \\ d_4
\end{bmatrix}
$$

The matrix with the a_{ij}'s and $1 - a_{ij}$'s is known as the *coefficient matrix* and, in this case, can be written as the sum of the identity matrix *I* and the matrix $-A$, i.e. as $I - A$. This matrix is to be multiplied by the column of x's, known as an *output vector*. (The reader can satisfy himself that multiplying a matrix by a vector will achieve the same result as shown in Table 3.1(b), by referring to any text on mathematical principles.) This multiplied result must be equal to the *final demand vector*. In other words, what is in Table 3.1(c) can be written simply as

$$(I - A) \cdot x = d$$

Of course, while such an arrangement may be very neat, it is not instructive unless it helps us answer some questions. Even at this elementary illustrative level we can begin to see what uses such an approach might be put to. If it were possible to "solve" the last equation above for x we shall be able to say what levels of output will be necessary in each industry in order to meet some expected demand, or some planned demand. If, say, we have a national plan in which we have an overall growth rate established and some pattern of demand planned, we shall be able to say what output each industry will have to aim for. As we shall see, there are many other uses. Actually "solving" the equation above is not complex once certain principles have been mastered. These principles generally lie outside the scope of this book. But their essence is that we can treat the equation

$$(I - A) \cdot x = d$$

as if it was an ordinary equation. To solve for x then we would simply write

$$x = d/(I - A) = (I - A)^{-1} \cdot d$$

It will be noted that, to find the requisite values of x we need only to find the *inverse* of the matrix $(I - A)$. Not all matrices have inverses and there are certain tests to find out whether any particular matrix is capable of "inversion". Those that are capable of inversion are called *nonsingular matrices* and well-established tests exist for determining nonsingularity. If the matrix passes this test further techniques exist for inverting it, although matrices do not have to be very large before the actual process of inversion becomes very complicated. It is in fact usually left to computers.

3.3 Input—output models: commodity by industry approaches

Section 3.2 illustrated some input—output concepts in the context of an input—output matrix proper. Following Victor (1972) we may extend the idea to a more general framework. Figure 3.2 shows various matrices, vectors and some totals (the totals appear as single figures and not as vectors or matrices — they are called *scalars*).

Instead of directly relating inputs to outputs, Fig. 3.2 relates to *commodities* to *industries*. We can see that there are several sets of interrelationships subsumed in Fig. 3.2. For example, the elements in matrix A relates industrial demand for commodities to be used as inputs. Matrix B looks at this relationship in a different way — it records the sales of each com-

Fig. 3.2

	Commodities 1,2..................N	Industries 1......................M	Final demand 1..............G	Totals
Commodities 1 2 ⋮ N		A	D	F
Industries 1 ⋮ M	B			G
Primary inputs 1 ⋮ P		C	E	H
Totals	K	L	M	J

modity by each industry. Matrix C will show the expenditure by each industry on each primary input. Matrix D will show, by category of final demand, the demand for each commodity. If final demands are not categorized, matrix D will just have one category of final demand and hence will become a vector. Matrix E relates final demand categories to expenditure on primary inputs. Looking at the "totals" column, we have vector F showing the total demand (industrial plus final) for each commodity; vector G shows the total outputs of each industry; vector H the total expenditures on each primary input; and scalar J shows the total expenditure on all commodities and all primary inputs. Looking, finally, at the final row we have K, a vector showing total outputs of commodities; vector L showing total inputs to industry; and vector M, showing total expenditure by category of final demand on all inputs.

3.4 Input–output models: including the environment

We can now consider how Fig. 3.2 can be extended to include the environment. Figure 3.3 repeats Fig. 3.2 but with "the environment" introduced by way of an entry "environmental commodities" and "discharges to environment".[2] One immediate problem arises in that, as we have seen, the entries in the other matrices are in money terms — e.g. a particular value of an input per unit value of output. Since, by definition, the environment as receiver of waste has no observed market valuation, we cannot extend these units to the matrices that contain the environment as source or destination of materials flows. Hence we have to bear in mind that waste discharges and the withdrawal of environmental commodities are measured in physical terms, and the measure used will be *weight*.

Looking at Fig. 3.3 we see that there are now six further entries in need of explanation, N, O, P, Q, R, S. Matrix N shows the amount of waste discharged as a result of the final demand for commodities. Matrix O shows the discharge of waste by industry. P will be a vector and will show the total amount of waste discharged by category of waste. Looking at the bottom row of Fig. 3.3, matrix Q will show the inputs of environmental commodities to economic commodities. Matrix R will show the input of environmental commodities to industries, and vector S will show the total input of environmental commodities to industry and final demand.

Fig. 3.3

	Commodities	Industries	Final demand	Total	Waste discharge to environment
Commodities					N
Industries					O
Primary inputs					
Totals					P
Environmental commodities	Q	R		S	

Progressing from this basic framework of analysis to an input—output table that can be used for practical purposes involves many complex steps. For example, consider matrix R in Fig. 3.3. This has elements r_{ij}, the input of the ith "environmental commodity" to the jth industry. But what this relationship looks like is another matter. A common assumption with primary inputs is to make these inputs proportional to industrial output, and this assumption has been used, for example by Victor (1972), also to describe the relationship in the R matrix — i.e. environmental commodity inputs are held to be proportional to industrial output. Making assumptions of this kind, the extended input—output model can be manipulated to answer such questions as "what effect would a change in final demand have on industrial activity and hence on demands for environmental commodities and on the amounts and types of waste discharged?" This type of question is clearly important. Rather than detail the actual way in which the various input—output-environment models that now exist can be manipulated, the next section briefly surveys some of the applications of these models.

3.5 Applications of input—output-environment models

Victor's "ecologic impact" tables

Victor (1972) has produced some estimates of the demand for water (an ecologic commodity in his terminology) by industry, and the discharge of wastes by industry, for the Canadian economy. The relevant figures are by weight, as explained above. For example, one dollar's worth of final demand for paper and paper products requires 1,245 lb of water, generates 0.33 lb of biochemical oxygen demand (a measure of the demand for oxygen by wastes disposed of to watercourses), generates 0.021 lb of phenols, 0.18 lb of sulphur dioxide, and so on. If we had some procedure for evaluating the relative importance of each waste discharged, we could consider deriving a "pollution league table" from such results. There could be various approaches. First, we might simply select pollutants widely regarded as being very important from an ecological point of view, and list industries according to the input—output coefficient that shows how much pollutant is produced per unit value of output. Suppose, for example, we select metals waste (item 13 in Victor's list of wastes), we find that rubber products generate 0.003 lb of metals waste per $1 of output, petroleum and coal products generate 0.004 lb, and chemical products generate 0.0038 lb. Unfortunately, even this separating out of the relevant industries does not supply us with sufficient detail because some metal wastes are more important than others. Unless the input—output table is sufficiently disaggregated we shall not be able to use this information for any policy purpose. Second, developing the first idea, we would need to allow for the size of total output in each industry, so as to assess the total waste from each industry. Finally, and this is Victor's approach, we can attempt to place a monetary valuation on the environmental commodities and discharges. To do this, of course, requires us to secure shadow prices reflecting society's evaluation of these items, and the conceptual basis for doing this was described in Chapter 1. But, as will repeatedly be seen to be the case, going from cost—benefit theory to practice is at the very least difficult, and is often virtually impossible in that, although *some* figure can be obtained, it has no meaning. Victor's study uses only relative weights — i.e. no attempt was made to put an absolute money value on items — and his weights are derived by asking an expert to assign them. As argued in Chapter 1, relative valuations can be made on any reasoned basis, and it can then be seen to what extent varying the valuations alters the final result. Victor (1972, p. 192) reports that a sensitivity test of this kind was undertaken and that "the results . . . were not greatly affected despite some fairly dramatic changes in the relative weights given to the ecologic commodities". Nonetheless, the failure to secure any wider consensus makes Victor's procedure very dubious, although there is no reason why it should not be extended in a more rigorous fashion since, in the end, some valuation has to be made and if it cannot be obtained from cost—benefit studies, nor from expert consensus, it will occur through implicit government action.

Victor's results, using his weighting system, show petroleum and coal products to have the highest (relative) ecologic cost, after which come coal, utilities, paper and paper products, non-ferrous metal basic products, iron and steel basic products, and so on. It may be asked why the elaborate structure of an input—output model is needed in order to obtain this result when the experts apparently already know the relative valuations. The answer of course is that it requires the input—output table to uncover the true demand by each industry for all other products, since many pollutants will already be "embodied" in the inputs to industries.

Victor's model applied to transport changes

Victor (1972) further applies his model to an hypothetical policy change with respect to transport. He asks what would happen to his index of ecologic costs if private automobile transport is reduced by 50 per cent and replaced with public transport. To do this, he alters the final demand vector so as to reflect this supposed change, and then traces the effects on the inputs and outputs of "ecologic commodities". Not surprisingly, the main effect is to reduce the demand for petroleum commodities and this in turn reduces "ecologic cost" by between 6.5 and 8 per cent (depending on which model is used).

Fazio and Cascio's model for Italy

One of the major uses for input—output tables in the environment field has been the assessment of the effects of antipollution measures on various of the more "conventional" economic magnitudes, such as industrial output, GNP, exports and imports, price levels, and so on. Generally, these models do not venture far from the more orthodox input–output models, and certainly do not include anything as venturesome as the environment matrices in Victor's models. Nonetheless, they permit answers to some vital questions. Thus, many countries have argued that antipollution measures are luxuries that cannot be afforded in terms of reduced national growth rates or price increases. The use of input–output models can be important in supporting or denying these arguments.

One model, by Fazio and Cascio (1972) has attempted to estimate the impact of antipollution measures on Italian output and prices. Concentrating on six, heavily polluting industries, the authors show that certain agreed antipollution measures will raise costs and prices as follows:

Industry	% Cost increase	% Price increase
Chemicals	5.0	5.0
Sugar	3.8	3.4
Alcoholic beverages	3.4	3.0
Plastics	3.0	3.0
Petroleum derivatives	2.5	2.5
Pharmaceuticals	2.0	2.0

The CONSAD study

A more ambitious project, relating to the United States, has been carried out by the CONSAD Research Corporation in the USA (CONSAD, 1971; Lakshmanan and Lo, 1972). The objective of this model is primarily to determine the regional impact of pollution control cost increases due to environmental policy measures. Because it is regional in orientation the input–output matrix is more complex than those described in sections 3.2 to 3.4 in that it is both inter-industry and inter-regional. It relates only to specific air pollutants, and three possible policy measures were considered. These were: (a) that all control costs would be borne by industry; (b) that the free play of markets would be allowed to determine the incidence of control costs, producers passing on that part of the costs they think "the market will bear"; (c) a cost-sharing policy in which government and industry share the control costs equally.

Some of the results are of interest. When the alternative strategies were considered for the period 1970–75 it was found that heavy polluting industries were able, if they had to, to bear the control costs without passing on significant price increases. According to the CONSAD study this generated net social benefits — i.e. pollution abatement benefits exceeded control costs — but it is difficult to place any faith in this particular result because of the general absence of any rigorous technique for estimating benefits. If industries are allowed to pass on cost increases (strategy *b*) the model predicted price increases of only 0.4 per cent, with consumers and producers bearing roughly equal proportions of the cost incidence. Under the cost-sharing strategy, consumers bear the same price increases as under strategy *b* *plus* their contribution to the government's tax revenue required to subsidize producers. This kind of analysis, defective though it may be in many ways, is useful in that it indicates the possible different distribution of abatement costs according to the different strategies adopted. If the model is disaggregated by region, it will also show the geographical incidence of costs, a factor of considerable importance as long as governments have regional policies. It is not a satisfactory means of assessing the entire incidence of pollution control measures unless the benefit measurement problem is overcome since benefits will also be distributed between producers, consumers and regions. Nonetheless, direct effects on consumption may be estimated as a rough indicator of this kind of effect.

Leontief's extended input—output tables
Professor Wassily Leontief has extended input—output tables, which he originated, to include a pollution abatement sector (Leontief, 1970). This is an important departure since pollution abatement is itself an industry requiring inputs from other industries. Also, *pollution coefficients* are estimated, relating tons of pollutant to some unit of value of industrial output. Only air pollution is considered in the model. No flow from the environment to industry is incorporated so that, like most of the other models, the principle of materials balance is not included in the model. Victor's models (Victor, 1972) are the exception to this general rule.

Figure 3.4 shows the general structure of Leontief's extended model. Thus, matrix A is the traditional input—output matrix relating inputs to outputs, consisting of elements a_{ij}. Matrix B relates industrial inputs to pollution elimination activities, which, as we noted, is a coordinal feature of Leontief's system. Matrix C relates pollution emissions to industrial outputs, so that the components here are the pollution coefficients. Matrix D relates antipollution activities to pollution, so that the elements will tell us how much pollution reduction occurs as a result of antipollution activity.

By manipulating the model, Leontief is able to assess the effect on the level of emissions in individual industries of particular levels of final demand. At the aggregate level, the model permits the estimation of the total level of pollution that will result if a given projected level of final demand occurs. The model can also estimate the price effects of particular

Fig. 3.4

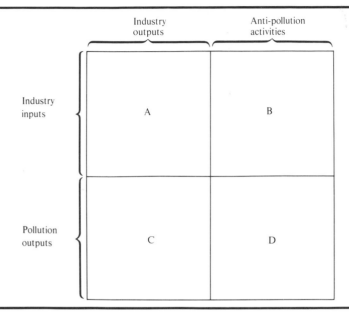

antipollution measures, a feature of input—output, as we have seen, that appears to be a desirable one from the point of view of governments.

3.6 Concluding notes

This chapter has been concerned with two things. First, it has attempted to show that the ecological principles of materials balance and that one-way energy flow govern the economic system as much as they govern ecological systems. Essentially, whatever is produced and consumed must eventually be disposed of. The significance of this principle for pollution is discussed in more detail in the next chapter. Second, a natural extension of the view that materials flow through the economy is to treat economic—environment interaction in terms of extended input—output models. We observed that the basic principles of input—output could be extended in this way and looked at just a few of the applications of the principle. We noted that not all input—output models extended in this way have observed the principle of materials balance. Nonetheless, they exist to answer some very important policy questions such as what impact pollution control measures will have. The models discussed here are but a few of those actually in existence. Almost universally, these models are still being developed. Some are operational and have been used, notably in America and Japan.

In principle, input—output models can be used to evaluate policies if they are extended to contain some valuation procedure. We noted that one attempt in this direction, that of Victor (1972) was rather weak, but that there is possible scope for extending the basic idea of consensus expert valuation. Some input models do contain explicit benefit—cost frameworks but, to date, no significant advances appear to have been made in this area. As we shall see, the problems of valuation underlie virtually all environmental analyses. Whether input—output models will be successfully applied to environmental problems depends first on whether the very detailed information they require will ever be available, and second on whether the well-known defects of input—output analysis are thought to render their results too untrustworthy. For example, the input—output coefficients are themselves assumed static, so that the use of such models to *predict* the effects of future patterns of final demand is widely held to be a tendentious issue.

Notes

1.   There are other approaches which attempt such a link. See, for example, Daly (1968). An excellent review of most of the relevant models is to be found in Victor (1972).

2.   Victor (1972) refers to these as "ecologic commodities" and separates them according to whether they are discharged to, or withdrawn from land, water or air. Hence, in Victor's analysis the matrices discussed below are *partitioned* to allow for this categorization. Since wastes discharged to the environment are not commodities in the normal sense, this usage has been avoided here.

4

The nature of pollution: economics and ecology

4.1 A classification of pollution

Confusion can easily arise in any discussion about pollution if terminology is not made clear. This is certainly true of the word "pollution" which is used in many different ways to refer to different things. Economists, in particular, tend to define pollution in a different way to, say, ecologists or biologists. It is not surprising, then, to discover that communication across different disciplines becomes obscured. One of the aims of this chapter is to attempt a taxonomy of pollution which will help to highlight different definitions. Definitions are, of course, value-free. They are simply declarations about how we intend to use words. But whether a definition is useful will depend on what role we intend it to play. If, for example, we choose a particular definition and then assert that all pollution is bad and should be eliminated, our definition will determine the extent of the proposed social policy. Clearly, then, it matters how we define pollution if we have policy ends in mind. Equally, we should have some basis on which to judge whether a particular pollutant is important or not. If our criterion is, say, unsightliness, then glass bottles become an important pollutant. They will also be important if our criterion relates to saving on "virgin" materials by recycling. But they are unlikely to be important if our concern is with ecosystem stability or with the general functioning of life-support systems.

To establish a taxonomy we shall make use of the concept of *assimilative capacity* discussed in Chapters 2 and 3. Now, this concept is quite widely used in environmental literature, but it is a slippery one. We observed that, if residuals are disposed of to the environment, then there exists some capacity in the environment, comprised of degrader populations, which will, over a period of time, transform the waste in such a way as to render it harmless, and/or return it as nutrients to the ecosystem. It will help if we can think of this assimilation process as being virtually instantaneous, but not so immediate that it will accommodate any amount of waste, or any quality of waste. That is, for any chosen period of time, there will be some limit as to the amount of waste the environment can assimilate. It will also help if we think of "the environment" as referring to some homogeneous system. In practice, it must refer to many different ecosystems which, nonetheless, are linked to each other.

The assumption of instantaneous assimilation is clearly unrealistic. In practice we know that degrader populations in rivers, say, take time to assimilate the wastes put into the rivers. During the actual process of assimilation we can expect the oxygen content of the water to decline and then, as assimilation is completed, to rise (the so-called "oxygen sag"). One physical measure of pollution relates to the river's oxygen content, often measured by the river's dissolved oxygen level or by biochemical oxygen demand (BOD) on the wastes. Hence, on this definition of pollution, there will be variations in the degree of pollution *during* the assimilation process. But, if the wastes disposed of to the receiving waters are within the assimilative capacity of the waters, we know that this pollution must be temporary. It is this temporary aspect that we shall, generally, ignore in the ensuing analysis, although we shall show how it can be incorporated. Proceeding in this way enables us to highlight several important features of the pollution process.

Figure 4.1 illustrates the fundamental physical features of assimilative capacity and pollution.

The diagram shows waste (W), in physical units, as a positive function of economic output (X). While it is *possible* for technology to change in such a way as to reduce the physical volume of waste per unit of output so that total waste falls as output increases, there seems little doubt that this is not what actually occurs. We therefore show the waste function as increasing with output (with linearity assumed only for convenience). Also shown is the assimilative capacity of the environment. When the amount of waste reaches W_E, with a level of economic activity X_E, the environment is not capable of receiving further waste. As we shall see, for certain wastes, this generates a process that is rather important for policy decisions about pollution.

Now, for certain types of waste, the assimilative capacity of the environment as we have so far defined it is, effectively, zero. For any time span relevant to policy decisions, glass bottles cannot be degraded by the environment because degrader populations do not exist. On the other hand, there are no biological effects on ecosystem populations from disposing of such waste, so that, physically, it would not seem to matter very much if we throw glass bottles away. But an economic definition of

Fig. 4.1

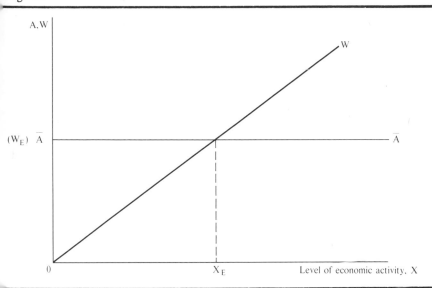

pollution would show that it does matter because at some stage, individuals will begin to express a dispreference for the unsightliness of glass bottles. As we saw in Chapter 1, this provides the basis for defining *external cost*. In this case, then, economic definitions will tend to dictate that action take place to inhibit glass bottle disposal, whereas physical definitions will tend to suggest that there is no pollution.

We thus establish our first category of wastes. These have the attributes that assimilative capacity (A) for them is effectively zero, while biological effects (B) are also zero. Economic effects (E) may or may not be positive in the sense that external effects may or may not be present. If they are present, "economic pollution" exists but physical pollution does not. If they are not present, neither economic nor physical pollution exists. This category is classified in Fig. 4.2.

Now consider a second category of wastes for which $A = 0$, but where

Fig. 4.2

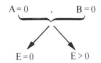

biological effects are significant. Such wastes might be mercury or cadmium, toxic metals which cannot be degraded by the environment $(A = 0)$, but which have direct toxicological effects on ecosystem occupants, causing disease, mutation and death. Economic effects exist, either because of the loss of commercial foodstuffs through poisoning, or because of toxic effects on humans (recall the food chain argument), or because of concern by humans over the effects on non-human species. In many cases, however, these effects will be temporally and geographically distant from the source of pollution. This is because many of these pollutants "travel" in ecosystem food chains, or in water and air currents, and because they are often cumulative, having no directly observable harmful effects until they have cumulated to a "threshold" level. The process of cumulation may take many years, perhaps a lifetime as far as direct consumption is concerned, and perhaps generations if we think of the build-up of some radioactive elements. These other features are considered in more detail for the example of cadmium in section 4.5. For the moment, we need to note that we have a further category of wastes, the features of which are noted in Fig. 4.3.

Fig. 4.3

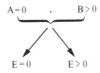

For completeness, we add the possibility that, if no-one cares about the biological effects of these wastes, there can be no economic effect. The difficulties of thinking directly in terms of economic effects for this category are discussed in section 4.4.

Finally, we consider the situation for which A exceeds zero and is not infinite. Here the relationship between the amount of waste (W) and the level of assimilative capacity is important. If W is less than A the system degrades the waste and there can be no biological or economic effects, at least not in the sense of permanent effects. In the short-run such effects can and do exist, as we noted above. Where W exceeds A, however, biological effects must occur, and economic effects *may* occur, depending upon whether any individuals are perturbed by the biological effects. The most we can say, then, is that external costs can be positive only *after* the assimilative capacity of the environment has been exceeded. Figure 4.4 shows the categorization for these pollutants and Fig. 4.5 shows how we can relate external costs to the physical components of Fig. 4.1.[1]

Fig. 4.4

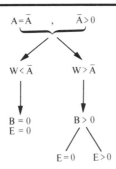

The top half of Fig. 4.5 repeats Fig. 4.1 and the lower half shows *marginal external cost* (this facilitates an analysis of the implications for policy in section 4.3). It will be seen that MEC starts at X_E. It could start further to the right. All that has been shown is that it cannot begin to the left of X_E, but we shall see that this is an important conclusion.

Fig. 4.5

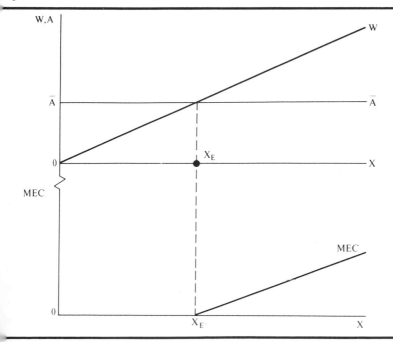

62

4.2 Dynamic ecological effects

Reference to Fig. 4.5 will show that X and W are flows. Suppose now that we operate the economic system such that, for these pollutants, the level of waste is above assimilative capacity — i.e. we operate to the right of X_E. What will be the effects of doing this? Chapter 2 emphasized a most important aspect of the effects of pollution of ecosystems. This was that *pollution makes the system less capable of withstanding further pollution.* What happens is that an excess of W over A has, as one of its biological effects, a reduction in the degrader populations whose function it is to assimilate waste. In other words, operating to the right of X_E must generate a downwards movement in A. What the magnitude of this movement will be will depend on the physical properties of the pollutants in question and the flexibility of the ecosystem. Now, if A falls, external effects *may* occur at lower levels of X than before. This is shown in Fig. 4.6. The downward shift in A from A_0 to A_1 causes MEC_0 to shift

Fig. 4.6

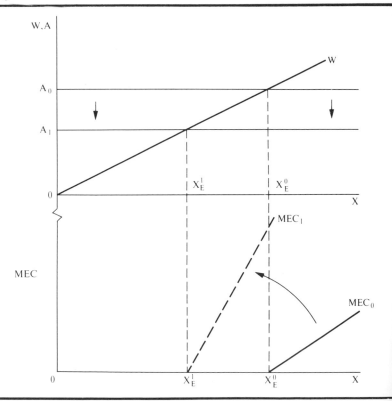

leftwards to MEC_1. Note that the slope of MEC_1 is now steeper than MEC_0 because a given unit of economic activity, and hence of waste, now takes place in the context of a lower assimilative capacity: the ratio A/X is now smaller. If the level of output in the economy is not adjusted, the level of A will be shifted further downwards and the process will be repeated. Even if output is adjusted from some level to the right of X_E^0 to a level below X_E^0 but above X_E^1, the dynamic process must continue. Only if output is reduced to X_E^0 (for the initial case) or X_E^1 (after the first downward shift of A) can this dynamic process be halted.

4.3 Social policy and dynamic ecological effects

We can now introduce social benefits into the picture in order to see whether the dynamic process noted in the previous section has any implication for policy. Figure 4.7 repeats Fig. 4.6 but adds marginal net social benefits (MNSB) where these are defined as marginal social benefits net of any private costs but not net of any external costs. In the case of a

Fig. 4.7

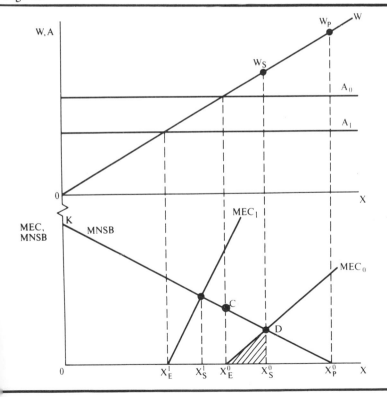

firm that imposes external costs but no external benefits, MNSB would be a marginal profits curve.

If we begin with the A_0 situation we can consider three "solutions" to the system. First, at X_P^0 we have the situation that will result from unconstrained private profit maximization since firms will be indifferent to the external costs they impose. This results in a level of waste W_P which is clearly in excess of A_0. Hence, the dynamic process must begin. If no action is taken to correct the level of output X_P^0 there will be nothing to stop the process until A coincides with the OX axis in the upper diagram, which means an MEC curve (in the lower diagram) coincident with the vertical axis. Presumably, this is one way of depicting the "doom" scenario that many popular analyses suggest could be the outcome of unconstrained economic activity. Here at least we have an analysis which shows the mechanics of the process.

Second, consider the social optimum, defined in the Pareto sense. For A_0 this occurs at X_S^0 since MNSB = MEC at this point (see below for the relevance of this equivalence). The "optimum externality" is shown by the shaded area between X_E^0 and X_S^0. But what is significant in this context is that this social optimum cannot prevent the dynamic ecological process noted earlier. For X_S^0 is consistent with a waste level W_S and this exceeds A_0. Hence the process again generates a "doom" solution, even if output is continually corrected to the new social optimum as each shift in A_0 occurs. Thus the move to A_1 entails a new Pareto optimum of X_S^1 but this too is not sufficient to prevent further downward shifts in A.

The problem obviously arises because the maximum levels of output that are "ecologically safe" (the X_E's) do not coincide with the levels of output that are dictated by Pareto optimality considerations. The difference between the two has been called "the ecological gap" (Pearce, 1973; 1974a; 1974b). The X_S points are optima in the Paretian sense since MNSB = MEC. If the polluting agency is a firm, MNSB = P − MPC, where P refers to price and MPC to marginal private costs. Hence MNSB = MEC is the same as saying P − MPC = MEC, or P = MPC + MEC. This, as we saw in Chapter 1, is the requirement for Pareto optimality. The X_E points are not "ecological" optima − rather, they are the points of maximum economic output consistent with the ecological constraint that the ecological gap should be zero. The latter constraint is established by the fact that ecological gaps greater than zero induce the dynamic ecological process we have described. The X_E points *are* optima if we say that the objective function is to maximize net social benefits subject to the constraint that the ecological gap be zero.

It is important to note that the effect of maintaining Pareto optimal levels of output in the current period is to generate an ecological gap, the disadvantages of which are felt in *future* periods. That is, the gap involves a process whereby A is shifted downwards, thus reducing the capability of the system to withstand future pollution shocks. This could easily entail a policy for future generations whereby they have to reduce output levels *below* even the X_E's in Fig. 4.7 simply to "mark time" and deal with the effects of the stock of past pollution. In short, the existence of the ecological gap provides us with a foundation for a process whereby the real burden of negative externality is shifted forward to future generations. If future generations matter at all — and it is difficult to see how this generation can morally assume the right to remove a future generation's right to exist (see Chapter 1) — then the process of valuing current social costs of pollution will systematically fail to accommodate this effect of the growing stock of pollution.

The argument so far is that X_E indicates an ecologically stable output, while X_S indicates the Pareto optimal output. Further, X_S systematically implies output levels higher than the ecologically stable levels. Clearly, however, if cost–benefit analysis could be carried out in some "ideal" fashion, it could be argued that it would accommodate the instability costs implicit in the ecological gap. As such, X_E and X_S would coincide. But inspection of Fig. 4.7 show that *this can only be true if MEC rises vertically*. Presumably, such an event would mean that social costs are infinite, and we have suggested that this is one way of talking about ecological crisis in the sense of some disintegration of the life-support system.

The suggestion here is that this outcome of the analysis is not at all absurd. For if ecological instability entails risks of large-scale non-survival it is pertinent to ask what utility number we place on the prevention of such an event. The question itself raises the prospect that, in this context, utility functions are unbounded. The fact that instability entails some positive probability of non-survival which may be less than unity does not affect the answer, since a non-member multiplied by a probability is still a non-member. Looked at in this way, our "ideal" cost–benefit analysis is redundant. To secure such an analysis requires prior physical knowledge of where on the output scale ecological crisis might occur. To engage in a further analysis which could only serve to identify the same output level would be to undertake a redundant exercise.

Now, it might be objected that no population, small or large ever expects to exist without *some* risk of non-survival. If so, no-one is likely to countenance systematic change in social systems so as to set pollution standards using X_E criteria instead of X_S criteria. That is, all communities, now and in the future, are unlikely to opt for the safety-first "optimum" X_E. There is clearly a trade-off in Fig. 4.7 between X_E^0 and X_S: X_S can only be achieved by accepting some system instability with its consequent survival risks; X_E^0 can only be achieved by sacrificing benefits of $X_E^0 X_S^0 DC$. And this trade-off will hold for each system analysed. Since the analysis of trade-offs is the very subject matter of economics, it would seem that economics should provide some rules for choosing a point somewhere to the right of X_E but not beyond X_S.

However, there are several reasons why externality approaches are likely to omit significant elements of social costs. The essential reason is that the assessment of instability risks has not, to date, even entered into the *a priori* reasoning of economic orthodoxy. To put it another way — the trade-off is between survival risk and flows of economic benefits. This trade-off cannot be presented in the form of comparable monetary figures. But it could, presumably, be presented in the form of some monetary figure for foregone benefits and some assessment of risk. Such an approach has parallels in all risk-taking activity, and the idea that people should be able to express monetary willingness to pay to avoid risks of death has been argued forcibly by economists. However, for the issue to be presented to people it must be necessary for the risks to be perceptible. But cost—benefit proceeds by the analysis of micro-decisions — and the impact of each decision on ecological instability is likely to be imperceptible. Therefore, the effect on survival risks will be imperceptible. Taken in aggregate, however, the risks must be positive and perceptible. Simply because partial analyses have no "systems orientation" the risk is that the trade-off will never actually be presented for anyone to be able to make a choice.

The non-applicability of economics to such *total* changes has, of course, been noted before. The suggestion here is that its relevance to environmental issues has not been noted, although Edel (1973) has recently put the point well: "Survival . . . is an either/or matter, not a question of degree. Ecology has thus been less concerned than economics for the determination of the exact optimum level of production. On the other hand, it has been more concerned than economics with how systems may change or even fail to survive."

We can approach the apparent incompatibility between cost—benefit approaches and "ecological" approaches depicted in Fig. 4.7 in another way. If we think of the shifts in MEC due to the dynamic ecological process as occurring in discrete time periods, we can add up the various costs and benefits associated with: (*a*) a policy of initially settling at X_E^0; and (*b*) a policy of repeatedly adjusting for Pareto optimal outputs. Under policy (*a*) we shall have gross benefits equal to the area under the MNSB curve up to output X_E^0 and, since there are no external costs, gross benefits equal net benefits. This flow of net benefits accrues each time period, without end. Under policy (*b*) we see that net benefits in the *initial* time period will be greater than they will under the "ecological" policy. They are in fact equal to the area under MNSB up to X_S^0 *minus* the shaded area of optimal externality shown. In the next period, however, net benefits are reduced to the area under MNSB up to X_S^1 *minus* the area under MEC^1 between X_E^1 and X_S^1. This second period net benefit is clearly less than the second period net benefit under the "ecological" policy. Similarly, the third period net benefit will be smaller still. We can conclude that the sum of net benefits over time will be less under the Paretian approach than under the ecological approach: (i) because the former policy results in a finite set of time periods over which benefits and costs are calculated; and (ii) because net benefits are smaller in every period except the initial one.

However, we now have two possibilities for arguing that the cost–benefit approach will yield the "right" result. The first is that, with a zero discount rate, an "ideal" cost–benefit will dictate X_E^0 as the initial optimum after all. It will do this because it will allow for the dynamic ecological externality argument and will build this into the cost–benefit analysis. Quite simply, as our argument above showed, net social benefits are highest (when aggregated over time) under a policy of opting for X_E^0 than under a policy of opting for X_S^0. That is, if our cost–benefit study is "dynamic" it will automatically identify X_E^0 as the dynamic optimum. Certainly, economics abounds with examples in which the "static" optimum (X_S^0) is not formally equivalent to the dynamic optimum (X_E^0). However, against this possibility must be posed all the doubts raised above as to whether a cost–benefit study ever would identify "systems effects" of the kind we are discussing.

The second possibility arises in a context where the discount rate is not zero. In our example only the initial period secures net benefits higher under the Paretian policy than under the ecological policy. But, of course, if the shifts are small, this situation might characterize quite a number of time periods before the "ecological" policy is shown to be superior. If this is so, and if future gains and losses are discounted heavily because of a high social discount rate, it is quite possible that the cost–benefit approach will dictate the "right" result, namely, one of repeatedly adjusting to find the Pareto optimal level of output. Now while this is happening, of course, nothing will alter the fact that the physical process of increasing instability is carrying on. Social and physical behaviour of the system will therefore be acting in opposite directions. But the reason society will not be worried about the ultimate fate of the system is precisely because it has discounted the future so heavily. Positive discount rates simply do mean that current society is revealed to care little or nothing about future society perhaps 100 years hence. *If* this view can be justified — i.e. if there is some sort of optimal date for "ending the world" — then X_E^0 in Fig. 4.7 really may not be a dynamic optimum at all and the cost—benefit approach could be correct. The issue, as we have seen. is reduced to one of justifying positive discount rates in terms of intergenerational equity.

4.4 Pollution and technological change

Although the preceding analysis has looked, in an extremely simplified fashion, at the dynamic ecological effects of pollution and their implication for pollution abatement policy, other dynamic elements are missing from the model. Not the least of these concerns technological change. The waste generation function in the upper part of the diagrams in sections 4.2 and 4.3 shows waste levels increasing with levels of economic activity. It is quite possible, however, for technological change to result in a reduction in waste per unit of output. This is in fact a fairly common feature of some new technologies in many industries such as the paper and pulp industry which is widely regarded as an industry that has particularly serious pollution problems. The improvement in the "pollution content"

Fig. 4.8

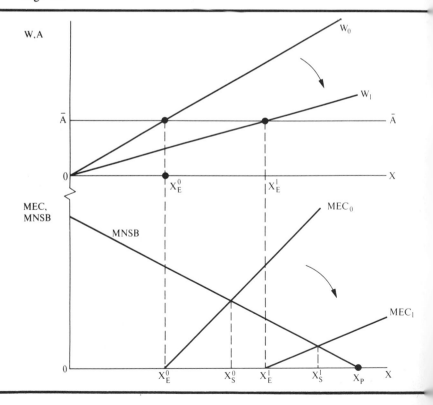

of these new technologies is not necessarily due to any social pressures or legislation, although that is quite often the case — especially with new automotive technologies — but is due simply to the fact that the new technology replaces old and much depreciated equipment which tends to be heavily polluting.

If technological change behaves in the manner suggested above, we would expect the W function to shift downwards, pivoting about its origin. This is shown in Fig. 4.8. The effect on the various optima is shown in the lower half of the diagram. If MEC responds to the change in the A/W ratio, we shall have the shift shown. There will be a new Pareto optimum as indicated. If the economy is operated in such a way as to secure Pareto optimality[2] we can see that the effect of technological change in no way alters the fact that an ecological gap continues to exist. Hence, if this policy is followed, technological change does not inhibit the operation of the dynamic ecological process noted above. On the other hand, if policy is designed so as to remain at the old social optimum, X_S^0 in Fig. 4.8, then, obviously, technological change will have secured a point closer to the ecologically constrained social optimum.

The effects of technological change, then, are ambivalent in that they are contingent upon whichever social policy is chosen. More than this, however, it has been widely argued that technological change does not operate in the fashion suggested above. Commoner (1971), for example, has suggested that changes in technology, on balance, *add* to the pollution burden. This is because the *amounts* of waste increase and also because their *nature* is altered. Effectively, what we have, in our terminology, is not just an increase in situations in which W > A, but also a shift away from those wastes for which A > 0 to those wastes for which A = 0 and B > 0. Our diagrammatic presentation does not permit us to show the qualitative changes. But we can bear them in mind by saying that what we have shown is what we might call "scale instability" — the ecological instability due to the level of economic activity — while what Commoner (1971) is drawing our attention to is "technological instability". This terminology is discussed further in Pearce (1974*b*).

4.5 Stock pollutants: the example of cadmium

In classifying pollution we noted that for one case where A = 0 and B > 0, there are other features which make conventional analysis complex. This section looks briefly at one such pollutant, cadmium, and tries to illustrate the problems that arise.[3]

The essential features of a chemical pollutant like cadmium are:

First, it is non-degradable or only slowly degraded, and hence persists in the environment. If the rate of emission is positive over time, the result is an accumulated *stock* of pollutant. Social damage from this stock may be considered to proceed in a stepwise fashion such that each increment in the stock may be judged harmless until some threshold is exceeded.

Second it tends to be invisible in its effects up to the identified threshold. In other words, damage is perceived only after the thresholds have been reached. Even then, the threshold level of stock will be related to social damage in a complex fashion: the incidence of harm may be geographically and temporally distant from the emission source. This contrasts with the "flow" pollutants which tend to be more immediate in their effect both in terms of location and time (although the much debated instance of sulphur oxide pollution in Scandinavia may be an example of a geographically distributed pollutant). Since damage is functionally related to the existing stock of residual, which in turn is already disposed in the environment in such a way as to be, virtually, non-recoverable, the damage associated with that stock is irreversible.

Third, if social policy toward cadmium and other "stock pollutants" is to be based on human response — i.e. observing how individuals change their behaviour in response to pollution — the invisible nature of the pollutant and its effects up to the damage threshold will militate against avertive measures unless some social learning process — whereby past damage guides future actions — operates. But this is likely only in the sense that governments take paternalistic action since individuals will, by definition, be unable to monitor their own "consumption" of pollutants.

Although cadmium is a "natural" element, human activity has added considerably to the amount of cadmium in the environment. Essentially, mining activities — especially zinc extraction — add to the stock of cadmium, as do many manufacturing processes. Cadmium has widespread uses, such as imparting a colour ("pigmenting") to plastics, and is used widely in electro-plating, in anticorrosive linings, in batteries, television tubes, and so on. In particle form, cadmium is emitted to the atmosphere from the various manufacturing processes, from zinc refineries, and from the burning of fossil fuels (coal contains small concentrations but this adds up to a substantial emission rate when we consider how much coal is burnt). The human "consumption" of cadmium takes place in various ways. Cadmium is inhaled from the atmosphere (cigarette smokers will inhale a great deal more because cadmium is in tobacco as well), and is ingested from water and food. Cadmium in food is in fact the major source of human intake. It is estimated (Nobbs and Pearce, 1976) that the average daily intake of cadmium is some 45–80 micrograms per day, of which 40–70 micrograms comes from food sources.

Now, of this intake of cadmium some 5 per cent is absorbed from the intestinal tract into the bloodstream, and, of this, some 90 per cent is retained in the bloodstream and accumulates in various organs of the body. To put it another way, about 4½ per cent of cadmium intake is stored in the body. A large part of this stored cadmium accumulates in the kidney and, if the concentration is high enough, will, after a fairly long time period, perhaps 30 or 40 years, result in various disorders of the kidney. The range of possibly implicated diseases is wide, and it would be foolish to suggest that a large degree of certainty exists about true cause and effect. Nonetheless, the problems range from hypertension to osteomalcia (bone-softening) and possibly to cancer and heart disease. How society chooses to behave in this context of extreme uncertainty is an issue to be determined by current attitudes to such risks, and by the extent to which current generations wish to shift forward to future generations these potentially hazardous problems. Thus, if cadmium is eventually shown to be truly implicated in many diseases, and if its stock level cannot be reduced, the consequences will be significant damage for future generations (and perhaps this one). If, on the other hand, cadmium turns out to be implicated in just a few diseases, it may well be that society, now and in the future, will judge the benefits of its use to outweigh these costs. One judgement has already been made by the authoritative Expert Committee on Food Additives jointly sponsored by the Food and Agricultural Organization and the World Health Organization. Referring to what they judge to be a critical level of concentration in the renal cortex of the body of 200 milligrams (mg) per kilogram (kg), they say:

"the Committee feels that present-day levels of cadmium in the kidney should not be allowed to rise further. If the total intake of cadmium does not exceed 1 µg/kg body weight per day,[4] it is unlikely that the levels of cadmium in the renal cortex will exceed 50 mg/kg, assuming an absorption rate of 5% and a daily excretion of only 0.005% of the body load (reflecting the long half-life of cadmium in the body). The Committee therefore proposes a provisional tolerable weekly intake of 400—500 µg per individual.[5] *However, because of the many uncertainties involved, this estimate should be revised when more precise data and better evidence become available. The continuing contamination of the environment from industrial and other sources is likely to increase the cadmium concentration in food, and in the future this may lead to hazardous levels. The Committee recommends that every effort should be made to limit, and even reduce, the existing pollution of the environment with cadmium."*

If we attempt to draw the external cost curve for cadmium pollution, we can begin to see some of the problems of actually applying the cost—benefit approach described in Chapter 1 and which is implicit in the selection of the X_S points in the diagrams in this chapter. The MEC curve would appear as a rather wide blur on our diagram, not just because uncertainty surrounds the effects of cadmium intake, but also because it is difficult to see what money valuation we are to apply to the very hazardous consequences if cadmium is truly implicated. On the other hand, we have no difficulty in defining the ecologically constrained level of output for this pollutant. It will be zero. But just to underline the problems of adopting such a "solution" we should recall that what is true for cadmium is also true for mercury, is possibly true for lead, for poly-chlorinated biphenyls, for many pesticides and for certain radioactive wastes. To opt for zero pollution in a context where the pollutants have an associated zero assimilative capacity is to opt for zero output of the goods resulting in that pollution, or for immensely costly pollution control policies. But because this kind of wider cost—benefit trade-off exists, it doesn't mean that zero pollution is a nonsensical policy prescription. For it can easily be the result achieved by considering the peculiar features of stock pollutants and their allied ecological effects.

Notes

1. The reader may note that Fig. 4.1 has not been adapted for the first two categories of pollutant. In the first case no formal relationship between E, B and A exists, so that the diagram is not strictly relevant. In the second case we could have shown the MEC curve — see Fig. 4.5 — beginning at the origin since $W = A$ at $A = 0$. But the complexity here is that much depends on how external cost is observed in this case, and we reserve a discussion of this to section 4.5

2. More strictly, the whole economy need not be aiming for Pareto optimality for points like X_S^1 to occur. All we need is for social policy, in so far as it relates to those industries which dispose of wastes that fit the category we are discussing, to aim for the equivalence of MNSB and MEC. This equivalence across the whole economy will secure Pareto optimality, but there are numerous instances of social policy being aimed at maximum net social benefits for certain sectors of the economy only. What this amounts to is a neglect of the second best problem discussed in Chapter 1.

3. This section draws heavily on Nobbs and Pearce (1976).

4. The weight of an "average" man is about 70 kg, giving an absolute value for daily intake of 70 μg. μg refers to micrograms.

5. That is 57—71 μg per day, which is *within* the range of observed existing intake.

5

Methods of securing the optimal amount of pollution

5.1 Control costs and damage functions

Previous chapters have shown the essence of the economic approach to pollution. As we saw, this centres on a comparison of monetary benefits and costs. The same idea underlies another frequently used approach. This compares the cost of abating pollution — called *control costs* or *abatement costs* — with the benefits of abating pollution, called *abatement benefits*. Looked at in another way, the benefits of abating pollution are the avoided external costs that would otherwise have occurred. A frequently used term for these costs is *damage costs*. Hence the comparison is between control costs and damage costs.

Figure 5.1 shows how the control cost/damage cost approach works. It is necessary to look at the diagram carefully because the cost curves have to be interpreted in a particular way. Consider first the top half of the diagram. TDC refers to total damage costs (total external costs), and these costs are assumed to increase, at an increasing rate, with the amount of pollution, P. The horizontal axis shows pollution levels, but we could equally well have chosen economic output levels since pollution will tend to be a direct function of economic output. The analysis is therefore in no way affected by what we measure on the horizontal axis. Now consider TCC, the total control costs. This curve slopes upwards from *right to left*. The reason for this is that movements along the horizontal axis in a left-wards position entail *less* pollution and the more we spend on controlling pollution the less we would expect there to be.

Now, the object of policy is to maximize net benefits, and we can show that this is formally equivalent to *minimizing the sum of TCC and TDC*. Let Y be the flow of output secured in the nation *with* pollution control, and Y^1 be the flow *without* pollution control. The difference will be

Fig. 5.1

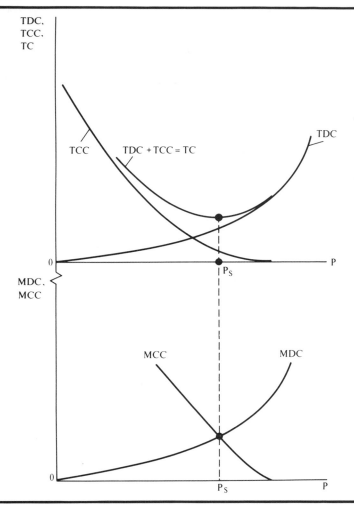

pollution control costs since pollution control absorbs real resources. Hence we can write

$$Y = Y^1 - TCC$$

With respect to the value of environmental services we can perform a similar operation. This flow will be S^1 without any pollution, and S with such damage. The difference, $S^1 - S$, will be the damage due to pollution. Hence

$$S = S^1 - TDC$$

Total social benefits are made up of Y + S, i.e.:

$$TSB = Y + S = Y^1 - TCC \pm S^1 - TDC$$
$$= Y^1 \pm S^1 - (TCC + TDC)$$

Now, pollution affects only TCC and TDC in the above expression. Hence to maximize TSB with respect to pollution control is the same as minimizing TDC + TCC.

This minimum point is shown in Fig. 5.1 as the pollution level P_S. (Note that the minimum does *not* coincide with the intersection of the two total curves — the reader can verify this for himself mathematically, or by drawing any two curves on graph paper and then adding them vertically.) It occurs at the point where *marginal* control costs and *marginal* damage costs are equal in absolute magnitude, though not in sign (MDC will be positive and MCC negative if we express them with respect to pollution levels).

5.2 Pigovian taxes

The economic approach to pollution problems requires us to think of pollution as an external cost and to identify the Pareto-optimal level of these costs. Invariably, this level will *not* be zero, so that some positive amount of pollution is justified. Figure 5.2 shows the essence of the cost—benefit approach. We concentrate, for the moment, on a perfectly competitive firm since this context describes the genesis of much of the literature on pollution control methods. Consequently, the demand curve in Fig. 5.2 is perfectly elastic. MPC gives marginal private costs which differ from marginal social costs (MSC) by an amount equal to marginal external costs (MEC) — i.e. the marginal costs of pollution.

The private optimum is at output X_P, but at this output external (pollution) costs of Ocd (the two shaded areas) are imposed. The social optimum is at X_S where the product price, P, equals MSC. Moving from the private to the social optimum saves external costs of abcd but leaves Oab external costs. Oab is then the "optimal" amount of externality. The question raised in this chapter is how do we secure the change from X_P to X_S? We shall also investigate whether such a change is always dictated by Pareto-optimality requirements.

One *prima facie* obvious method of securing X_S is to tax the generator of pollution according to the external cost he imposes on others. Such a tax is called a "Pigovian" tax after A. C. Pigou whose early work *The Economics of Welfare* (Pigou, 1932) is a landmark in the development of applied welfare economics. In Fig. 5.1 we see that P = MPC maximizes *private* profits — i.e. maximizes the area under the demand curve and above the MPC curve. But *social profits* are clearly less than private profits

Fig. 5.2

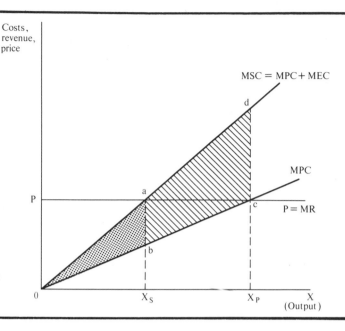

by the area Odc, the total external cost. The Pareto objective is to maximize social profits (B) — i.e. to maximize

$$B = R(X) - C(X) - E(X)$$

where R is revenue, C is cost and E is external cost. These social profits will be maximized when no addition to B can be made by increasing or decreasing output — i.e. when

$$\frac{\Delta B}{\Delta X} = 0$$

Hence we can write

$$\frac{\Delta B}{\Delta X} = \frac{\Delta R}{\Delta X} - \frac{\Delta C}{\Delta X} - \frac{\Delta E}{\Delta X} = 0$$

as the (first-order) condition for maximizing social profit. We can rewrite this in terms of the notation in Fig. 5.2 as:

$$MR = MPC + MEC$$

If we now set a tax T equal to MEC, we obtain the condition

$$MR = MPC + T$$

That is, social profit is maximized by setting a tax equal to marginal pollution costs at the optimal output. The firm will now bear the external costs in the form of a tax which it will obviously treat as a private cost. In this way the external cost is said to be "internalized". The firm's new marginal private cost curve becomes

$$MSC_t = MPC + MEC = MPC + T$$

and it will now maximize its (after tax) profits at output X_S which is the Pareto-optimal output.

Criticisms of the "Pigovian" solution to pollution problems are numerous. First, consider the situation depicted in Fig. 5.2 but this time in the context of *imperfect* competition. Figure 5.3 shows the various cost and revenue functions facing the firm. The firm's *private* optimum is at output X_P with price P_P. But a Pareto optimum exists where $P = MSC$ — i.e. at output X_S — since only at this output are the combined producers' and consumers' surpluses maximized — i.e. only at output X_S is the area bounded by the MSC curve and the demand curve maximized (area Oab). Now, in contrast to the perfectly competitive case, the required optimum involves an *expansion* of output. Since a tax will add to the firm's private costs it must induce the firm to move in the wrong direction — i.e. to

Fig. 5.3

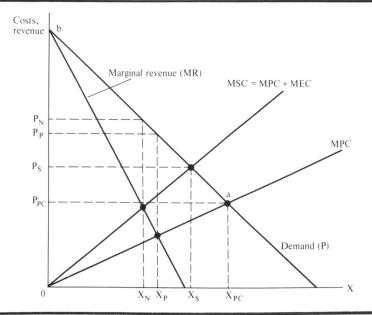

reduce output. We can see this clearly in Fig. 5.3 since a Pigovian tax will make MSC the firm's (after tax) cost curve.

The firm will now maximize profits by setting MR = MSC and this produces a reduction in output to X_N and an increase in price to P_N. Inspection of the diagram shows that the tax has now only reduced combined surpluses in comparison to the "ideal" output at X_S, but it is also worse than the situation in which the firm maximized private profits irrespective of the externality. This argument was noted by Buchanan (1969).[1]

What has gone wrong? Essentially, we have a second best problem. We are applying a Pigovian tax in a situation which is non-optimal quite regardless of the externality problem. The starting point is the output, price combination X_P, P_P, whereas the optimal position (regardless of externality) is in fact X_{PC}, P_{PC}, the price and output that would result from making the imperfectly competitive firm behave as if it were a perfectly competitive firm with P = MPC. There are in fact two types of imperfection in Fig. 5.3: there is the divergence from the social optimum caused by monopoly power (the difference between X_{PC} and X_P), and there is the divergence from the optimum caused by the externality (the difference between X_{PC} and X_S).

Strictly, the idea of a Pigovian tax is not falsified by the existence of imperfect competition as long as we recognize that other sources of imperfection require correction before Pigovian taxes are applied. It might also be argued that, for some industries, the divergence between X_P and X_{PC} would be small anyway and that, for practical purposes, the preceding analysis presents no real problem as far as applying Pigovian taxes is concerned. Where the imperfections are substantial, however, a Pigovian externality tax could move us in the wrong direction, or, at least, to the wrong output, as far as finding the optimal output is concerned.

We can develop the preceding argument by considering what would happen if the pollution tax causes the firm to change its production technology to one that is less polluting (Pearce, 1974). If firms are profit maximizers we must assume that their existing pre-tax technology is the least private cost one. Consequently, any switch into cleaner technology must shift the firm's marginal private cost curve upwards, as shown in Fig. 5.4. At the same time, the cleaner technology will shift the marginal external cost curve (shown as MEC) downwards. We show these shifts as MPC to MPC* and MEC to MEC*. For convenience we write

$$MPC^* - MPC = c$$
$$MEC - MEC^* = d$$

If we suppose that the firm has a flexible technology, the firm will make

Fig. 5.4

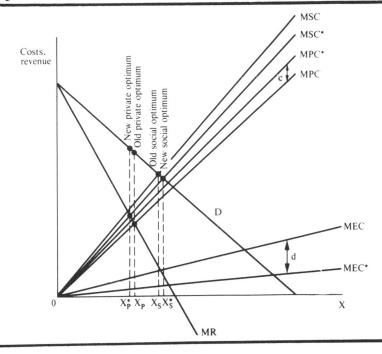

the switch in question only if c < d. That is, it will switch to a cleaner technology only if the extra costs of doing so (c) are outweighed by the extra savings in pollution tax which are equal to the reduced external costs (d). The firm now has a new marginal social cost curve MSC* which must lie below the original one. MSC* also becomes the firm's new marginal private cost curve (after tax) so that firm maximizes its profits at X_P^*. Now, the effect of the tax has been to move the firm from X_P to X_P^* – a *reduction* in output. But this is a movement in the wrong direction when compared to both the old and the new social optima. We conclude that once we have established those conditions under which a firm will switch technologies, those conditions dictate that a Pigovian tax will move us further away from the social optimum and not nearer to it. Of course, once again, if the imperfection due to monopoly power is corrected first, the tax will work correctly.

Finally, we can demonstrate that the same conclusion applies to the control cost/damage function approach described at the beginning of this chapter. This is as we would expect, although it is much less apparent in the control cost/damage function approach. Figure 5.5 repeats the previous information concerning the costs and revenue facing the firm, but

Fig. 5.5

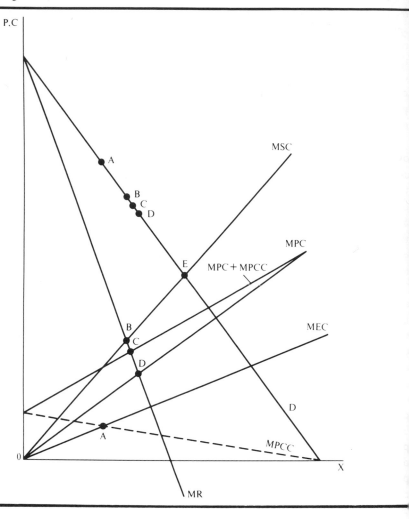

we add marginal pollution control costs (MPCC). We assume that pollution is a positive function of output so that MPCC rises as we approach lower output. The interpretation of this is that it is less expensive to go from, say, a heavily polluted environment to a slightly less heavily polluted one, than it is to go from a mildly polluted environment to a virtually non-polluted one. This, as we shall see in Chapter 6, is in accord with what little we know about control costs. In Fig. 5.5 we can observe the following points. Point A is where the combined sum of damage costs and control costs is minimized — i.e. where MPCC = MEC. This is the "optimum" dictated by the approach which requires us to trade-off damage costs against control costs, as section 5.1 showed. Point B is achieved by setting a pollution tax equal to marginal damage cost, as required by the Pigovian solution. Point C is the point achieved by making the polluter bear all the control costs, and point D is the private optimum of the firm with all externalities ignored. Point E is the social optimum. We can see that point A is further from the social optimum than all the other points. Incidentally, drawing MPCC further north will not solve the disparity since our starting point must always be the private optimum of the firm.

Even if the problems brought about by market imperfections could be overcome, the Pigovian tax solution faces other problems. In particular, it appears to require actual estimation of the external cost (damage) function: otherwise the tax cannot be computed. Detailed consideration of the problems of estimating monetary damage functions is postponed until Chapter 6. For the moment we need only observe that research in this direction has been substantial but that the state of play cannot be considered such as to inspire sufficient confidence in the orders of magnitude obtained to suggest that they be used in actual tax policy decisions. There is in fact a serious quasi-political problem that arises in this context and one that appears not to be generally recognized. Suppose a tax system is devised for, say, a water basin area, and that the taxes imposed are related to some estimate of pollution damage. Since such estimates must, of necessity, be open to dispute — the differing estimates of damage caused by particular pollution sources are testimony to this — it would be an obvious strategy for the taxed firm (or individual) to challenge the basis of the tax by securing an alternative estimate, just as an individual might dispute the basis of an income tax return. The result will be a political bargaining situation (unless the tax is introduced as an unchallengeable piece of legislation) the outcome of which will depend less on what damage actually is, than on relative bargaining strengths. Of course, similar problems may arise with other "corrective solutions", but the point here is that it is wrong to assume that tax solutions can be based on damage cost estimates which are known with any degree of certainty.

It has been suggested that some of the problems of tax solutions can be overcome in the following way (Beckerman, 1972). Figure 5.6 repeats the control cost/damage function diagram introduced in section 5.1 (Fig. 5.1): MEC is the marginal external (damage) cost curve and MPCC is the marginal control cost curve. If the problems raised by the second best issue previously discussed can be ignored, P* will be the Pareto-optimal level of pollution. A tax t* will secure P*. Now suppose that MPCC is not known, and that MEC is known only *ex post* and for given levels of pollution: that is, damage can be estimated for an achieved level of pollution, but the *ex* *ante* damage *function* cannot be known. In this state of uncertainty, Beckerman proposes than an iterative procedure be employed. Suppose a tax of t_1 is introduced. This will induce polluters to move to point P_1. If social costs are computed for this point *only*, the taxing authority will, according to Beckerman, be able to establish whether actual marginal social cost (S_1) is less than t_1, in which case the tax is too high (or greater than t_1, in which case the tax is too low). In this way the taxing authorities can change the tax in an "iterative" fashion until it is exactly right.

Unfortunately, this proposal is more than unlikely to be consistent with the requirements of an optimum Pigovian tax. First, it is damage costs that are more difficult to estimate than control costs, so that a proposal which requires us to know damage cost but not control costs economizes on the more readily obtainable source of information at the cost of placing a heavy burden of reliance on the source that is *more* difficult to estimate. Second, it is far from clear that, *in practice*, "point" estimates of damage are any easier to secure than estimates of complete functions. This is even more true when we realize that the Beckerman proposal requires us to estimate more than *one* point estimate. The research effort involved here could well exceed that for estimating an entire damage function. Third, the initial estimate of pollution cost with the initial experimental tax rate (t, in Fig. 5.6) cannot be an estimate of *marginal* pollution cost, as Beckerman suggests, because we require knowledge of the *range* of the

Fig. 5.6

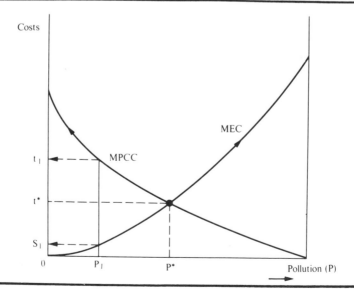

damage function in the neighbourhood of t, to estimate this ("marginal" does, after all, refer to "change in"). We conclude that there is little net merit in the iterative Pigovian tax as advanced by Beckerman.

There is, however, one respect in which a pollution tax is held to be superior to other control mechanisms. It is *the least cost method of achieving a given standard of environmental quality* (Baumol and Oates, 1971). Figure 5.7 illustrates the general argument. Suppose we have three firms, A, B, C, with marginal pollution control cost curves $MPCC_A$, $MPCC_B$ and $MPCC_C$ (notice that the horizontal axis now measures pollution *reduction*).

Fig. 5.7

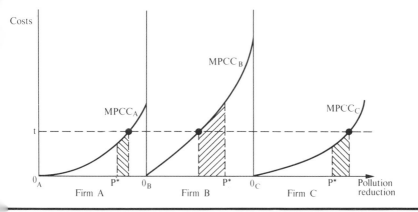

Suppose an environmental quality standard is set such that it involves a reduction equal to $3P^*$. If we seek to enforce the standard, each firm will be required to secure an amount of pollution reduction P^*. The total costs of achieving this uniform standard will be equal to the area under $MPCC_A$ between O_A and P^* *plus* the area under $MPCC_B$ between O_B and P^* *plus* the area under $MPCC_C$ between O_C and P^*. But it is possible to achieve the reduction of $3P^*$ by imposing a tax of t on each firm. The effect is to make firms A and C secure *more* pollution reduction than the standard does, but to make firm B secure *less*. The rationale, of course, is that firm B faces the highest marginal costs of pollution reduction so that it should not have to aim at the standard P^*. Finally, the difference between the aggregate cost of achieving $3P^*$ by the standards approach and the taxation approach can be seen to be equal to the sum of the shaded areas for A and C, *minus* the shaded area for B. But the shaded area for B exceeds that of the other two areas combined, so that the tax solution is in fact cheaper overall in terms of resource costs.

5.3 Bargaining solutions

The Pigovian tax solution clearly requires the intervention in the market of some government authority to assess and administer the tax. If pollution externalities are widespread, or are "pervasive" to the system as might be suggested by the materials balance model of Chapter 3, the activities of government will then also be extensive, reaching down into most aspects of economic activity. Now, while an elaborate structure of pollution taxes could be thought of as being no more intrusive than, say, the imposition of business corporation tax, those who are concerned to minimize government activity in this respect have tried to show that in fact a Pigovian tax structure is not required. Advocates of the virtues of the free market tend to argue on the following lines. First, if pollution is an external cost then there need be nothing to stop those who suffer from negotiating directly with those who cause the pollution to reduce it. In this way a "bargain" may be struck over pollution in just the same way as it is over the sale of commodities in the free market. Second, while it is self-evident that a polluter who is concerned to maximize his *private* profits will not voluntarily offer compensation to a sufferer, it is open to the sufferer to offer a "payment" to the polluter for him *not* to pollute.

The idea that those who "innocently" suffer should "bribe" or "subsidize" the polluter not to pollute appears distinctly odd at first. After all, the argument might be extended to murderers and thieves: if we agree to pay them *not* to murder or burgle us, they could capitalize on a potentially very profitable activity of threat-making. But one defence of the polluter in this respect could be that, whereas society has already deemed the murderer and thief a criminal with no moral right to his activity, pollution tends to be the by-product of a legitimate activity, namely, producing commodities for the consumer. In this way, we could argue that there is nothing intrinsically "wrong" with the polluted bribing the polluter. Indeed, where property rights are vested in the polluter it could be argued that the polluter has the prior right to use the environment in the way he does and that sufferers, by requiring the polluter to install expensive pollution equipment are imposing an external cost on him. The morality of this argument is debatable, not least because we are faced with a trade-off of "rights". The sufferer can argue that he has a right to enjoy peace and quiet, or freedom from air pollution, or whatever, just as English law actually does vest such rights to owners of "riparian" land — the land adjoining watercourses. The polluter can argue that he has the right to produce his product as best he can. There are no "natural" rights in the sense of being able to demonstrate the absolute moral validity of statements like "property owners have a natural right to use their property as they see fit". As a moment's thought shows, my right to behave as I think fit may be quite inconsistent with your right to behave as you think fit. Indeed, rules of social behaviour often derive from exactly such conflicts. But if we have no absolute and final source of categorical moral imperatives, we have no particular reason to set historically determined property rights above any others we might care to name. Consequently, the argument that existing property rights may justify the sufferer bribing the polluter are likely to prove sterile. Equally, of course, arguments that sufferers have the right to be compensated rest on similar foundations. This does not mean that both have *equal* rights − our concern is merely to show that theories which rest on the arbitrary selection of one set of rights rather than another must themselves be arbitrary. What is finally decided on this issue must rest on the value judgements society does choose to apply.

But if polluters can be bribed by sufferers will the result be Pareto-optimal? It can be demonstrated that such a bribe solution is consistent with Pareto optimality under certain conditions (Coase, 1960). Figure 5.8 shows the polluting firm's marginal *profit* curve (MB) and the sufferer's marginal loss curve − i.e. MEC. We select just these two curves because they are the relevant bargaining curves of the two individuals: the firm will accept any bribe higher than MB for a unit reduction in output and the sufferer should, in theory, be willing to pay any unit bribe less than the suffering he would otherwise have to bear. We assume in Fig. 5.8 that perfect competition prevails.

Fig. 5.8

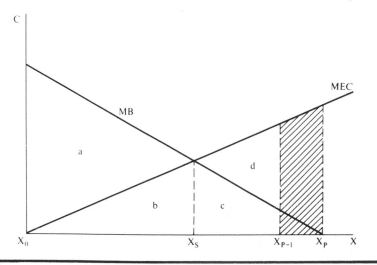

Now, if property rights are vested in the polluter, we can assume that the starting point of the analysis is point X_P where the firm is maximizing private profits. At this point, external costs are equal to area b + c + d. Social benefits are equal to area a + b + c, so that *net* social benefits are equal to area a − d. But the social optimum is clearly at output X_S where net social benefits are maximized and are equal to area a. Beginning at X_P, the sufferers should be willing to pay some amount up to a maximum, shown by the shaded area, to secure a one-unit reduction in the firm's output to $X_P - 1$. Exactly what amount will be paid if bargaining occurs cannot be determined: all we know is that it will be, at most equal to the shaded area, and, at least equal to the small triangle under the MB curve between X_P and $X_P - 1$. The actual amount will depend on relative bargaining strengths.

The same analysis can be applied to further reductions in output, until we reach point X_S. At this point it is no longer possible for the sufferer to bribe the polluter to reduce output — his marginal losses are less than the marginal gains he is asking the polluter to give up. Consequently, X_S is a natural equilibrium outcome of the bargaining process and, of course, is also a social optimum in Pareto terms. Consequently, bargaining secures a social optimum provided property rights are vested in the polluter.

Does the reverse apply? If property rights are vested in the sufferer the natural starting point will be the origin X_O. Now, for the firm to produce any output at all it must offer the sufferer compensation for losses. This can do because, initially, its marginal gains from expanding output exceed the sufferer's marginal losses. Accordingly it can compensate the loser up to point X_S, but not beyond. In short, the bargaining process appears to work in the situation where property rights are vested in the sufferer, but the direction in which cash payments flow is reversed. In the event that polluter and sufferer come together, the "market" will, it seems solve the problem. Such a solution would also seem to be evidence of the desirable elegance of the competitive market system, which perhaps accounts for its attractiveness to many economists.

But in reality the bargaining solution faces many problems. We can look at the salient ones in turn. First, consider what would happen if we translated the analysis of Fig. 5.8 into the context of imperfect competition. Under imperfect competition the firm's demand curve slopes downwards. This is shown in Fig. 5.9. The bargaining curve of the polluting firm remains its marginal profit curve MB, and that of the sufferer the MEC curve. Whether the starting point is X_P, the private optimum, or O, the zero output point that results from property rights being invested in the sufferer, the equilibrium point is at X_B. And X_B is also the point that would be achieved by a Pigovian tax. We can demonstrate this simply:

For bargaining equilibrium,   MEC = MB

But   MB = MR − MPC

Hence   MEC + MPC = MR

Or   MSC = MR

Fig. 5.9

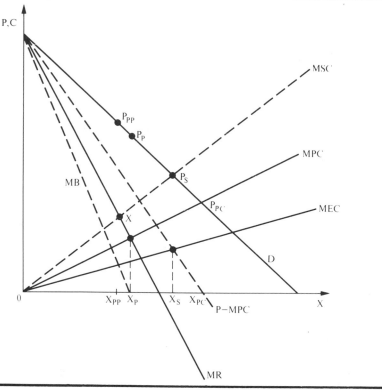

That is, the bargaining result is equivalent to that output/price combination that would result from setting marginal revenue and marginal social cost equal to each other. But this is the result of applying a Pigovian tax to a situation in which firms already maximize private profits. We have seen that, under imperfect competition, this result is Pareto non-optimal. Hence, the bargaining solution is equally inefficient.

Figure 5.9 does, however, show one other possible bargaining curve. This curve P − MPC is obtained by subtracting marginal private costs from price. Now, the difference between P and MPC is in fact equal to the combined surplus (producers' plus consumers'), so that we could interpret P − MPC as a "marginal surplus curve". If this curve now becomes a bargaining curve (the interpretation of which we consider in a moment) and MEC remains the sufferer's bargaining curve, it can easily be shown that equilibrium bargaining will in fact be socially optimal:

If $\qquad\qquad$ P − MPC = MEC

on rearrangement, $\quad$ P = MPC + MEC = MSC

which is the requirement for a social optimum. It would appear then that bargaining *is* optimal under imperfect competition if the bargain takes place such that P − MPC = MEC. In fact, such a bargain would, in all probability, be a tripartite affair since P − MPC contains the surplus of producers and the surplus of consumers. Hence, two parties are involved — firms and consumers — in bargaining with sufferers. The logic of such a situation can be seen, but, as we shall see, bargaining is *less* likely to take place as the numbers involved increase, so that the tripartite aspect of the above bargain is likely to militate against its occurrence.

A second problem with the "bargaining" solution is that it tends to pre-suppose a well-defined situation in which there are one or two sufferers and one or two polluters. In these circumstances it is possible to think of bargains taking place. Indeed, it is perhaps significant that much of the literature devoted to externality problems deals with cases which must be regarded as being fairly trivial — arguments over lawn-mower noise, bonfires in the garden and so on. The suggestion is that such cases could be the subject of some sort of bargain, but that the significant forms of pollution externality could not be. How, for example, would a city's residents bargain with the many sources of air pollution? How would they identify who is responsible and how would they band together to carry out the negotiation? We can perhaps summarize these problems by saying that bargaining is certain to have significant *transactions costs* (T) as far as the important pollution contexts are concerned. If transactions costs are positive, government intervention could be justified if the costs faced by the government in securing an optimum are less than the transactions cost of the bargaining parties (Turvey, 1963). This point is important because it suggests that the existence of transactions costs does not necessarily mean that governments *should* intervene, at least not if the objective is a Pareto optimum. Governments are likely to face serious administrative costs (G) if they have to intervene, for, in order to identify the optimum, they will require knowledge of the MB curves and the MEC curve in Fig. 5.9. Further, government intervention would be justified only if these administrative costs are less than the welfare gain (W) to be secured. Equally, of course, bargaining will only be worthwhile if the transactions costs are less than the gain to be secured.

We can summarize the bargaining/administrative costs problem by saying:[2]

(a) If T < W, bargaining will occur;
(b) If T > W, bargaining will not occur;
(c) Government intervention is justified in situation (b) if G < T, *and* if G < W.

This leaves the possibility that T *and* G are greater than W, in which case the externality would have to remain uncorrected, unless some *other* policy has a cost (S) less than G or T and can secure some welfare gain greater than S. Indeed, this may very well define the attractiveness of environmental standards (more on which below). Far from the existence of transactions and administrative costs justifying minimal or non-existent government intervention, we have an argument for a different kind of government intervention through the use of environmental standards.

Mishan (1971) points out that the analysis used to demonstrate the Pareto equilibrium becomes less determinate when we introduce income effects. The relevance of these effects can arise in two ways: (a) because direct utility comparisons are sought (a departure from the strict Pareto analysis); or (b) because property laws are changed. Figure 5.10 repeats the MEC and MB curves from the previous analysis, but *two* MEC curves are shown. The curve MEC_O relates to the situation in which the starting point is the origin X_O — i.e. to the situation in which property rights are

Fig. 5.10

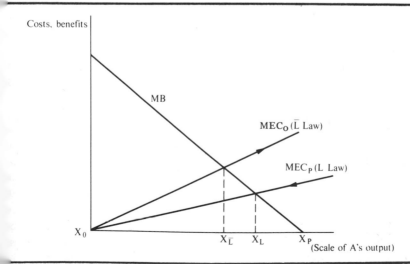

vested in the sufferer (this is Mishan's $\overline{L}$ law, the law that prohibits nuisance and hence vests rights in the sufferer). The curve MEC_P relates to the situation in which the starting point is output X_P, the polluter's private optimum, which means that property rights are vested in the polluter (Mishan's L law). Now, if we begin at X_P the sufferer will be *better off* as he moves from right to left on the diagram. Hence his willingness to pay the polluter at X_P to reduce pollution must be less than his requirement in compensation for moving *to* X_p from say X_{p-1}. That is, MEC_p must lie below MEC_O. If the starting point is X_O, the sufferer's willingness to pay to *avoid* moving to X_{O+1} will be less than the compensation he requires to tolerate the increased pollution.

As Fig. 5.10 shows, the social optimum depends on the state of the law. If the L law (permissive) prevails, more pollution results than if the $\overline{L}$ law (prohibitive) prevails.[3] If pollution does significantly affect individuals' welfare (and this is a much disputed proposition) then the divergence between the two "optima" will be significant and we cannot conclude that a bargaining solution will achieve a *unique* optimum regardless of who owns property rights, which was one of the original theorems of the bargaining literature. On the other hand, we have not developed any argument which establishes who *should* possess property rights.

We may briefly look at some of the remaining difficulties of bargaining solutions.

First, we have already noted that, if property rights are invested in the polluter, he can secure gains *in excess of* what his maximum private profits would otherwise be simply by bargaining to receive bribes in excess of the private gains he surrenders by reducing output. As a number of writers have pointed out, this makes threat-making a profitable activity and could therefore lead polluters to channel resources into this activity. Not only would this be a misallocation of resources in itself, but it distorts economic incentives since it would mean that the distribution of income could be altered "coercively" in such a way as to reflect the pattern of threat-making power in the economy rather than some pattern of marginal productivity (Mumey, 1971).

Second, bargaining solutions tend to presuppose that the external cost in question involves readily identifiable parties. We have already seen the problem that arises when groups of sufferers become large and when sources of pollution become difficult to identify. But suppose we now consider applying the "bargaining" solution to say cadmium or mercury admissions, pollutants of the Class 3 variety discussed in Chapter 4. Since the externality involved is: (*a*) uncertain in magnitude; (*b*) liable to occur at considerable geographical distance from the source of emission; and (*c*) liable to occur at a point in time quite divorced from the time of emission, it is scarcely likely that polluter and sufferer ever *could* come together to bargain.

Third, we argued in Chapter 1 that, whether we like it or not, *some* distributional judgement is implicit in conventional cost—benefit criteria and that distributional judgements cannot be avoided. Hence the distributional effects of externality bargaining solutions are of interest. Where property rights are vested in polluters it can be seen that bargaining will amount to a transfer of *income* from sufferer to polluter. If sufferers tend to belong to below-average income groups, and polluters to above-average income groups, this transfer would be judged regressive on an ethical rule that the rich are less deserving than the poor. Whether this argument holds in practice requires empirical evidence which is in short supply. But the following points are relevant. First, the rich tend to be more capable of adjusting to negative externalities by moving their location to more amenable areas. As such, we would expect high pollution concentration areas to overlap significantly with low income areas. This appears to be the case (see Freeman, 1972). Second, whether low income groups *perceive* the pollution is questionable. There is evidence to suggest that pollution abatement is a luxury good — i.e. that its income elasticity of demand is above unity. If so, whether pollution is distributed so as to impinge (physically) most on the poor may not be relevant if the poor do not care about it. Third, the sufferer may nonetheless have a powerful case in equity simply because he is the sufferer. That is, the existence of the externality itself may prevent him responding in the fashion he would consider most desirable. This is particularly true if the externality causes some income loss in the form of property value depreciation: the effect on value indicates, in part at least, the existence of a negative externality, but it also inhibits the sufferer from responding to the externality unless a direct means of *actual* compensation exists. Research into these areas is still very limited, but there is some good reason to suppose that equity considerations militate against bargaining type solutions.

Several writers (Portes, 1972; Starrett, 1973; and Baumol, 1972) have pointed out that normal presentations of externality contexts assume "well-behaved" marginal external cost and marginal profit functions such that a unique, stable equilibrium is secured. Figure 5.11 shows some possible results of assuming "non-convexity". In Fig. 5.11(*a*) we show a decreasing MEC function which cuts MB from above. In this situation it can be seen that point E is not an optimum (total external costs exceed total private benefits) nor is it a stable equilibrium since, to the right of E, polluters can compensate sufferers to accept pollution increases, and to the left of E, sufferers can bribe polluters back to zero output. In Fig. 5.11(*b*), MEC slopes downwards but cuts MB from below. In this case

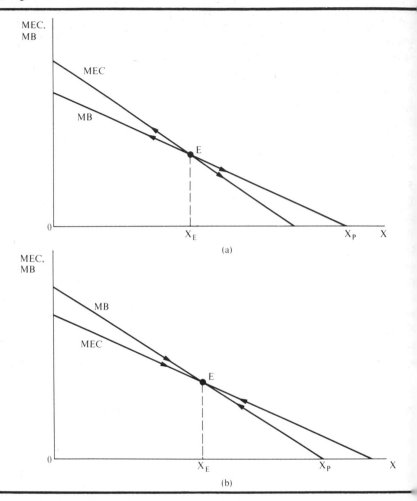

(a)

(b)

E is both stable and an optimum. If, for the moment, we ignore the possibility of multiple equilibria (see Portes, 1972),[4] it could appear that only the situation in Fig. 5.11(a) causes any difficulty for the bargaining solution. Even there we may note that, if property rights are vested in polluters, and X_P is therefore the starting point, the absence of a bargain will be Pareto optimal if total external costs at X_P are less than total private benefits. More to the point, we must ask whether a declining MEC is at all realistic. Starrett suggests that, for the situation in which sufferers are firms, it is. The argument is essentially that firms cannot lose more than their fixed costs. If the externality causing the firm's loss reaches an amount equal to the firm's profits calculated as an excess over *variable* costs, the firm will close down causing a discontinuity in the MEC curve such that MEC = 0. It is not clear, however, whether this particular argument gives rise to any serious problem. It is perhaps better to think of this case as setting a limit within which any externality correction policy can take place. Nor does it mean that the MEC curve has to slope downwards over its whole length, merely that we have an eventual discontinuity. Baumol (1972) has, however, provided a more general point about non-convexity. Again, the analysis is in terms of inter-firm externalities but the results appear to hold for all categories of externality. Baumol's argument is considered in the next section.

5.4 More on Pigovian taxes

Baumol's argument is that the very existence of external effects may be sufficient to induce a non-convexity situation (Baumol, 1972; Baumol and Bradford, 1972). The argument proceeds as follows. Consider two industries, P which produces some commodity with pollution as a side effect, and S which produces and the commodity does not pollute but suffers the pollution from P. In Fig. 5.12(*a*), taken from Baumol and Bradford (1972), line OA shows the output possibilities of industry P. For 4 units of work (i.e., 4 units of leisure) 10 units of output are secured. For 8 units of work, 20 units of output are secured. In Fig. 5.12(*b*) the output possibilities of industry S are shown. Line OB shows input/output combinations when industry P does not produce at all. Line OH shows reduced outputs

Fig. 5.12

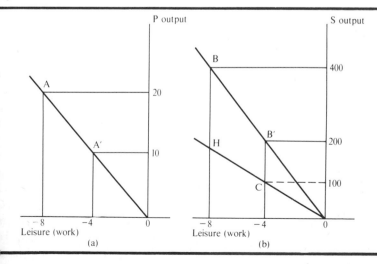

| (a) | (b) |

per unit input when industry P does produce, such that S suffers the externality. Now consider the combined production possibilities. We can choose to produce at A in Fig. 5.12(*a*) in which case we shall have the combination (−8L, 20P, 0S), where L is leisure. Or we can choose B in Fig. 5.12(*b*), in which case we have (−8L, 0P, 400S). But if we choose to put *some* labour into producing some of both commodities, we shall face the effects of the externality. Thus, if we put 4 units of labour in each we shall have 10 units of P, but only 100 units of S (not 200) because output line OH is now operative. Hence, we shall have the combination (−8L, 10P, 100S). If we plot the output combinations to produce a production possibility curve we obtain Fig. 5.13.

Fig. 5.13

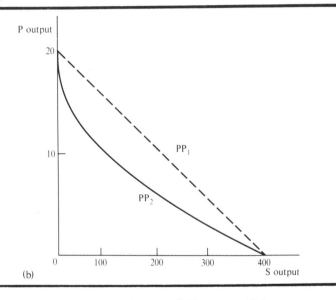

(b)

Line PP₁ shows the production possibility curve if there are *no* externalities: it is a constant returns curve as we would expect. Line PP₂ shows the production possibility curve if the externality exists. *The externality itself has generated non-convexity in the production possibility curve.*

In Fig. 5.12 the total loss of the S industry increases at a constant rate. In terms of the diagrams in section 5.3 this means that the MEC curve is horizontal. Baumol's result, that the production possibility curve is concave, is *strengthened* if *either* the S industry experiences a decreasing returns output function when the externality is present, *or* experiences an increasing returns output function when the externality is *not* present. In each case the MEC curve will be rising. For MEC to fall, however, the S industry must *either* experience an increasing returns function with the externality (Starrett's case) *or* experience a decreasing returns function without the externality. But even if MEC falls, the production possibility curve remains concave up to that output where MEC = 0 for industry S.

What is the significance of non-convexity in the production possibility curve? Figure 5.14 illustrates a totally concave production possibility curve and superimposes a "social welfare function", SWF. Line BB is a relative price line. The optimal position is at A where social welfare is maximized. The problem now is that prices no longer have any normative significance in this context. To see this, consider a point like K. K is achievable since it lies on the production possibility frontier and, at the relative prices prevailing at A, K appears more desirable. That is, if the prices given by BB are P_S and P_P respectively, it is easy to see that

$$(P_P X_P^K + P_S X_S^K) > (P_P X_P^A + P_P X_S^A)$$

where X refers to quantities. But, in fact, K lies on a *lower* social welfare curve than at A. Equally, then, if a tax is imposed on industry P we can have no guarantee that it will take us to an improved position. Baumol (1972) generalizes this to saying there is likely to be a *multiplicity* of local

Fig. 5.14

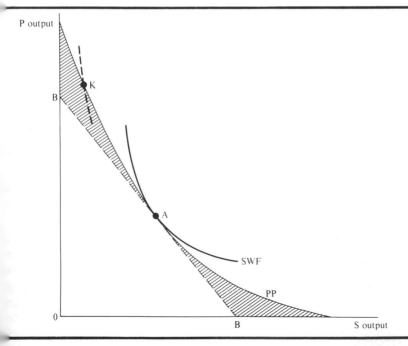

optima. He illustrates the point with a simple geographical example. If we have two locations one of which is safe from pollution generated in the other one, then we can locate households in one location and the polluting factories in the other location. Since we can operate with either location in this respect, we have at least two local optima, "for either of these arrangements keeps the smoke and people apart". As we increase the number of locations, the sources of externality, and the other variables that will affect least cost allocations of people and factories, we must expect the number of such maxima to grow considerably. Now, as is well known, a move that *appears* to improve welfare in such circumstances may well be costly if it precludes a move to a higher maximum, just as the move from A to K in Fig. 5.13 only *appeared* to be a good one. In short, a Pigovian tax is liable to move us in any direction if non-convexities exist. We *cannot* say it will produce an improvement without the kind of knowledge that simply will never be available. And Baumol's conclusion is all the more forceful when we relate it to the "materials balance" view of the economy which showed externalities to be *pervasive* to the economic system.

5.5 Environmental standards

In practice, most environmental policy is implemented via the laying down of standards. These may be expressed in terms of the quality of the receiving environment (e.g. a given watercourse should be maintained at some level of dissolved oxygen), or in terms of the quality of the effluent being dispersed to the environment. Most of the economic literature on environment tends to argue that standards are an inefficient way of implementing environmental policy. The reasons for this view are basically twofold: first, standards tend to be based on factors which do not relate to any objective assessment of benefits and costs, and, second, even where a standard is agreed, its implementation tends to require legal sanctions and these, it is argued, are not the least-cost method of ensuring that standards are observed. We may consider each argument in turn.

The source of many standards tends to lie in some explicit or implicit agreement between the affected parties as to what is "acceptable" or "reasonable". In this way, a standard may be made more rigorous if there is a public outcry about some aspect of pollution, or may be relaxed if there are representations from the polluters that the standard is "too costly" to implement. As such standards tend to be politically determined, perhaps with health criteria setting the minimum desirable quality of the environment but with pressure-group bargaining determining how far above this minimum the standard is set. The economist's complaint is that such a process is ascientific: it does not relate standards to benefits and costs. The response, of course, is that the costs of pollution control are not accurately known, and the benefits are highly uncertain as far as their measurability is concerned. Indeed, in many cases, we do not even know what the physical effects of pollution are: e.g. we do not know very much about the health effects of noise nuisance, or of air pollution, or precisely how toxic metals travel in ecosystems. In these circumstances the advocates of standards argue that attempts to establish precise regulations based on monetary assessments of costs and benefits are misguided.

The force of this argument is clearly considerable, but one point must be borne in mind when deciding whether to choose a tax or a standard. Any standard must imply something about benefits and costs. In Fig. 5.15 we show total benefits of pollution control and total costs of pollution control. If we know both curves, the optimum standard is at C_S since this is where net benefits are maximized. If we now say that we do not know the benefit curve and we set a standard at, say, C_1, then that decision implies that we regard the benefits as being *at least* equal to $C_1 C_1'$, the cost of implementing the standard. That such a process is potentially misleading can be seen if, without knowledge of the benefit curve, we set the standard at C_2 in Fig. 5.15 since the costs of implementing this standard exceed the benefits. In this way it is always useful to remember that standard setting does imply something about our assessment of the benefit side of the picture. It is because of this that many tax-advocates dislike standards: they suggest that it is better to make some attempt to find the position of the benefit curve, whatever margin of error may be involved.

It is possible, however, that standard setting based on "quality thresholds" would overcome this objection. For some pollutants at least it

Fig. 5.15

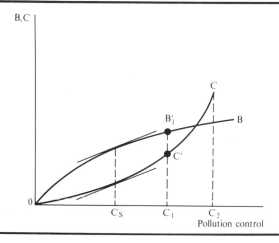

Fig. 5.16

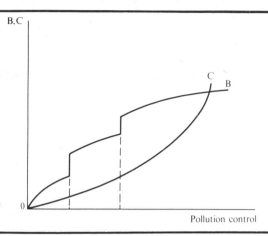

would appear that benefits respond in a "jumpy" fashion. Figure 5.16 illustrates the point. As soon as the quality of the environment reaches a certain level (pollution is reduced by a certain amount) it is capable of sustaining more life forms. Perhaps the river now supports a wider variety of fish. At another level it becomes both safe and pleasant to swim in, and so on. In other words, depollution benefits do not appear in the form of the smooth curve of Fig. 5.15 but like the "jumpy" curve of Fig. 5.16. If we now set a standard based on one of these threshold quality levels, we see that there is a good chance of that standard coinciding with a point of maximum net benefits, even though we do not know the benefit curve.

If some ("political") setting of standards is accepted, is legal enforcement of those standards the best mechanism of ensuring they are observed? We have already shown that setting standards in such a way that each polluter has to meet the same standard is economically inefficient. However, a standard is determined, setting taxes so as to secure the overall standards, is the least-cost method of achieving that standard (Baumol and Oates, 1971; Baumol, 1972). We must be clear what this approach means. The "taxes versus standards" literature tends to concentrate on the issue of how taxes and standards are determined. This is slightly misleading because the pollution tax is really an *instrument* for *achieving* a particular standard — ideally that standard which maximizes net social benefits. Consequently, arguments can only centre on two issues: (*a*) whether the Pareto-optimal standard can be known with any degree of accuracy; and (*b*) whether, *whatever* standard is chosen, a tax or a legal regulation is the best means of securing that standard. The answer to (*a*), as we saw, is that attempts to estimate benefits may prevent us from making serious errors in setting standards, but the risks of this kind of error are not large. In light of the immense difficulties of estimating benefits, it seems unavoidable that we work with standards determined by the best information available. The answer to (*b*) must depend on the relative advantages and disadvantages of taxes and regulations. To these we now turn.

First, then, we have the argument that taxes are the least-cost method of securing a given standard, and this argument clearly favours the use of taxes.

Second, we have to consider the distributional aspects of taxation and regulation. It is sometimes argued that pollution taxes merely serve to shift the burden of the tax onto consumers. On economic efficiency criteria, however, such a shift does not matter because the tax reflects the external cost embodied in the product in question, and product prices should change so as to reflect the different external costs embodied in different products. In other words, the very object of pollution taxes is to change relative prices. The indifference of some economists to who bears the burden of the taxes is explained by the fact that they want to see product prices changing in this way. In any event, the imposition of a standard still requires that the firm meet the real costs of achieving that standard, and consequently we would expect firms to shift some of this burden forward.

Burrows (1974) has, however, suggested that taxes and regulations differ in their distributional consequences because taxes turn what otherwise would be a "free" input — environmental services — into one with a price attached to it, whereas regulation does not. Figure 5.17 illustrates

Fig. 5.17

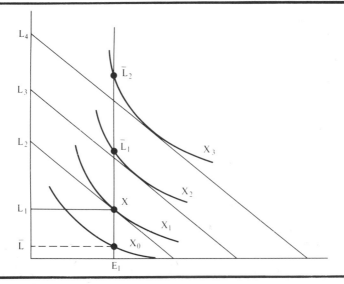

the general argument for an imperfectly competitive firm. The diagram shows two inputs — labour and the "environment". The isoquants show levels of output and we assume that the firm would, given relative input prices, including the tax on the use of E, but no other constraints, produce the level of output X_1 with input amounts L_1 and E_1. We assume that the marginal cost of expanding output is constant — i.e. the distances $L_1 L_2$, $L_2 L_3$, $L_3 L_4$, etc., are equal. If now E is "free" but the firm is required to use only E_1 of it, we see that the marginal cost of expanding output along $E_1 X$ is equal to $\bar{L} L_1$, $L_1 \bar{L}_1$, etc. That is, *below* output level X_1 the marginal cost of expanding output is less under regulation than under taxation, but *above* X_1 it is higher. If we translate this finding to the firm's total cost and revenue functions, we obtain Fig. 5.18. Where the total cost curve under pollution taxation is TC_T we see that it changes to TC_R under regulation. The profit maximizing output of X_1 does not change, but the profit level does, from an amount a to an amount a & b. Effectively, as Burrows points out, regulation has caused a redistribution from the owners of environmental outputs (i.e. the environmental inputs of the firm) to polluters. There is then a distributional asymmetry between taxes and regulations. Burrows (1974) observes that a uniform standard will mean that those suffering from pollution will now suffer equally, where before they may not have done. With a tax, however, the suffering will depend on

Fig. 5.18

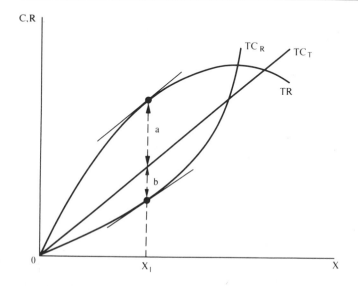

polluters' abatement costs, and he argues that "it does not seem quite *equitable* that this should be the case". If equity is to be equated with equal suffering this is a justified conclusion. On the other hand, if we think in terms of the benefits of the new situation compared to the previous unregulated and untaxed situation, the distribution of benefits is not necessarily clear. Thus, with a uniform standard, the distribution of benefits will vary with the difference between the new uniform standard and the previous levels of quality which, in turn, would have varied with polluters' technology and levels of output. With a tax the same consideration applies but with the new quality level for individual polluters varying with their abatement cost functions. In addition, without empirically investigating *who* gains from pollution reduction, it is impossible to say whether a particular unit reduction by one polluter is more desirable on equity grounds than a unit reduction by another polluter.

Third, we noticed that taxes were least-cost solutions to securing a given environmental standard, and that such a result depends on setting the tax level in such a way that it induces each firm to carry out its own optimal level of pollution abatement. If we assume that firms know their marginal abatement cost functions, then the authority setting the tax will have to guess at the initial level of tax and see whether it achieves the overall environmental standard laid down. If not, the tax will have to be changed. But one of the well-known problems with such procedures is that they induce firms to instal abatement equipment in response to the initial pollution tax which, if it is changed, then leaves the firm with the possibility of having over-invested in such equipment. Regulations have their own sources of inefficiency, but they may be less than those of the tax solution. Essentially, a standard which is set equal for all firms will run up against the problem already noted: firms cannot respond according to their differing marginal costs of adjustment. Of course, one might begin with a whole set of standards (Burrows, 1974), varying these according to whether their combined effect is to secure the overall standard laid down, and according to individual circumstances. There is, in short, no clear answer to the issue of choosing between taxes and regulation for achieving given standards, at least as far as costs of implementation are concerned.

Fourth, it is often argued that taxes leave the firm with the widest possible choice of mechanisms for reducing pollution, ranging from output changes to the introduction of "clean" technology (UK Royal Commission on Pollution, 1972). This cannot, however, be an additional benefit when compared to regulated standards since exactly the same choices are open to the polluter in the latter case. The possibility of evading standards by "secret dumping" is of course equally open if a tax is applied, so that this argument is equally inapplicable.

Fifth, taxes will provide an incentive for the polluter to seek less polluting technologies which may reduce pollution *below* the environmental standard. The reason for this is simply that the tax effectively prices all environmental inputs, whereas the regulated standard implies a zero price below the chosen standard and an infinite price above it. Such an argument is slightly odd in one respect since it implies that the standard set is not the right one, and this, if true, is easily corrected. On the other hand, there are clear advantages to using an instrument which encourages a continuous reappraisal by the polluter of the alternative technologies open to him. Arguably, taxes do this but standards do not.

Sixth, we need to inquire as to the amount of information required by each mechanism. If a standard is set and each firm is required to meet that standard irrespective of variations in their costs of abatement, the information required will consist of data on the quality of the receiving environment and some knowledge of the quality of effluent from individual polluters, the latter arises because the standard has to be apportioned between polluters. Polluters are assumed to know their own costs of abatement so that this information is not required by the authorities for the implementation of the standard. For the tax solution the information is the same: as long as firms know their abatement cost schedules they will adjust the amount of abatement to the tax. The authorities must monitor the quality of the receiving environment, but may not have to monitor individual effluent levels which could be a substantial advantage. The reason for this is that the rate of tax depends only on the quality of the receiving environment. If the tax fails to achieve the right standard then it is varied upwards or downwards, but it is the same tax for each firm. On this count then, the tax solution appears to have a slight advantage in terms of information costs. If, however, the disadvantages of the iterative approach to getting the right level of tax are to be avoided, then the authorities must know the polluters cost of abatement functions.

Seventh, there will be administrative and enforcement costs associated with both regulation and taxation. Administering the standard is common to both instruments, but there may be additional costs with a tax because of the need to transfer funds, firms having to make tax payments presumably on some annual basis to a government organization. This involves additional use of the firm's accountants and extra labour in the government department administering the tax, as Burrows (1974) points out. Enforcing a regulated standard clearly involves some legal sanctions which the authorities must be prepared to implement if the standard is to be honoured. One of the serious problems with those environmental standards that already exist is that, all too frequently, they are allowed to lapse because of the complexity of imposing sanctions on those who fail to honour the standard. A similar problem arises with a tax. Polluters may of course simply not pay it, in which case some legal process would be involved, but it is not clear why non-payment of a pollution tax should be any more common than, say, non-payment of corporation tax.

Notice that standards which are set in such a way to take account of differences in firms' abatement costs will involve substantial increases in the amount of information required, mainly because the authorities will now have to know about firms' cost functions in order to assess any cases of "special pleading" (Burrows, 1974).

It seems clear that the only conclusion on the issue of taxes versus regulations for achieving given environmental standards is that there can be no unambiguous recommendation to use one instrument rather than another. Regulation and taxation have their own costs and benefits and, without empirical evidence on actual policies, the net benefits of one measure or the other cannot be clearly known. Even then, one suspects strongly that thinking in terms of taxation or regulation for all cases is the wrong approach: it seems right to argue that standard setting is unavoidable given the limited knowledge of the relevant data for implementing full "Pigovian" taxes and the doubts expressed about the efficiency of such taxes, but it may well be that a given standard is best secured by taxes in some cases and by regulation in others.

5.6 The sale of pollution rights

It has been suggested by Dales (1968*a*, 1968*b*) that many of the problems of securing a given environmental standard can be overcome if an official authority is established for the sale of "pollution rights", or "environmental usage certificates". Thus, if a predetermined standard is established, and if the relationship between waste emissions and that standard are known the authority would require that each polluter buy a certificate entitling him to emit a certain amount of waste over a specified period of time. The number of certificates issued would be determined by the pre-established standard for the receiving environment, and by the requirement that the authority retain a small proportion of the certificates for other uses, to be described.

The essence of this approach is that the certificates will command a price in the market since polluters will have to bid for them in the first place, and will also be entitled to sell or buy certificates from each other, subject perhaps to the authority acting as a broker in such exchanges (this enables the authority to know who owns certificates). We can think of the demand for such certificates as being given by the demand curve in Fig. 5.19. This demand curve will in fact be the aggregate of all polluters' marginal pollution control cost curves. If the resulting price of certificates

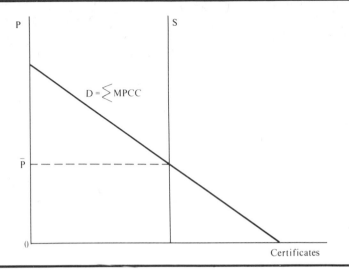

exceeds control costs it will pay the polluter to instal abatement equipment and buy fewer certificates. If the price is less than pollution control costs, it will pay the polluter to buy certificates and discharge waste rather than instal abatement equipment. The price will initially be established by this aggregate demand schedule and the supply schedule which will of course be fixed and totally inelastic, being determined by the authority's initial quality standard. Now, if certificates can be freely sold between polluters, the turnover will be determined by the number of firms moving into the authority's area (and thus requiring certificates if they wish to discharge waste) and by the number who are leaving the area, or who are closing down, or who have installed abatement equipment and who have thus reduced their demand for certificates. The certificate issue can also be related to damage costs, although this is not necessarily an integral part of the pollution rights plan. Thus, if the price established is $\bar{p}$, this can be related to a marginal damage cost function, if known. If $\bar{p}$ fails to correspond to the predetermined quality standard (P*), then the authority can buy or sell certificates to change the standard. For example, if $\bar{p}$ is less than the required price to establish P*, the authority buys back certificates, thus raising the price by shifting the supply curve marginally leftwards. This in turn will now correspond to a higher environmental quality. If the authority wishes to lower the standard it will sell certificates thus lowering their price and making it more profitable for some polluters to discharge waste rather than treat it.

Notice that as new firms come into the area and/or the output of individual existing firms grows, the demand curve in Fig. 5.19 will shift to the right, thus raising the price of certificates. Note also that polluters, though required to buy certificates if they wish to discharge waste, need not be the only buyers: conservation groups could also buy them and simply withhold them for polluters. This will raise the price to polluters and hence increase the level of environmental quality. As Stein (1971) has pointed out, however, this aspect of the sale of pollution rights is likely to be less attractive in practice since those who suffer from pollution are invariably not organized to engage in this kind of activity. It is in fact the same problem as arose with the so-called "bargaining solution". The real attraction of the plan is its flexibility. It is the trade in certificates which enables relatively easy adjustments to changes in the pollution context to take place — standards can be varied by relatively simple (open market) sales and purchases by the authority, and the dynamic context in which firms change and substitute for each other is accommodated by sales of certificates between polluters. The scheme is of course a pollution tax scheme.

The scheme has one disadvantage which is serious, however. Lambelet (1972) has shown that if any polluter is capable of influencing the price of certificates, their price will not relate to marginal pollution control costs in the proper fashion.[5] The same of course will hold if the authority is faced with just a single polluter. In part this suggests that the authority be empowered to cover a wide area so that the overall price of certificates is governed by aggregate demand and supply and not by the actions of individual price-makers. But this will tend to make the concept of a pre-established environmental quality standard meaningless — it is necessary to think in terms of fairly small regions. Because of this, the presence of oligopoly or monopoly among the purchasers of certificates will render the scheme inferior to the tax scheme discussed in previous sections.

Notes

1. Note that if marginal external costs are large enough the output where P = MSC will lie to the left of the output where MR = MPC. In this case, the tax gives a move in the right direction but the firm will adjust its output below this new optimum.

2. We might add that if bargaining costs, T, are of the lump sum variety — i.e. are a constant sum — their existence cannot affect the optimal *level* of the polluter's activity because fixed transactions costs have no effect on marginal profit or marginal loss curves. Such fixed costs would of course affect the actual level of net welfare gain. See Burrows (1970).

3. We have simplified Mishan's approach somewhat. Mishan has a similar divergence in the marginal private gain curve. He also distinguishes the initial difference between the loss curves (and gain curves) from the welfare effects of the actual bargaining process.

4. Multiple equilibria could arise if the damage function is non-linear and this can be true of inter-firm externalities where firms affect each others' cost such that damage done by one firm depends in part on the level at which other firms are producing. See Kneese and Bower (1968). Increasing private returns for polluters do not, incidentally, give rise to rising MB functions so that we rule this possibility out here.

5. Let the price of certificates be P_c, and pollution levels P. For the ith firm, where this firm can influence the price of certificates, we have

$$TC_i = C_i + F_1(P_i)P_i + F_2(P_i)$$

where TC refers to total costs, C to all "normal" costs such as labour, etc., F_1 relates certificate prices to the pollution level of firm i (i.e. $p_c = F_1(P_i)$), P is pollution and F_2 relates pollution control costs to pollution. Then the aim is to minimize this expression, giving

$$F_1(P_i) + P_i \cdot F_1'(P_i) + F_2'(P_i) = 0$$

i.e.

$$p_c + P_i \cdot F_1'(P_i) = -F_2'(P_i)$$

i.e.

$$p_c + X = MPCC$$

But $X > 0$, so that the price of certificates cannot be equal to marginal pollution control costs.

6

Cost-benefit analysis of pollution: the practice

6.1 The framework

Chapter 5 showed that the cost–benefit approach to pollution requires the estimation of control cost and damage cost functions. This chapter investigates some of the difficulties of securing actual monetary estimates of these functions. There is now a vast literature which describes various attempts to place money values on pollution damage. Rather than survey the entire field we choose to look in some detail at the attempts to value *noise nuisance*. This should give the reader the "flavour" of the cost–benefit analyst's approach, particularly as some of the methods of placing money values on noise nuisance are applicable to other problems such as air pollution.

The literature on estimating control costs is comparatively small. The actual process of collecting these estimates is laborious, though very essential. The time and effort that is needed to survey firms, to make allowances for variations in the age of capital equipment, and so on, perhaps explains why major research funds are generally required before the exercise can be carried out. We describe later some of the procedures used and some of the results obtained, and we look at some of the suggested aggregate measures which purport to indicate the national cost of pollution control.

A word on the "philosophy" of attaching money values to damage is required because it appears to attract considerable criticism. First, there is the purely pragmatic rationale for valuing damage in money terms. Since pollution control costs are expressed in money units, units which should, ideally, reflect the value of the resources used up in pollution abatement, we would have no complete way of identifying the "trade-off" between abatement and damage if damage was not also valued in money terms. We could of course say something like "a further expenditure of £X will secure Y units of pollution reduction" and leave someone to judge if this is worthwhile. But this would of course amount to placing a money value on the pollution reduction: if they replied that it is worthwhile they will imply that $Y.p > X$ where "p" is the "shadow" price of pollution. If they declare it not worthwhile they will imply that $Y.p < X$. Second, Chapter 1 suggested that monetary valuations will at least indicate what consumers think about the damage. Ideally, the shadow price, p, will indicate their preferences. As we saw, there are numerous problems with this view, but it is perhaps better to attempt monetary valuations rather than leave the decision to some anonymous government agency, or to the influences of pressure groups. Finally, while it is often argued that putting money values on social costs make them appear as if they are "on the same plane" as material items of welfare, *not* putting a money value on them can be a recipe for ignoring them altogether. The advocate of environmental protection as a prime item of social policy would do well to reflect that it is pressure from environmentalists that has led to social cost valuations being made. If money values are not put on these items, or, rather, if the attempt is not made, it is easy to imagine that when environmental lobbies are not powerful (and there are signs that such issues as the "energy crisis" are reducing their power) the situation could revert to one where environmental problems are simply overlooked.

Nonetheless, many of the criticisms of the attempts that are made at money valuations are valid. It would be naivete of the highest order to imagine that the process of monetary valuation is watertight and sound.

6.2 Property price approaches

The essence of the property price approach to noise nuisance evaluation is that individuals can "buy" peace and quiet by choosing to locate their homes in peaceful areas and by choosing to work only for employers who locate their activities in such areas. Accordingly, observation of the behaviour of people who vary in their sensitivity to noise should enable us to estimate their implicit (positive) valuations of quiet and hence their implicit (negative) valuations of noise. If, to take an extreme example, a consumer is able to choose between two houses, identical in every respect except that house A has a peaceful location and house B a noisy location, then the existence of noise-sensitive people should mean that the price of A (P_A) exceeds the price of B (P_B). The differential $P_A - P_B$ would provide a *prima facie* measure of the extra value of peace and quiet attached to house A.

This generalized approach requires us to accept: (*a*) that individuals *are* free to choose in the manner supposed (modifications with respect to this assumption will be discussed later in the chapter); (*b*) that noise is not a ubiquitous "public bad" but a localized public bad — i.e. we must be able to argue that peaceful areas still exist such that individuals can locate their activities in them; (*c*) that "noise" or "quiet" can be measured quantitatively in a fashion similar to the quantification of the amounts of other commodities;[1] and (*d*) that the effects of noise on house prices can be disentangled from the many other effects on house prices. Clearly, it is *technically* feasible to separate out such effects using well established statistical techniques.

Figure 6.1 illustrates the essentials of the property price approach. VC is a demand curve for houses and the stock of houses is assumed fixed at ON. Hence the ruling market price is P_0 where supply and demand are equated. We now suppose that QN houses are affected by noise such that the sensitivity of consumers to noise nuisance causes the demand curve to fall to V_1C_1, setting a price of P_1 for noisy houses. Note that the QN noisy houses are occupied by persons with a low apparent valuation of noise. But the OQ quiet houses are now relatively more valuable, so that the demand curve for them shifts to V_2C_2. The position of V_2C_2 is established by considering the marginal willingness of pay to avoid noise for the Qth person. This is given by the distance ab = D, the distance between the demand curves VC and V_1C_1 for the Qth person. If this marginal willingness to pay is not altered, then the Qth person must be willing to pay $P_1 + D$ for a quiet house. Hence, adding D to P_1 gives point C_2 as the

Fig. 6.1

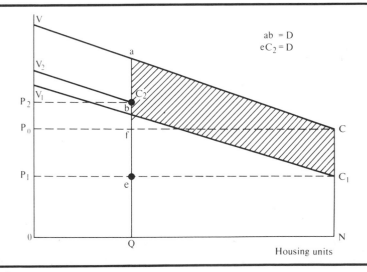

demand by the Qth person, and similar analysis for other consumers gives us V_2C_2 as the demand curve for quiet houses, setting a price of P_2.

The *observed* house price differential (HPD) after noise has been introduced and the market has adjusted is

$$HPD = P_2 - P_1$$

But the actual change in welfare, as measured by the change in consumers' surplus, is given by the shaded area in Fig. 6.1. We can analyse this area as follows:

$$Area\ aCC_1b = afC + feC_1C - ebC_1$$

Writing S for consumers' surplus, ΔS for the change in surplus, S_0 for the surplus at the original price P_0, and S_1 for the surplus at the new price of noisy houses P_1, this becomes:

$$\Delta S = S_0 + (P_0 - P_1)QN - S_1$$

or

$$(P_0 - P_1)QN + (S_0 - S_1)$$

This shows us that the relevant measure of welfare loss is the HPD between the *initial* "no-noise" situation and the new price of noisy houses, *plus* the change in surplus (on the QN noisy houses) between the initial "no noise" situation and the new noise situation. But it is important to observe that this is *not* equivalent to the measure obtained by the simple formula quoted earlier of the difference between the new price of quiet houses (P_2) and the new price of noisy houses (P_1).

We may conclude that any property price approach must:

(i) ensure that the HPD is measured across the correct prices;
(ii) allow for changes in surplus

We may observe the following inequality from Fig. 6.1:

$$(P_0 - P_1)QN < \Delta S < (P_2 - P_1)QN$$

That is, an HPD approach using only the difference between the no-noise and noise situations will *understate* noise costs, and an approach using the differential between the new price of quiet houses and the new price of noisy houses will *overstate* noise costs.

This conclusion must cast doubt on those empirical studies which have used market price data *alone* to measure the economic cost of noise, although Walters (1975) has suggested an approach which does require only market price data.

Now one adjustment mechanism open to the consumer in the face of noise nuisance is to move house to avoid it. The most sophisticated HPD models have in fact incorporated the relocation decision into the property price analysis. There are numerous modifications to the basic HPD/relocation models. We concentrate on two such models, those of the Roskill Commission Team (CTLA, 1971) and Walters (1975).

The "Roskill" model
We may first categorize the types of persons affected. These are:

1. People who are "natural movers" — i.e. who will be moving anyway for reasons unconnected with noise. If noise increases as these people sell their houses, we can expect house prices to fall by an amount $D = P_0 - P_1$ (in Fig. 6.1). For these people, consumers' surplus, S, is zero (CTLA, 1971, p. 268; Flowerdew, 1972, p. 37).
2. People who move *because* of noise. Now, for many of these people, the value they place on their homes exceeds the market valuation by the amount S. Hence they lose both D and S by moving. In addition, of course, they will incur removal costs R. For these people, then, it must be the case that the cost of noise, N, *if they remained*, exceeds S + D + R. Consequently S + D + R is a minimum estimate of the costs to this category of sufferer.
3. Those who *stay* and tolerate noise. They suffer a cost, N. Technically, N < S + D + R for these people, and, of course, N could be zero (or even negative if these are noise-lovers! But it is so unlikely that we rule this out).
4. Those who move in to the noisy area to replace natural movers and those who have moved because of noise. If these people are fully aware of the new circumstances, it would be reasonable to assume that they are at least compensated by D, the depreciation on property, that they now buy. In fact, of course, D could exceed their requirement for compensation, in which case there would be *benefits* for this category. The general assumption, however, has been to set costs equal to zero for this category.
5. Those who lived outside the previously quiet area and *would have moved in* but for the noise. These people experience a welfare loss, as Pearce (1972) points out. It seems fair to say that property price models have ignored this category of loss entirely.

Heggie (1972) has presented a diagram which usefully illustrates the gains and losses for categories (1) to (5) above. Figure 6.2 below is adapted from Heggie (1972, p. 106). An existing stock of "quiet" housing is assumed, the demand for which is given by D_0. S_0 shows the supply of houses *for sale* — i.e. the *flow* of offered properties from the given stock available per unit time period. Now, since householders will offer properties for sale on the basis of their subjective valuations, S_0 has to be thought of as "the implied surplus derived by the present owners" (Heggie, p. 107). This is most important to an understanding of the model. The intersection of S_0 and D_0 at P_0 gives the equilibrium market price.

Now, if noise affects the entire stock, it has two effects. First, the demand curve shifts to D_1 as noise-sensitive people switch their demand to quiet properties elsewhere and are replaced by in-movers. Second, the supply (implied surplus) curve S_0 shifts down to S_1 now that existing owners are prepared to dispose of their properties at reduced prices. The gap, $S_0 - S_1$, can be thought of as "the price which property owners are prepared to pay to be rid of the noise nuisance". (Heggie, p. 107.)

Fig. 6.2

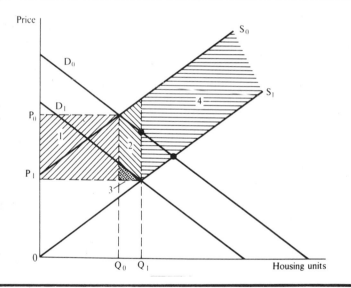

We can immediately distinguish the relevant categories of resident:

1. The "natural movers" are OQ_0 because, at the pre-noise price P_0, their subjective valuations (given by S_0) lie below P_0. They clearly suffer a total loss of $OQ_0 (P_0 - P_1)$, given by area 1 in Fig. 6.2.
2. The "induced movers", Q_0Q_1, sell at P_1 because of noise, their subjective valuations having exceeded P_0 but now lie below P_1. Their loss is therefore given by areas 2 + 3 in Fig. 6.2.
3. The "in-movers" replace the "induced movers" so that they too are shown by Q_0Q_1. This category *gains* a surplus shown by area 4, the excess of their willingness to pay over P_1.

4. The "non-movers" beyond Q_1, suffer a loss given by the area between S_0 and S_1, shown as area 4 in Fig. 6.2.

All in all, the net losses, in terms of the areas in Fig. 6.2 are:

Area 1 + Area 2 + Area 3 $-$ Area 3 + Area 4
= Area 1 + Area 2 + Area 4

The informational requirements of the model are then:

(a) An estimate of the "natural" rate of emigration, "e", from the now noisy area.
(b) An estimate of D.
(c) An estimate of R.
(d) An estimate of S.
(e) An estimate of N.

For an estimate of "e" the CTLA Research Team initially used a figure of 7 per cent per annum, based on independent evidence to the Commission, but subsequently revised this to 4.1 per cent per annum (CTLA, 1971, p. 268).

The estimate of D was obtained from estate agents round Gatwick Airport, London's second airport. (Gatwick was thought to be similar to the four sites chosen for short-listed consideration.) D was thus a direct estimate of how estate agents thought noise *alone* would affect house prices. The estimates of D vary according to house price category. Three categories were chosen — high, medium and low — with absolute price levels being estimated from rateable values.[2] Estimates of D varied, then, for each house price category and for each noise zone. The estimates of D were validated, *ex post*, by reference to Inland Revenue data (Flowerdew, 1972, p. 41).

The estimate of R was obtained independently from professional removers and was taken to include the "disruption" costs of moving. The actual figure used was 16 per cent where $R = 0 \cdot 16P$ (CTLA, 1971, p. 268).

The estimate of S was obtained from a survey of householders. S was assessed as a sum of money required by householders to induce them to move, not as the sum householders might pay to retain their peace and quiet. The former is (roughly) equivalent to the compensating variation measure of surplus and the latter to the equivalent variation measure of surplus detailed in Chapter 1. The latter will be less than the former since it is restrained by *ability* to pay. Actual estimates of S were obtained by a questionnaire approach to people living in areas considered to have close resemblance to the actual sites under consideration. People were asked to give an estimate of the market value of their property and then to say how much they would require to induce them to move. The difference between the latter and the former gave the *householder's surplus*, as it was called. The final average surplus was 52 per cent of property price — i.e. S = 0·52P (CTLA, 1971, Appendix 23).

Finally, an estimate of N is required. N is that "sum of money which would just compensate ... [the house owner] ... for the nuisance suffered and make him as well off as he was before" (CTLA, 1970, p. 366). But the actual estimation of N was quite complex. In particular, we need to know N because it determines the proportion of residents who move *because* of noise (i.e. they move if N > S + R + D, but stay if N < S + R + D). There are in fact two relevant measures of S which affect the decision rule to move. It is argued later that the relevant measure of S for purposes of measuring noise *costs* is that compensation required by the householder such that his initial welfare situation is restored; i.e. the sum of money he requires in order to move. But in terms of the *movement rule*, S will be the (smaller) measure of how much the consumer is *willing to pay* to buy back quiet and stay where he is. This point is made in Paul (1971) and Walters (1975). The procedure for estimating N was as follows: the distribution of annoyance scores over the population in each NNI was taken from the Wilson Report (Wilson, 1963). For each distribution the median is associated with the value D such that D is *assumed* to measure noise disbenefit. Thus, in Fig. 6.3 we have a distribution of annoyance scores for a given NNI. The median annoyance score can be immediately identified from the distribution, and this in turn is assumed to correspond

Fig. 6.3

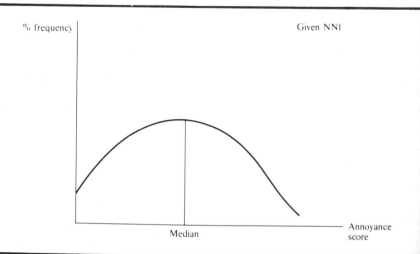

to a monetary disbenefit equal to the value of D for that NNI. This procedure is repeated for other NNI, enabling a table such as Table 6.1 to be derived.[3]

Table 6.1

Annoyance score	NNI for which the score is Median	Corresponding depreciation (%)		
		Low	Medium	High
1	32	2	4	6
2	40	4	9	15
3	49	10	15	26
4	55	13	20	35
5	60	15	22	38

These disbenefit measures can now be fed back to the distributions within each NNI, with the percentage depreciation being expressed in absolute terms in each case. These are the absolute values of N, and they will now appear as a distribution for each NNI category, just as in Fig. 6.3, except that the horizontal axis will now measure the *monetary values of N attached to each annoyance score* by the previous procedure. The effect is shown in Fig. 6.4 using NNI = 40−45 and the medium-price house category as an example.

Now, to obtain estimates of those who move (N > S + R + D) we look at the distribution of householders' surplus. Thus, to continue our example, S = 0 for 11 per cent of people in medium-priced houses (S is invariant with respect to NNI), D = 9.4 per cent for the average priced house of £6,000, and R = 16 per cent of property price. Hence, S = 0; D = £564, and R = £960. Hence S + R + D = £1,524. Now, N > £2,000 for 21 per cent of people in the 40−45 NNI, medium-house price category, so that some 21 per cent of people have N > S + R + D, and these people are predicted to move.

Accordingly, by securing independent values of S, R, and D, and by deriving N from D, the model is able to predict the *sizes* of the relevant categories noted above.

To complete our description of the "Roskill" noise cost model, we need only consider how *time* is entered into the analysis.

First, N is really a sum of money required by those who stay to tolerate noise for ever. Since some people who initially stay will later move, we

Fig. 6.4

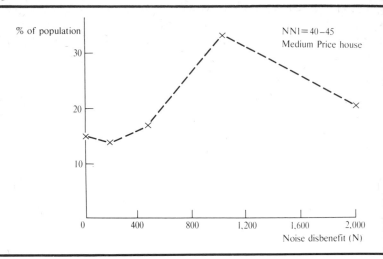

need to convert N to an annual value. This was accomplished by the following formula (Flowerdew, 1972, p. 38):

$$N = \sum_{t=t_1}^{t_2} n \cdot \frac{(1+g)}{(1+r)} t - t_0$$

where n is the compensation value for nuisance in year t_0, the date to which costs and benefits are discounted; t_1 is the date at which the noise nuisance begins; t_2 is the date at which the nuisance ends; r is the rate of discount, and g is the rate at which noise disamenity valuation rises (see below).

Second, it was accepted that the *relative* valuation of "peace and quiet" would rise over time, because of a presumption that the income elasticity of demand for quiet exceeds unity. Thus, if real incomes can be assumed to rise at x per cent per annum, the real value of quiet can be assumed to rise at some rate nx per cent per annum, where n is the income elasticity of demand for quiet. In fact, the house depreciation data themselves suggest a relationship whereby noise costs vary as (approximately) the square of income, making n = 2 in the above formulation. In the CTLA study, a value of n of about 1.7 was used, so that g in the equation in the previous paragraph was 0.005 (5%) for the real income growth rate of 0.03 (3%).

Criticisms of the "Roskill" methodology There can be no question that the Roskill Commission Research Team methodology has had a profound world-wide impact on cost—benefit work on the valuation of disamenity

Precisely because it is so widely used it is important to establish the limits of its validity. The criticisms that have been made have concentrated on the methodology, the data inputs, and the estimation procedures used. In this chapter we look only at the methodological criticisms.

Divergence between private and social discount rate   The price depreciation, D, in the "Roskill" model is a change in a capital value, which in turn is a capitalization of a flow of benefits from the property over time. Hence, house prices, and therefore D, reflects the discount rate relevant to the housing market. In an "ideal" world this rate will be equal to all other market rates and to the social time preference rate which is arguably the relevant rate for discounting in cost—benefit analysis. In reality, however, the rates will differ. Consequently, there is a bias in the use of property price data (Heggie, 1972). The direction of the bias depends on whether the housing market discount rate (h) is above or below the social discount rate (s).

In general,

if h > s, D will *understate* the social costs of noise.
if h < s, D will *overstate* the social cost of noise.

If h and s are known, corrections to property price models can easily be made.

The role of expectations   The validity of the "Roskill" model depends critically upon the "rational" behaviour of householders and on a perfectly functioning housing market. Rationality is, of course, fundamental to all economic analysis, but it is always pertinent to ask if irrationality exists and, if so, how it affects the validity of the model. Sources of market imperfection are even more important. It will be seen that many of the methodological criticisms of property price models centre on the imperfections of housing markets.

One such problem is the expectations of the in-movers. As we saw, these people have losses less than or, at most, equal to zero. Indeed, as Fig. 6.2 shows, they should experience a gain due to the fact that their subjective valuations lie above the depreciated property price P_1. But the validity of this point depends on the expectations of the in-mover, with respect to noise, being fulfilled. Since, virtually by definition, in-movers do not experience their new surroundings for any significant period of time there is no reason to suppose that they predict correctly the net advantage of the environment. As Paul (1971, p. 311) points out, planning authorities frequently restrict residential building around airports: there would be little point in this if the authorities did not expect in-movers to make precisely the kind of mistake noted above.

Noise-pervasiveness   If noise nuisance occurs in such a way as to affect *all* areas, or all areas to which noise-sensitive residents can move, then the change of residents predicted by the "Roskill" model will not occur. That is, if noise behaves like a global, or near-global, public bad, property price differentials will not emerge even though noise-sensitive residents are clearly worse off (Mishan, 1970).

How far noise-pervasiveness of this kind prevents the previously described model from operating as it is supposed to depends entirely on evidence about which residents move and which do not even though they would like to. As yet, such evidence is limited in amount, but there is some evidence to suggest that noise-sensitive residents do not move as expected (Griffiths and Langdon, 1968).

Indeed, we may generalize this point by looking again at Fig. 6.2. The S_1 curve there is the implied surplus curve showing residents' willingness to sell if they are *not* compensated for noise nuisance. That is, $S_0 - S_1$ measures their willingness to pay for quiet. To find the compensation requirement we would have to refer to a different supply function lying consistently *below* S_1 in Fig. 6.2, such a function showing the implied surplus if *compensation is* paid. Reference to this curve will then mean that induced movers and non-movers should have their disbenefits more *highly* valued. This general point is emphasised in Heggie (1972).

Asymmetry in social costs   Cost—benefit analysis requires us to regard a social cost that has an associated cash flow as being conceptually indistinct from a social cost without an associated cash flow. This, in the "Roskill" model, D and R correspond to *actual* financial losses, while S and N do not. In general, this asymmetry will not matter, but it will matter in the case under consideration if those social costs associated with *actual* losses constrain the resident from behaving as the model predicts, or if it alters the methodology of valuation. Thus, the model predicts that if $N > S + D + R$, residents will move. But the act of moving requires the resident to purchase another residence: the oddity of housing as an economic good is that it cannot (in general) be dispensed with altogether, whereas other goods can. Consequently, the affected resident must pay a price for his new (quiet) property which will be comparable to the price of his existing house *before* the noise nuisance occurred. Now, unless compensation is *actually* paid for at least the loss in D, the affected resident may be prevented from moving by the fact that noise has affected his *wealth* situation in a detrimental fashion (Pearce, 1972. See also Whitbread and Bird, 1973).

Further, as Paul (1971) has pointed out, because of the above argument, D can, at best, only measure what people are *willing to pay to buy back quiet*. This sum, as we saw, is constrained by income. But the relevant measure is *the compensation required to tolerate noise*. Only the latter will measure N as it is defined in the model. But N is derived from D (see above) so that, unless the compensation and willingness to pay measures coincide, the use of D to estimate N will bias the estimate of noise nuisance. Since we know compensation requirements exceed willingness to pay measures, the use of D to estimate N will *understate* noise nuisance.

The use of D to estimate N   We have already observed one source of error in using D to estimate N. A more general point is that there is no *particular* reason to suppose that the median of the noise annoyance distribution is associated with the measure D. That this assumption was never substantiated was accepted in the final *Report* of the CTLA (CTLA, 1971, p. 270). The earlier argument used by the CTLA Research Team (CTLA, 1970, p. 368) was that there would be an equal number of buyers and sellers of houses the residents of which thought N exceeded D. Consequently, if we plotted a distribution of such people, 50 per cent would think N > D, and 50 per cent would think N < D. Hence the median of such a distribution should coincide with D. As Paul (1971) points out, however, this is not the relevant distribution: what matters are all those residents in noise-affected houses, not just those in houses bought and sold after the noise has occurred. Those who stay and suffer the noise also lose part of their surplus. Heggie, (1972, p. 108) has emphasized the same point.

The relevance of NNI   If the measures of noise in common use are, for one reason or another, unsatisfactory, the economic models based upon them will also be open to error. One recent attack on the use of such measures as NNI has been advanced by Hart (1973), and directly contradicts the assumption that NNI (and hence other noise measures, since such measures tend to be transformations of each other, albeit complex ones — see Walters, 1975, Ch. 2) is a cardinally indexed entity.

The NNI index is expressed as

$$NNI = \overline{PNdB} + 15 \log N - 80$$

and $\overline{PNdB} = 10 \log (1/N) \Sigma_i\, 10\, L_i/80$

where   L = peak noise level in perceived noise decibels (PNdB) for the ith aircraft;

$\overline{PNdB}$ = logarithmic average of noise loudness;

N = number of aircraft heard on an average summer day;

80 = a constant corresponding to zero annoyance.

Hart (1973) begins by doubting whether the implications of such an equation can be correct. It implies, for example, that annoyance doubles if N quadruples from 1 to 4; but also only doubles if N rises from 20 to 80, or from 80 to 320 (Hart, 1973, p. 142). This is clearly an absurdity. Hart then shows that, using the original data from Wilson (1963), only 20 per cent of the variation in noise annoyance between people was ever explained by noise loudness and numbers of aircraft.[4] Hart traces this unsatisfactory explanatory power to the method of assessing annoyance scores themselves. He argues that the questionnaire technique actually used could never have elicited correct answers (Hart, 1973, pp. 142—3), particularly because they were asked in such a way as to preclude the *number* of aircraft from affecting annoyance in a sensible fashion. Hart also points out that annoyance ratings are *ordinal* but NNI is a *cardinal* index. But ordinal measures are determinate only up to monotonic transformations, while cardinal scales are determinate up to linear transformations. Basing a cardinal measure on an ordinal scale is illicit. Finally, Hart observes that 80 dB can no longer be regarded as corresponding to zero annoyance. Hart suggests that deviations from 70 or 75 dB would be more sensible, which means that current NNI measures will *understate* noise nuisance.

The Walters model
The most sophisticated development of the property price approach is to be found in Walters (1975). The outcome of Walters' approach is an actual valuation of noise which, it is argued, can be applied to most noise-generated or noise-abatement programmes. The significant feature is a valuation *per unit of noise* which is held to apply regardless of where on the noise scale (NNI, CNR, etc.) the increase or reduction in noise occurs. Clearly, if such a unit value of noise could be derived it would simplify immensely the problem of intergrating noise nuisance valuation into standard cost—benefit approaches.

The essentials of the approach can be described.

First, a utility maximizing model is developed, in which "quiet" appears as one of the commodities the consumer can choose. Essentially, a constant returns Cobb—Douglas utility function is assumed, giving rise to a unitary elastic demand curve for quiet. In this way, quiet (and hence noise) is not seen as an attribute of housing as in other property price models, but as a continuum such that the consumer can choose the *amounts* of noise he wishes to experience given his preferences for other commodities. This is important, because in other models, dubbed "attribute" models by Walters, the consumer is judged to be choosing between noise and quiet which in turn are seen as polar extremes of each other. But clearly, consumers can choose to move location to experience slightly less (or even more) noise, much less noise, or a complete absence of noise. Hence, "it is misleading to suppose that an efficient analysis of noise can be conducted with an 'all-or-nothing' attribute model" (Walters, 1975). Because of this deficiency in the attribute model, Walters aims to find a demand function for "quiet": this he does by deriving such a function from the utility maximizing model. If this demand function can be estimated, we have a direct means of valuing noise. Strictly, we secure only a minimum estimate since what is paid for quiet reflects the consumer's willingness to pay for the marginal unit of quiet only. We require, of course, an additional estimate of the consumer's surplus on intra-marginal units of quiet. In practice, as Walters emphasizes, noise changes tend to affect only small proportions of the housing stock, so that, he argues, we can legitimately ignore consumer's surplus unless the change is non-marginal.

Walters' (1975) utility maximization model proceeds as follows. Consider a (constant returns) Cobb–Douglas utility function for each individual i — :

$$U_i = X_i^{1-b} \cdot Q_i^b$$

where X is some composite consumption good, Q is the quantity of quiet, and b is a constant less than unity. Then b is the "noise sensitivity coefficient" of individual i.

Let the price of X = 1 and let the *price of quiet* be P such that P measures the willingness to pay of the consumer for the marginal unit of quiet. Then, each individual has the (same) income:

$$Y_i = X_i + P \cdot Q_i$$

Maximizing the Lagrangean

$$L = X^{1-b} \cdot Q^b + \lambda(Y - X - P \cdot Q)$$

and solving the resulting equations gives the *demand functions*

$$X = Y(1 - b)$$

and[5]

$$Q = \frac{b \cdot Y}{P}$$

We note that $Q = \dfrac{b \cdot Y}{P}$ is the *demand function for quiet*.

Hence,

$$P = \frac{bY}{Q} = \frac{bX}{Q(1-b)}$$

Aggregating across N individuals, $i = 1, 2 \ldots N$,

$$P = \frac{\sum b_i \cdot X}{Q \cdot \sum(1-b_i)} = k \cdot \frac{X}{Q} \text{ where } k = \frac{\sum b_i}{(1-b_i)}$$

We can also write

$$\frac{1}{N} \sum b_i = \frac{P}{N \cdot Y} \cdot \sum Q_i$$

So that $\bar{b} = \frac{P \cdot \bar{q}}{Y}$

The average noise sensitivity coefficient, b, is directly measured by the average amount spent on quiet expressed as a proportion of income.

Now, the "compensation" measure advocated by Walters for any noise-generating or noise-abating project is:

$$C = \Delta NNI \cdot NDSI \cdot P_H \cdot H \cdot \frac{1}{100} \qquad [1]$$

where $NDSI = 100 \cdot \frac{P}{P_H}$ \qquad [2]

and \qquad H = number of houses affected.

(NDSI refers to a "noise depreciation sensitivity index".) We can show that the formula for C reduces to an equation where C is given by the depreciation on property prices:

Substituting [2] in [1]

$$C = \Delta NNI \cdot 100 \cdot \frac{P}{P_H} \cdot H \cdot \frac{1}{100} = \Delta NNI \cdot P \cdot H$$

Now,

$$P = \frac{b \cdot Y}{Q} = \frac{b \cdot P_H}{NNI}$$

provided we substitute P_H for permanent income and NNI as a direct measure of quiet. Hence

$$C = \Delta NNI \cdot \frac{b \cdot P_H}{NNI} \cdot H$$

$$= \Delta NNI \cdot \frac{D}{NNI} \cdot P_H \cdot H$$

where $\dfrac{D}{NNI}$ is the percentage depreciation per unit NNI. That is, NDSI is simply the percentage depreciation per unit of NNI.

From the model we can see that the proportion of income each consumer spends on quiet (b) is a direct measure of the value of quiet at the margin. If the amount of quiet experienced by a consumer changes, that consumer will adjust his behaviour in such a way as to maintain the *amount he spends* on quiet constant: this result is a direct outcome of the unitary elasticity of the demand curve for quiet, and, in turn, this unitary elasticity results from the specific form of utility function assumed. In this way, the distribution of B across individuals is invariant with respect to the price of quiet, and the relative supply of quiet.

Accordingly, we require a direct measure of $P \cdot Q/y$, and this will be the "value" of quiet. Since income measures are not usually available as an independent piece of data in property price studies, Walters proposes, as the derivation above suggests, the use of house prices themselves as a measure of "permanent income". This he justifies by the fact that the elasticity of demand for housing itself tends to be minus unity (Walters, 1975), such that the amount people spend on housing tends to be a constant proportion of their total income. In this way we can alter the problem to one of looking at the expenditure on quiet as a proportion of house prices. Now, if the price of quiet can be thought of as being a constant, the effect of a change in the *supply* of quiet (through noise-generating or noise-abatement investments) will be such that the depreciation in the market price of noisy property will measure the change in expenditure on quiet. In short, for a *given* income level and *given* noise level, D, the house price depreciation, will measure b, the value of quiet. In practice, Walters accepts that imperfections in housing markets, wrong expectations and so on, will mean that the value of B would not be the same for each income category in each noise group. There will in fact be a distribution of b within each income group and noise level. Walters' procedure is to take $P \cdot Q/y$ (the observed expenditure, which in turn equals D) to be the mean or median of this distribution of b. This was in fact the assumption of the "Roskill" Research Team.

We now need to see how Walters' model can be applied. Borrowing an example from Walters (1975), if we have 20,000 houses affected by noise such that NNI increases from 30 to 45 and the average price of a house is £8,000, we obtain, assuming an NDSI of 1 (justified by looking at various studies of the effect of noise on house prices) the compensation required:

$$C = NNI \cdot NDSI \cdot P_H \cdot H \cdot 1/100$$

where H is the stock of houses affected. i.e.:

$$C = 15 \cdot 1 \cdot £8,000 \cdot 20,000 \cdot 1/100 = £24 \text{ m.}$$

The salient virtues of Walters' model are: (a) that it is relatively easy to use since it requires knowledge only of average house prices in each noise affected area and the change in noise levels, and; (b) that it rests on a specified behavioural model. Its weaknesses are: (a) that its particular specification rests upon the assumption of a constant returns utility function, and there can be no specific rationale for this. Indeed, as Walters himself notes, the particular utility function assumed is inconsistent with an income elasticity of demand of 2 implied in house price depreciation data; (b) that the information used to establish some general values of the NDSI is itself weak, so that it might be better to attempt a recalculation of NDSI for each study − i.e. essentially to estimate D for each specific case; (c) that the observed value of b for any homogeneous income group is taken to be the mean of the b_i distribution and information is lacking by which to substantiate this assumption (although Walters suggests it is consistent with some of the socio-psychological data); and, finally, (d) that it presupposes a particular equilibrating mechanism in the housing market which seems unlikely to occur in practice given the immense constraints on movement and adjustment.

6.3 Empirical aspects of property price models
The estimation of property price depreciation (D)
If a house price can be thought of as the present value of the flow of services from a property, and if that flow of services can be thought of as including all the environmental features of the house and the surrounding area, then any price depreciation on the property must reflect some change in the "mix" of the features of the property. In addition, D will be the market's valuation of those changed features. Since the house price, and D, are present values, expectations about the future should, strictly be accounted for in these prices. As we saw above, this is an arguable point but in the "Roskill" model it was stated that "the market price for property reflects not only current circumstance but also buyers' and sellers' expectations about the future. People buying a house affected by aircraft noise would be very naive if they did not expect an increase in the noise at least for the next ten years or so" (CTLA, 1970, p. 368).

In the "Roskill" model, D was estimated separately for Gatwick (London), and for Heathrow (London). These estimates were validated by returns from the District Valuer of the Inland Revenue. The Gatwick data were held to be relevant to the Third London Airport problem because of the closer similarity of Gatwick to the possible TLA sites. The method of estimating D was one of asking estate agents to say what the relative house price depreciation was in noisy and non-noisy areas. If the responses can be relied upon, it should be noted that the estimates of D will be estimates which relate to the effect of *noise alone*. This is because of the fact that samples can be devised to deal with house prices in areas where the airport affects employment but not noise levels, and in areas where both employment and noise are affected (this arises because access factors tend to be distributed geographically round an airport in a different fashion to noise contours).

Table 6.2 below shows the results obtained for Gatwick in terms of agents' responses:

Table 6.2   Percentage depreciation

	35—45 NNI			45+ NNI		
	Low-price house (£4,000)	*Medium-price house* (£4,000—8,000)	*High-price house* (£8,000)	*Low-price house*	*Medium-price house*	*High-price house*
Highest estimate	10	15	25	15	25	50
Average estimate	5	9	16	10	17	29
Lower estimate	0	3	5	5	10	12½

Source: CTLA Research Team. "Noise Cost Sensitivity Analysis — Variation in Values of House Price Depreciations Caused by Noise". Document presented to CTLA Stage V Proceedings, 1970.

It will be seen that the variation in estate agents' responses is substantial i.e. the variation when looking down the columns in Table 6.2). Although Flowerdew (1972, p. 41) states that "agreement between estate agents was satisfactory", the actual figures suggest a wide variation. However, the Inland Revenue data tended to confirm the *average* depreciations used (i.e. the middle row of Table 6.2).

Table 6.3 shows the depreciation figures for Heathrow and Gatwick.

Table 6.3   CTLA — Gatwick and Heathrow: Value of D (%)

			35–45 NNI		45–55 NNI		55+ NNI
Low price	Gatwick	(G)	4.5	G	10.3	G	N/A
£4,000	Heathrow	(H)	0.0	H	2.9	H	5.0
Medium price		G	9.4	G	16.5	G	N/A
£4,000–8,000		H	2.6	H	6.3	H	10.5
High price		G	16.4	G	29.0	G	N/A
£8,000		H	3.3	H	13.3	H	22.5

Source: CTLA, 1970.

Several points are in order. First, it can be argued that D is related to NNI in a linear fashion, although in the case of the Gatwick data this is tenuous since only two observations exist from which to secure a relationship. Nonetheless, the other data tends to support the linearity proposition. Further, if we look at the *change* in %D for given house price levels as we move from one NNI band to another the changes are very similar in magnitude. Thus, a move from 40–50 NNI to 50–60 NNI on the Heathrow data shows changes of: 2.9 and 2.1 per cent for low-priced houses; 3.7 and 4.2 per cent for medium-priced houses; 10.0 and 9.2 per cent for high-priced houses. The importance of this linearity is that it justifies the use of noise measures such as NNI as cardinal indicators of "quiet" (Walters, 1975). Second, if it is legimate to extrapolate to lower NNI figures we can observe that D will continue to be greater than zero for values of NNI less than 30 in the case of high- and medium-priced houses (Gatwick — CTLA). Now, most studies have excluded values of NNI below 35 NNI. If the depreciation data can be relied upon, they indicate that positive social costs exist at levels of noise significantly below 35 NNI — a most important consideration in cost—benefit studies.

One unresolved issue concerning the effects of noise on property values has been noted by Pearce and Nash (1973). They observe that *road traffic noise* appears not to have significant effects on property prices. Diffey's study (Diffey, 1971) concluded that "there is no negative effect due to noise on house prices", while Towne (1968), carrying out a similar study in the USA, states "the analysis . . . strongly suggests that the occupant's annoyance is not reflected in rent". On the other hand, aircraft noise does, as we have seen, appear to affect house prices. If aircraft noise is in some way intrinsically more annoying than road traffic noise, this asymmetry would not be noteworthy, but, in fact, psychological and sociological studies (see Wilson, 1963) suggest that people are *more* sensitive to road noise than to aircraft noise. Pearce and Nash conclude from this that "there is a 'hidden element' of noise nuisance which is felt by residents but which is not valued by the house price differential approach". If this is correct, and only further research will show this, it suggests that house price approaches will systematically understate noise nuisance costs.

Whitbread and Bird (1973), however, doubt if Diffey's results are conclusive since noise differences between the areas studied were not very pronounced, and some attributes of affected properties (physical condition in particular) were excluded. They also suggest that a low income elasticity of demand for amenity would explain the low sensitivity of house prices to noise in Diffey's study because the houses in question were occupied by low income groups. Nonetheless, it isn't clear if Diffey's finding that noise and property prices were *positively* correlated would turn into a *negative* correlation — as property price models predict — with these factors corrected. Also, some other studies support the view that property prices need not be affected by disamenity (Crecine *et al.*, 1967). A study of freeway noise and property values in Toledo (Colony, 1967) showed: (*a*) that, statistically, no effect of noise on property values could be demonstrated; (*b*) that estate agents ("realtors") thought noise reduced property values by 20—30 per cent; and (*c*) over 60 per cent of residents said they would not live near an expressway again. The inconsistency of these results is not satisfactorily explained.

The estimation of consumers' surplus (S)
We observed that approaches which look at house prices changes *alone* are deficient in that they fail to allow for changes in consumers' surplus. Consequently the estimation of this surplus, S, is important. The CTLA Research Team (CTLA, 1970 and CTLA, 1971, Appendix 23) considered various ways of estimating S. Strictly, one requires to observe a set of prices freely negotiated between house owner and developer. If these could be observed they might indicate the distribution of house owners' subjective valuations. These could then be compared to actual market prices, and the difference would be a measure of S. However, practical difficulties prevent this approach being used — primarily, no such "free" negotiations can take place in reality — so that a questionnaire approach was adopted. Six areas in the south of England were chosen for the survey, each of the areas supposedly being unaffected by development. Respondents were asked to consider a hypothetical "large development" and to say "what price would be just high enough to compensate . . . for leaving this house and moving to another area" (CTLA, Further Research Team Work, 1970). The price quoted was then recorded and the difference was the consumer's surplus.

Table 6.4   Consumer's surplus

Inducement	% response CTLA
<£150	11
£150—450	2
£450—950	14
£950—1,500	19
£1,500—2,500	11
£2,500—4,500	18
£4,500—10,000	12
>£10,000	5
Would not sell	8
	100

The responses to the CTLA surveys are shown in Table 6.4.

It will be noted that a significant number state that they would not sell "at any price". It is certainly tempting to think that very large offers would have been sufficient to induce these respondents to sell: their failure to state a definite sum has led to them being called "infinites" because they appear to imply infinite sums for compensation. But this may not be the correct conclusion to draw. It may simply be that people do not think or behave like the economist's "rational man" on all occasions: that is, they may not conceptually be able to translate the many intangible items covered by "householders' surplus" into money terms. If this is true it presents severe methodological problems for cost—benefit studies, but it is at least as consistent a view as supposing that there must be some finite figure for compensation.

As to those finite values reported by respondents, Mishan (1970) criticizes the use of these on the grounds that respondents were given no indication of how far they would have to move to avoid the (hypothetical) development scheme. Whitbread and Bird (1973) adopt a similar stance when they argue that the valuations of S are unreliable because respondents were unable to identify from the questionnaire what the alternatives were before them.

One important deficiency of surveys is that the very *fact* that the survey is taking place makes the respondent believe that there is a connection between disamenity and money values which is capable of being assessed (Hedges, 1972). It also remains true that hypothetical questions are almost certain to induce unreliable responses because the respondent knows he is not being asked to engage in *actual* decisions.

6.4 Applications of property price models

This section summarizes some of the applications to which property price noise-cost models have been put.

(a) The Third London Airport

Four short-listed sites were considered as the location for London's third airport (now postponed indefinitely). These were Cublington (C), Nuthampstead (N), Thurleigh (T), and Foulness (F). (For an overview of the cost—benefit study of the third airport see Dasgupta and Pearce, 1972.) The methodology used was that described previously as the "Roskill" approach. The final measures of noise costs (£m.) were as follows (CTLA, 1971): Cublington, 22.7; Foulness, 10.2; Nuthampstead, 72.2; Thurleigh, 15.6. The figures are discounted to 1982 which was the then estimated year of opening the airport. These figures differ from those in CTLA 1970 due to small changes in population and NNI statistics, but mainly to the allowance of a 5 per cent per annum increase in the relative price of "quiet" as discussed earlier. These figures relate to "off-site" noise — residents "on site" would clearly be required to move physically.

In terms of numbers of households, the figures are: Cublington, 28,464; Foulness, 20,334; Nuthampstead, 94,185; Thurleigh, 25,028; so that the average noise cost per household is approximately: Cublington, £800; Foulness, £500; Nuthampstead, £765; Thurleigh, £620.

It must be emphasized that these figures cannot be used as an index of noise costs because there is clearly a distribution of costs about the average. They are produced here merely to indicate the kinds of magnitudes involved.

The orders of magnitudes are confirmed by the estimates for Luton airport (CTLA, 1971, p. 259) which gives an average of £810 per household. Walters (1975) has separately estimated noise costs for the four sites on the basis of his own approach which, it will be recalled, does not require the categorization of residents but which uses a general estimate of D. Walters' results require some further explanation. Using the Third London Airport data, Walters obtains the relationships, set out in Table 6.5 where H = number of households above 35 NNI:

Table 6.5

H (1)	Mean NNI (2)	Variance of NNI (3)	Total NNI ('000) (4) = (1) × (2)
C 29,400	42.1	4.29	1,238
F 20,300	41.8	3.51	849
N 94,800	40.2	2.46	3,811
T 25,600	42.4	8.05	1,066

We require the variance of the NNI to allow for the fact that average NNI may be similar for any two sites, but noise costs will vary significantly if one site has its NNI concentrated in one particular range.

Walters then calculates total NNI above NNI = 27 since 27 is taken to correspond to zero annoyance. Using the CTLA research team cost estimates, this gives noise cost per unit NNI above 27, as in Table 6.6.

Table 6.6

Total NNI above 27	CTLA noise cost	Cost per unit NNI above 27
C 444,000	£22.7m.	£51.1
F 301,000	£10.2m.	£33.9
N 1,251,000	£72.2m.	£57.6
T 394,000	£15.6	£39.6

Walters then shows that cost per unit NNI and variance (V) have the relationship

£ cost per unit NNI (above 27) = 65.6 − 3.5V

Now, with these relationships in mind, we have *two* approaches to estimating noise costs. First, we can use the formula:

$C_A = P \cdot NDSI \cdot H \cdot D \cdot NNI \cdot 1/100$

derived earlier. In this formula we can substitute the figures for total NNI above 27 derived above for H·D·NNI. This is approach A. Approach B makes use of the noise cost/NNI variance relationship noted above and which is derived from the "Roskill" data. On this approach, B, noise costs are estimated as

$C_B = (65.6 - 3.5V)$. Total units NNI above 27.

The table below shows the results (£m.).[6]

	C	F	N	T
Walters (A)	22.2	15.1	62.5	19.7
Walters (B)	22.4	16.0	71.3	14.7

We can see the very close similarity between the results of approach B and the original "Roskill" results. This of course is logical since approach B is nothing other than a simple way of reaching the "Roskill" results. Walters' own approach is seen to produce results very close to the "Roskill" results in two cases, but the margins of difference are quite large in the case of Nuthampstead and Thurleigh.

(b) Retrofitting aircraft

Walters (1974) has suggested some "back of the envelope" calculations concerning the desirability of retrofitting aircraft. For the USA he uses a figure of $2 billion as the cost of retrofitting the entire US airlines' fleet, and a figure of 4 million households affected by noise. Taking an average house price of $25,000 and an NDSI of 0.7 (lower than the value Walters uses for the UK) gives a "willingness of pay" figure of $1.4 billion, so that "there is certainly no overwhelming case for retrofitting the whole United States' fleet" (Walters, 1975). It is worth noting, however, that if such calculations are of the right order of magnitude, they indicate that a fairly substantial proportion of aircraft should be retrofitted.[7]

A more detailed UK government study (Board of Trade, 1970) used estimates of house price depreciation as a direct indicator of noise disbenefits. The benefits of a UK retrofit programme, relating to Heathrow only, were estimated to be, on this basis, between £24.9 m. to £32.6 m., with £28.8 m. as the "most likely" estimate. The costs of retrofit were considered on two bases: first, on the basis that UK residents bear the costs; second, that UK residents and foreign residents bear the costs equally through increases in air fares. In the final analysis the second alternative was dropped. The total cost was put at £34.9 m., so that, on the "most likely" benefit measure, retrofit would have net *costs* of £6.1 m. and could not be worthwhile.

The study was extended to consider a retrofit programme which would include foreign airlines. This was held to double benefits but to leave costs *to the UK* unaffected. Hence, such a programme yielded net *benefits* of £27.9 m. on the "best estimate" of house prices.

It is worth emphasizing again that the conclusion drawn from the initial study is not necessarily the interesting one: what is required is the schedule of costs and benefits such that the optimal amount of retrofitting can be estimated. That this amount is not 100 per cent of aircraft does not imply that it is zero.

6.5 The exclusion facilities approach

Starkie and Johnson (1973*a*, 1973*b*, 1973*c*, 1975) have proposed a different approach to the valuation of noise costs. They point out that, besides moving to escape noise or staying to suffer it, there is a further option open to householders, namely to insulate against it. In this way, the "Roskill" model can be modified to allow for this option. Essentially, where the movement decision in the "Roskill" model depended on

$$N \lessgtr S + D + R$$

Starkie and Johnson argue that those who stay to tolerate noise must obey the inequality

$$S + D + R > N < G + N' \tag{1}$$

where G is the cost of "exclusion facilities" such as house insulation, fencing (if it is motorway noise), etc., and N' is the valuation of "residential noise" — i.e. that noise left over even after the introduction of insulation.

Similarly, those who stay but buy exclusion facilities must obey

$$N > G + N' < S + D + R \tag{2}$$

Starkie and Johnson used the cost of double-glazing — which varies with window size — as a surrogate for price, thus providing the basis for estimating a demand schedule.

The logic of equations [1] and [2] is simply that households will buy exclusion facilities if the value of noise reduction so secured is more than the expenditure on the facilities, i.e. if

$$N - N' > G$$

in which case there will be a surplus gained on G. In this way, "expenditure on exclusion facilities represents a minimum valuation of the good 'peace and quite'" (Starkie and Johnson, 1975). If variations in the price of exclusion facilities can be observed, we can obtain a demand curve the area under which would be a minimum measure of surplus, and hence a value that can be entered into a cost–benefit analysis.

It must be noted that the approach will produce unrepresentative valuations for average households if there is a significant number of movers: the model operates, by definition, only for those who stay. Starkie and Johnson (1975) argue that the bias in this respect is small since they estimate that there are very few households that move because of noise. This is in contrast with Walters' (1975) suggestion that movement rates in noisy areas are probably 20 to 30 per cent above the "natural" movement rate. On the other hand, the Heathrow area has a high proportion of tenants who, Starkie and Johnson argue, are constrained in terms of their ability to move.

Since Starkie and Johnson's population sample was fairly homogenous, it was assumed that its members had similar incomes. By indirect means, this average income was estimated at £1,800, and total willingness to pay for insulation of three bedrooms was £45 and for two living rooms was £47, for a given average reduction in noise of 14 dBA. This suggests a willingness to pay of about 5 per cent of income for the total insulation of a house with three bedrooms and two downstairs rooms. Starkie and Johnson further suggest that this is a maximum value since sound insulation has joint-good aspects – it serves also as heat insulation – which means that the expenditures for noise *alone* can be thought of as being less.

Starkie and Johnson's figure of 5 per cent of income as the value of "quiet" compares to Walters' suggestion that the range of values is between 2 per cent (for low income groups) and 7 per cent (for high income groups).

Starkie and Johnson's approach is an interesting one and it is clear that further useful work could be carried out in this general direction. The problems with it are: (i) that it cannot be relied upon to provide an average valuation of noise if there is a significant number of people who move because of noise; (ii) it provides an average value of N–N' but leaves residual noise unvalued, although this may be thought of as cancelling out with the joint good aspects of insulation; (iii) it provides us only with an average valuation for a specified range of noise reduction so that we have no marginal valuation which can be applied to other ranges; (iv) expenditure on double-glazing gives us an estimate of what householders are willing to pay for the joint product of noise insulation, thermal insulation and house protection.

6.6 Pollution control costs: sector level
As we saw, the cost–benefit approach to pollution control requires us to estimate the relative magnitudes of damage costs and control costs. While

the estimation of damage costs is perhaps more hazardous, it has received a disproportionately large share of attention of researchers. In consequence, the apparently more "concrete" pollution control costs are frequently unknown.

At the conceptual level one immediate problem arises. Industry is engaged in a continual process of replacing depreciated capital equipment. If, overnight say, some new antipollution legislation is passed, it should be possible to see how much extra expenditure on capital equipment is required to meet the new legislated requirements. But, at the same time, if the legislation is thought to be permanent, capital equipment designers will tend to incorporate the antipollution requirements in their new designs. At the same time, however, their new designs will also incorporate other technological change. A new machine may, as a result, be cheaper than the old machine, but still contain antipollution technology in it. Has the antipollution element embodied in the new machine a negative cost? Technically we require to know what the new machine would have cost without the antipollution content and what it costs with that content. The difference will be the capital cost of abatement. All too often, this kind of estimate is impossible to secure.

Other abatement expenditures are easier to identify. Thus, many abatement costs are not embodied in machinery at all, but exist quite independently in the form of purification plant, precipitators, screens, and so on. Of course, if, for any reason, abatement interferes with the usual rate of production of the good in question, any costs to this effect are legitimately included in the cost of abatement. Care has also to be taken to secure the true cost of abatement: many of the costs reported by industry, for example, can reflect tax and capital allowances granted by government to industry when antipollution equipment is purchased.

A further point of importance is that, in cost–benefit work, we are interested in the true *social* cost of abatement. Technically, we need to know the present value of the social benefits that *could have been* obtained had we used the funds in some other use. In practice, as in virtually all cost–benefit work, the money price of the abatement capital is taken to measure those benefits, although, clearly, consumer's surplus will not be included by adopting this approach. Looking at social costs also means that we are not interested in items such as interest payments paid on money borrowed to buy the equipment – such payments will be transfers between one individual in society and another, and hence do not reflect real costs. Finally, it will be necessary to add to capital costs, the operating costs that will occur in a fairly continuous time stream.

Generally, marginal pollution control costs tend to increase with the amount of pollution abatement. That is, controlling a sizeable proportion of emissions can be achieved for a specific cost, but to improve the proportion say from 60 to 70 per cent leads to substantial increases in cost. To completely "purify" an industrial process tends to be extremely expensive. Tables 6.7 and 6.8 give two illustrations. In Table 6.7 we show the pollution abatement costs associated with various programmes to "clean up" the Delaware Estuary in the United States. The estuary is surrounded by highly concentrated industrial complexes and a pollution of some 6 million people. The study of the estuary that gave rise to the control costs estimates in Table 6.7 considered five objectives that might be aimed at: objective number 5 aimed only to prevent further pollution and would have kept the estuary at its quality level pertaining in 1964; objective 4 aimed for slight improvements on the 1964 quality level; objective 3 would have secured a higher level of quality set by aiming for the preservation of fish populations for a set level of probability; objective 2 is similar to objective 3 but with a raised level of probability of fish survival; objective 1, the highest objective, aimed to secure a water quality level suitable for many "water-contact" recreational uses, and levels of dissolved oxygen in the water that would permit the safe migration of fish.

Table 6.7

Objective	Uniform treatment Total costs $m.	Zoned treatment Total costs $m.	Cost Minimization Total costs $m.
1	460	460	460
2	315	250	215
3	155	120	85
4	130	80	65
5	—	—	30

Source: Kneese and Bower (1968), p. 230.

Obviously, the costs of achieving each abatement level will vary with the type of abatement policy adopted. Strictly, as any economist will point out, the type of policy should always be that which minimizes costs for a given objective. Hence, column 3 in Table 6.7 shows the cheapest way of achieving objectives 1–5. Other methods have to be considered if cost-minimization implies some administratively unacceptable programme: for example, concepts of fairness might be relevant such that there will be objections if some areas are zoned for purification and others are not. The marginal costs of abatement are not strictly something that we can derive from Table 6.7 because the objectives are not defined in terms of some continuous quality index, or in terms of benefits. We noticed this problem with noise evaluation procedures — we should really be speaking of the costs of achieving a given increment in benefit, where benefits are on a cardinal scale. With noise we saw that there is an argument to suggest that indices such as NNI are "cardinal" in this respect, although the proposition is disputed. With water quality we have no such relationship. Nonetheless, with this caution in mind, and treating objectives 1–5 in Table 6.7 *as if* they represent points on a cardinal scale, we see that the marginal costs of abatement do rise as we increase the quality objective. In so far as they are meaningful, as we go up the quality scale, marginal costs of abatement proceed in the sequence 35, 40, 130, 245.

Table 6.8 shows the control costs associated with removing waste from water systems polluted by the US steel industry. Notice that these abatement costs are presented in a very different fashion to those in Table 6.7. First, they relate to "pounds of pollutant" removed and not to some defined measure of water quality. Naturally, we expect water quality to improve as pollutants are removed, but the relationship is not the same as that we have noted in Table 6.7. Second, we may note that abatement costs are presented in an "inverse" form — in terms of amounts of pollutant removed per $1 of expenditure and not in terms of costs per unit of pollutant removed or of costs per unit of quality objective achieved. The letters A . . . E refer to abatement technologies, so that A represents existing treatments, B will indicate a supplementary treatment to secure more depollution, and so on.

In general we see that, bearing in mind once again the fact that we do not strictly have a measure of benefits or water quality in Table 6.8, marginal abatement costs tend to rise with higher levels of purification. Thus, if we take sintering, and consider the five processes, we see that an extra $1 on technology B will remove an extra 6.10 lb of suspended solids; a further $1 (C) will remove only 0.47 lb; a further $1 (D) only 0.16 lb; and the final $1 (E) will remove 0.28 lb. Marginal abatement costs would appear to drop slightly with the final process, but the general upward trend is there.

6.7 Pollution control costs: national level

We noted in section 6.6 that one practical problem of measuring abatement costs is the absence of a uniform index of quality or benefit against which to measure them. The same problem arises with national estimates of pollution control costs. For example, an ideal analysis would tell us what it would cost to secure a given uniform quality of environment in

Table 6.8 Pounds of pollutant removable from water per dollar of cost in the steel industry (USA)

Production subcategory	Treatment process*	Pounds removed per $ of costs							
		Suspended solids	Ammonia NH$_3$	Phenol	Cyanide	BOD$_5$	Sulphide	Oil and grease	Fluoride
Blast furnace (Ferromanganese)	A	284.50	6.15	0.19	1.65	—	3.71	—	—
Blast Furnace (Ferromanganese)	B	3.70	7.40	0.03	3.80	—	4.60	—	—
Blast furnace (Ferromanganese)	C	0.11	0.23	0.01	0.04	—	0.04	—	—
Sintering	A	164.00	—	—	—	—	2.80	11.40	—
Sintering	B	6.10	—	—	—	—	—	—	—
Sintering	C	0.47	—	—	—	—	2.90	2.00	0.94
Sintering	D	0.16	—	—	—	—	0.13	—	0.20
Sintering	E	0.28	—	—	—	—	0.01	0.11	0.23
Blast furnace (Iron)	A	108.20	—	—	—	—	—	—	—
Blast furnace (Iron)	B	6.40	0.79	0.12	0.20	—	2.60	—	0.49
Blast furnace (Iron)	C	0.17	0.50	0.02	0.06	—	0.02	—	0.49
By-product coke (Biological)	A	0.07	1.65	0.58	0.18	1.48	0.62	0.16	—
By-product coke (Biological)	B	—	5.06	0.02	0.40	1.16	0.14	0.06	—
By-product coke (Ph/Ch)	A	0.07	1.65	0.58	0.18	1.48	0.62	0.16	—
By-product coke (Ph/Ch)	B	—	8.16	0.03	0.56	1.40	0.14	0.14	—
By-product coke (Ph/Ch)	C	0.12	0.18	0.01	0.08	0.36	0.03	0.02	—

Source: US EPA,   * See text.

different countries. This would enable us to make a meaningful comparison of these costs, bearing in mind that each country would have a different starting point in terms of the current quality of their environments. In practice, each country has different environmental objectives so that any comparison of costs must be interpreted as being a comparison of the relative costs of achieving *different* objectives. If we observe, say, country A spending less than other countries, we cannot conclude, as is often done, that country A is less "concerned" with the environment — i.e. has a lower objective. For the difference may be due to the fact that country A starts off at a higher quality level and hence has less of a problem to solve compared to other countries. Also, there may be every reason *not* to have uniform standards between countries.[8] Lastly, different countries have different assimilative capacities, so that expenditures need not be so great in a country with high assimilative capacity as in one where it is low.

Table 6.9   Pollution abatement costs as percentage of GNP

	Investment	Operating costs	Total
United States (1971—80)	0.7	1.5	2.2
Germany	0.9	0.9	1.8
Italy	0.4	0.2	0.6
Japan	2.2	n.a.	n.a.
Netherlands	n.a.	n.a.	1—1.5
Sweden	0.7	n.a.	n.a.

Source: OECD: *Survey of Pollution Control Cost Estimates, Made in Member Countries*, Paris, 1972.

Table 6.9 shows pollution abatement costs as a percentage of GNP for six countries for the period 1971—75. The magnitude of these costs is modest. The USA costs, for example, amount to one-quarter the size of defence expenditure, less than a third of the size of education expenditure and less than a third of the size of health expenditures.

The expenditure shown in Table 6.9 can be broken down into expenditures on alleviating water pollution, air pollution and solid waste problems. These are shown in Table 6.10. It will be seen that countries vary significantly with respect to the types of pollution problem they consider it

Table 6.10 Percentage of total additional expenditure on pollution control over programme period[1]

	Air	Water	Solid waste	Total
United States	56	29	14.5	100
Germany	15.5	71.5	13	100
Sweden[2]	9[3]	85.5	5.5	100
Netherlands	26	59	15	100
United Kingdom	22	78	—	100
Italy[2]	32	65	2.5	100

1. Programme periods are 1971–75 for Germany and 1971–80 for the remainder.
2. Investment only.
3. Without thermal plants.
Source: Barde, 1973.

necessary to abate. In the USA most of the effort is expended on air pollution, but in the UK it is mainly devoted to water pollution.

Pollution control cost estimates at the national level have to be treated with considerable caution. Observing that given objectives can be secured at only 1 or 2 per cent of GNP is in no way a cause for complacency. As we have seen, such small expenditures are consistent with the objectives being rather limited. Moreover, control costs may be defined differently. The estimates in Table 6.9 and 6.10 do not, for example, include any expenditures on noise abatement, nor on improving the physical features of urban environments, nor on landscaping or preservation of national parks and wilderness area. In the absence of some kind of aggregative cost–benefit analysis, we have no direct way of saying whether the low recorded percentages are too low, or even too high. Nor must we fall into the trap of making a "league-table" out of pollution expenditures: the figures do not warrant this.

Notes

1. The point is an important one. For an individual, the price of any commodity is the same however many he buys. If apples in the market are priced at x pence each, the amount spent is a simple multiple of quantity bought and the constant unit price paid. But, given the way noise measures

are constructed, one would expect units of noise to differ according to how many of them one already has. That is the (negative) price of 1 unit of NNI (the "noise and number index" — a measure of noise which attempts to incorporate both loudness and frequency of occurrence) added to an existing 50 units should be higher than the (negative) price attached to an additional unit on top of 40 NNI. In this respect we would expect the price — NNI relationship to be nonlinear. Walters (1975) argues that the evidence from the information collected in the investigation of London's third airport supports the assumption on linearity — i.e. a constant price per unit of noise measure. Since the information on which this argument is based is itself questionable, and since other investigations do not appear to support the linearity hypothesis (though they do not really refute it either), Walters' argument is, as he readily admits open to doubt.

2. The actual formula was $P = a + bV$ where V is rateable value and P is price.

3. Taken from Paul (1971) who provides perhaps the most explicit account of the Roskill procedure for estimating N and of the use of N in predicting who moves.

4. N and PNdB are linked via annoyance scores. Observations of different PNdB, N combinations were correlated to annoyance scores, so that given levels of N could be shown to be equivalent to particular levels of PNdB in terms of annoyance. This was then used to construct the graph below, showing that a fourfold increase in N, *regardless of the initial size*

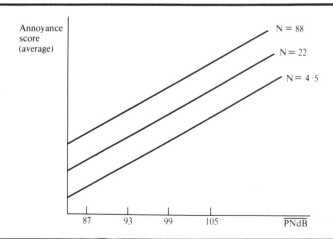

of N, is equivalent to about 9 dB. The measure PNdB + 15 log N was found to be equal to 80 for an annoyance score of zero, so that 80 must be subtracted to get the NNI equation.

5.   Note that therefore $Q \cdot P = b \cdot Y$, i.e. expenditure on quiet, equals bY. Hence $\dfrac{\delta(Q \cdot P)}{\delta Y} = b$, and $\dfrac{Y \cdot \delta(Q \cdot P)}{Q \cdot P \cdot \delta Y} = \dfrac{b}{b} = 1$. This is the income elasticity of demand for quiet. It is noted in the text that this is inconsistent with Walters' argument that the income elasticity of demand for quiet appears to lie in the range 1.7 to 2.0.

6.   The estimates are those of the author since Walters shows only some of the results and the two approaches are not entirely separated in Walters (1975).

7.   The Boeing and McDonald—Douglas Companies estimate total cost of retrofit to be some $9.5 billion, compared to Walters' figure of $2 billion. See US Environmental Protection Agency *The Economic Impact of Noise*, Washington, 1971.

8.   This issue of international uniformity is not pursued here. Readers are referred to Cumberland (1972) and to several of the other essays in OECD (1972). Extensive, if occasionally esoteric, work on international aspects of environment is contained in OECD (1974).

7

The depletion of non-renewable resources

We saw in Chapter 3 that pollution and the depletion of natural resources are, to a considerable extent, obverse sides of the same coin. The more resources extracted from the "environment" the more residuals there must eventually be for disposal back to the environment, and, hence, the more potential pollution there is. In this chapter we investigate the environment from the natural resource standpoint, concentrating only on non-renewable resources such as minerals and energy sources.

7.1 Classifying resources

Resources can of course be classified in any number of ways. But we shall generally find it useful to think in terms of the intertemporal characteristics of a resource (Common and Pearce, 1973): that is, what does its use now imply for its use in the future? The answer to this question depends critically upon what type of resource is under consideration, so that discussions that treat the concept of resources as if it refers to some completely homogeneous entity can be misleading. We can recall the concept of an intertemporal production frontier from Chapter 1 for use here. This production frontier tells us how much of a resource will be available in a later period if we select a particular usage now. Consider some alternatives. If we have a resource that is totally fixed in supply and which cannot be reclaimed for re-use, the intertemporal production frontier will appear as in Fig. 7.1. The total stock, ab, could be used in the current period, or in the later period. In between are endless combinations, but future availability (Q_{t+1}) will always be equal to the total stock (Q) minus current usage, (Q_t) i.e.

$$Q_{t+1} = Q - Q_t$$

so that the production frontier is a straight line.

Fig. 7.1

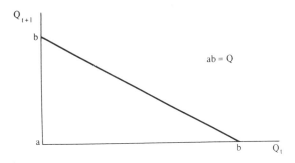

Now suppose we have a resource which even if used in the current period can be completely reclaimed and re-used in a future period. Here we have the extreme of 100 per cent recycling of past stock. In this case, the fixed stock could all be used in the current period and is still available in the next period. We have to assume of course that the periods in our analysis coincide with the period over which the resource stock has a useful economic life in its initial form — i.e. it must be disposed of in such a way that it can be reclaimed and reprocessed for the next period. This will give us the frontier shown in Fig. 7.2.

Fig. 7.2

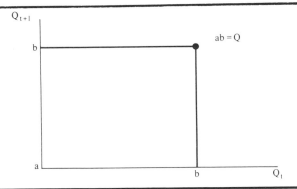

One hundred per cent recycling is, of course, so remote from reality that we can safely treat Fig. 7.2 as an extreme for illustrative purposes only. Figure 7.3 illustrates what happens if only *some* of the resource in question can be recycled. If all the initially available resource is used up in the current period, there will still be an amount, say ac, which is available for the next period.

144

Fig. 7.3

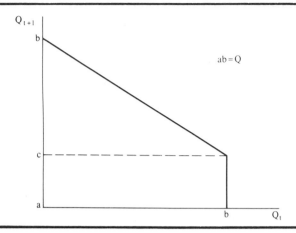

Later sections in this chapter investigate the implications of these production frontiers for the concept of optimal use of resources over time. For the moment we can observe one vitally important fact which derives from the production frontiers. *In the absence of a 100 per cent recycling society, or in the absence of complete substitution between renewable and non-renewable resources, there must exist a trade-off between the use of resources now and the use of resources in the future.* We argued in Chapter 1 that no *logical* rationale can be provided for ignoring future generations. Indeed, we suggested that the conventional framework of economics obliges present generations to consider the welfare of future generations. As such, the nature of the trade-off implicit in the use of natural resources is vitally important.

In classifying resources, then, we require a classification with the emphasis on intertemporal transformation, an emphasis justified by the future-orientated nature of the natural resource problem.

Intertemporal transfer depends upon storage. Storage may be "natural" or induced by deliberate action. Solar energy is naturally stored and is released at a reasonably constant rate through time. If it could be trapped and held over future periods this would constitute deliberate storage. Past solar energy appears in minute part in the form of "inventoried energy" — coal, oil and gas — which can be stored either before the extraction process (simply by refraining from consumption) or after. A particularly important form of storage concerns the retention of some stock in the current period in the form of seed or potential parent population for regeneration in the next period: this form of storage defines *renewable* resources. But storage also depends upon whether the resource appears as a flow of material or energy or is the result of energy-flow. Thus, the principle of materials circulation (Chapter 3) tells us that even when materials are used in some productive process they are potentially reclaimable provided they have not gone through chemical transformation such that they cannot be reconstituted. Thus recyclable materials are "naturally" stored in the above sense. On the other hand, energy flows are unidirectional, and this applies whether the energy source is inventoried or otherwise. Such energy flows cannot be recaptured and, although not destroyed (the first law of thermodynamics), are dispersed uselessly.

Figure 7.4 illustrates the basic categories. The four groups of interest are: stock-energy resources ($R_{S,E}$), stock-material resources ($R_{S,M}$), flow energy resources ($R_{F,E}$), and stock-renewable resources ($R_{S,R}$).

Energy produced by nuclear fission in consumer reactors fits category $R_{S,E}$, being dependent on fixed stocks of materials such as uranium. The possibility of breeder reactors means that nuclear energy produced by this means would belong to category $R_{S,R}$. Energy production via nuclear fusion, of course, raises the possibility of virtually limitless energy sources.

(a) Stock-energy resources

Resources in this category, such as coal, natural gas, oil, are fixed in total stock, and the capacity rate of flow varies with respect to the extraction effort applied to them. Intertemporal trade-offs are secured by abstention from current consumption, and the intertemporal production frontier is linear. As long as usage is positive, the fixed stock must be exhausted in finite time. In addition, the physical transformation of energy inputs is such that recycling is not possible.

(b) Stock-material resources

As with stock-energy inputs, total supply is fixed and intertemporal transformation can be achieved only by abstention from current consumption. Unless the physical transformation process is such as to render materials into non-recoverable wastes, however, recycling is possible, and does of course take place in many industries — waste paper, lead, copper, etc. We include water as a stock material resource.

(c) Flow-energy resources

The rate of capacity flow tends to be fixed for these resources, but actual usage also tends to fall very short of the capacity flow. Thus only a minute proportion of solar energy is impounded by photosynthesis and animal use. Similarly, the potential for tidal and hydroelectric energy is substantial, but actual usage is small. Flow-energy resources exhibit several highly important features not present with other resources:

Fig. 7.4

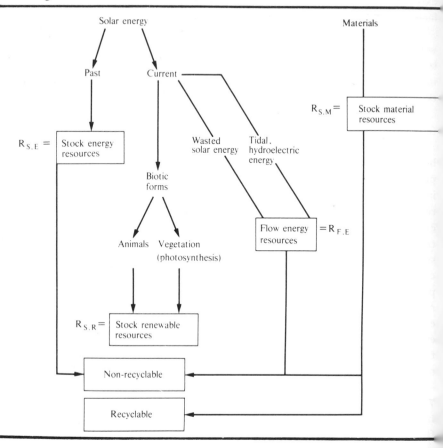

1. They cannot be intertemporally traded since storage is possible for only very short periods.

2. Although optimal usage might then appear to correspond with capacity usage, this ignores possible economic—ecologic trade-offs of the kind considered in Chapter 2.

All activities designed to alter an ecosystem will of course have eco-system effects, but some activities generate appreciable and fairly immediate results. This is certainly true of hydroelectric energy, so that increases in this source of energy capture will involve ecological effects. Unfortunately, the nature of these effects is not always predictable, so that there is no way of assessing the social worth of such projects in a future generation orientated cost—benefit framework. Capture of "spare" solar energy on the other hand is not likely to have such effects, although existing technology appears to suggest that solar energy "traps" would have to cover vast tracts of land to be of economic use.

Whether such trade-offs can be assessed in comparable terms determines whether economics and ecology will ever secure a common basis in science, and it is the absence of such a common basis at the moment does much to explain the poor communication between ecologist and economist.

(d) Stock-renewable resources

An important category of resources has a fixed stock at any point in time, but the stock is renewable through biological reproduction. Agricultural produce and marine resources comprise this category. Labour also falls into this category. Reproduction may be "natural" (most marine resources, labour) or "managed" (fish farms, forest products, agricultural crops and livestock). Intertemporal trade-off is determined by reproduction rates and the size of the potential parent population. Current consumption of potential parent populations will of course reduce consumption in the next period, but not consumption in the subsequent period if next year's stock is used for reproduction. Where reproduction is natural, population adjustment mechanisms will tend to operate in the event of resource depletion in any one year. There is, of course, ample evidence to show that these adjustment mechanisms have not been allowed to operate for some marine resources with consequent elimination and near-elimination of species.

7.2 Optimal usage: basic concepts

If it is possible to establish the existence of an intertemporal social welfare function, a function showing us the relative desirability of distributing resource consumption between different time periods (see Chapter 1) it would be possible to identify the amounts of a resource that should be consumed in each period. Basically, we would have a familiar exercise in constrained utility maximization but with time entering the analysis. If we take one of the production frontiers (or transformation functions) from the previous section and superimpose a welfare function, we obtain a diagram such as Fig. 7.5 which shows that the optimal distribution of resource use over the two time periods in question, t and t + 1, is given by OR_t and OR_{t+1} respectively. There are no intrinsic difficulties in extending the analysis to more than two time periods.[1]

Figure 7.5 deals with the case of the non-recyclable fixed stock resource such as fixed energy stocks. Figure 7.6 shows the analysis for a completely recyclable resource, or for R_F type resources where storage is not possible. In this case it can be seen that there is a prima facie case for

Fig. 7.5

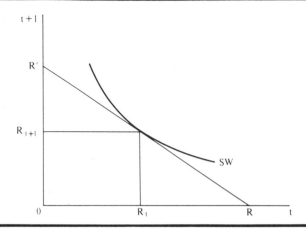

consuming the entire flow in each time period. This conclusion will be modified to the extent that such an action interferes with ecosystem stability. If there is some ecological limit say R_t^e $(= R_{t+1}^e)$, then the economy will be required to operate at a lower level of resource use than that implied by capacity flow or by total available stock. Social welfare will appear to be lower but only because the shadow price attached to ecological instability is not included in the analysis.

We may also consider the case where some recycling takes place, as in Fig. 7.7. We saw that the effect of recycling is to impart a vertical section

Fig. 7.6

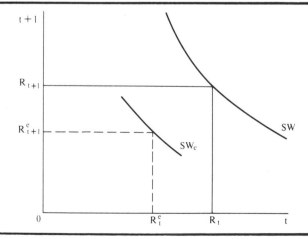

Fig. 7.7

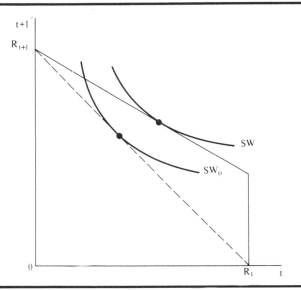

to the transformation function. Figure 7.7 compares this transformation function to one where no recycling takes place (the broken line). It should be evident that social welfare is higher if recycling takes place, and that the more recycling there is the higher is the level of welfare that can be achieved. This conclusion is modified in Chapter 8. For the moment it is necessary only to note this simple demonstration of the potential importance of recycling.

7.3 Optimal usage: basic results

Determining the optimal allocation of a given exhaustible resource between different periods of time is a highly complex problem, at least as soon as even faintly realistic assumptions are introduced. Examples of the highly sophisticated mathematical approaches to these problems can be found in Heal (1975), Kay and Mirrlees (1975), Koopmans (1973), Anderson (1972) and Vousden (1973). This section makes no attempt to describe these contributions. We concentrate only on some basic results which have generally served as the foundation of further theory. We shall also attempt to summarize some general points which should help us to decide whether resources are being used "too fast".

We saw in Chapter 1 that, under highly restrictive conditions, a perfectly competitive economy will allocate resources in such a way as to secure a Pareto optimum. This basic result also holds when we extend the analysis to include time. Consequently, if resource owners behave competitively, and if the rest of the economy is also competitive, we could argue that the free play of market forces will secure an optimal allocation of resources over time. In a world where the future is certain, a producer (resource owner) should be indifferent between securing unit of profit now and securing $(1 + r)$ units in one year's time, where r is the interest rate ruling in the economy. That is, his concern is with the *present value* of profits, not with their absolute magnitude regardless of when they occur (see Chapter 1). Hence what he aims to maximize is profits (V) where

$$V = (P_0 - C_0) + \frac{(P_1 - C_1)}{1 + r} + \frac{(P_2 - C_2)}{(1 + r)^2} + \cdots + \frac{(P_T - C_T)}{(1 + r)^T}$$

In this expression, P is the price of the finished resource, C is the marginal cost of extracting the resource from the environment, and r is the interest rate. The difference between P and C is the profit or "royalty". (The Appendix, p. 162, to this chapter derives some results from this formula, but using continuous and not discrete time.) T is the point in time at which the resource is exhausted.[2]

Now, one result of maximizing the expression V, is the following:

$$(P_0 - C_0) = \frac{(P_1 - C_1)}{1 + r} = \frac{(P_2 - C_2)}{(1 + r)^2} = \cdots \text{etc.}$$

That is, the present value of the marginal contribution that the resource makes to profits must be equal for each point in time. If it was not so, then resource owners could increase profits by shifting production between periods — producing more now, or withholding production now in favour of the future.

Now, since profit maximizing behaviour is Pareto optimal in a perfectly competitive world, the above marginal allocation condition also describes the requirement for socially optimal allocation of the resource between time periods. The preceding analysis would therefore seem to suggest a prima facie case for leaving resource allocation to the market, and for not worrying if we observe high positive rates of extraction, contrary to what we might call the "conservationist" case.

As always, however, the real world bears little resemblance to the perfectly competitive conditions that underlie the analysis so far. But this does not mean that deriving the perfectly competitive marginal conditions is a waste of time, for one approach that can be adopted is to see how far reality diverges from these "ideal" conditions, which can be treated as a benchmark. If the divergencies all act in one direction, we should be able to reach qualitative conclusion as to whether resources are being used too fast or too slowly. We now consider the various types of market imperfections that may occur and try to assess in which direction they cause a divergence from the optimal path of natural resource use.

Monopoly
Unless there are substantial differences in economies of production, monopolists will tend to restrict output and keep prices higher than they would be under perfect competition. If resource owners are monopolists we would therefore expect, in accordance with our previously stated marginal conditions, that resource production will be too *low* compared to the optimum.[3] If monopolists obtain substantial economies of scale, however, this may offset this bias.

Now, observation of many resource markets suggests that monopoly is in fact important. Certainly, as the industrialized world knows to its cost, most oil-producers have developed a powerful cartel (OPEC — The Organization of Petroleum Exporting Countries) which has unilaterally and successfully pushed the price of crude oil up threefold in under 1 year. Other cartels exist in copper, bauxite, rock potash (essential for fertilizer supplies), and even to some extent in natural rubber (which is now regaining lost markets as synthetic rubber, made from oil, increases in price). Some resources, such as nickel, are monopolistically owned by single companies. In consequence, the monopoly argument is an important one and can be taken to mean that resource use in practice is likely to be *less* than the optimal rate.

The discount rate
The Appendix to this chapter shows the relationship between resource prices and interest rates. In general, resource prices will grow at the same rate as the rate of interest if resources are optimally allocated through time and no imperfections exist. But the interest rate in question is the *private* discount rate. If the *social* rate of discount is different, resources will not be optimally allocated. Determining the social discount rate is itself a complex issue, but it is widely held that the social rate lies *below* the private rate. If this is true, the rate actually used in resource markets is too high, which will clearly work to the favour of *current* production but against *future* production. Hence the rate of extraction will be too fast. In this context we may note that social projects can be argued to have lower risk than private projects because the former have their risks spread over the whole population such that, if the project fails, the costs of failure are small relative to average per capital incomes. If this is correct, resource owners will have higher than desirable discount rates since they have to bear all the costs of uncertainty. Further, the resource owner must face

tax on his sales and on his capital gains. Hence his after-tax returns will be below his pre-tax returns, but the latter will be nearer the social discount rate. Hence his required rate of return — his discount rate — will be higher than the social rate of return. We conclude that social discount rates are likely to diverge from private discount rates in such a way as to induce over-rapid depletion of resources.

Absence of forward markets

The view that perfectly competitive markets will optimize the rate of resource usage over some selected time period requires that there exists perfect forecasts by resource owners of future prices. The only way of ensuring such accurate prediction is by having forward markets — markets that enable buyers and sellers to agree prices for transactions that take place some time in the future. While some forward markets exist for exchanges in the relatively near future, no such markets exist for the forward purchase and sale of natural resources in the longer run. Hence it must be recognized that future prices are not known with certainty and are therefore *expected* prices. Now, if owners overestimate future prices they will wish to supply more of the resource later and less now compared to a situation in which they forecast accurately. Hence, overestimation of future prices will lead to too low a rate of resource exploitation. But there may be an equilibrating mechanism at work which corrects this slightly — for the effect of such an overestimate will be to raise current prices, thus slowing the rate of expected price increase, and hence reducing the planned "bunching" of supplies in later periods. Kay and Mirrlees (1975) note that such an equilibrating mechanism is not readily observable, or that, if it exists, it may operate with extremely long time-lags. They do suggest, however, that an actual market price below the marginal cost of extraction could not exist for long, in which case there is reason to suppose that, if prices are incorrectly forecast, the bias will be in favour of overestimation and hence toward underexploitation of resources.

But it is also pertinent to ask over what period expectations, however formed, will operate. Economic decisions about the future are notoriously "myopic" — planners generally look only a little way ahead. If the time-horizon, T, over which we wish to plan resource use does not coincide with resource-owners' planning periods, there is the real problem that resource owners will plan a resource depletion rate which is far more rapid than the "global" plan requires (Nordhaus, 1973). To some extent we might expect this divergence to be minimized by the fact that resource owners can sell their rights to exploit resources, thus passing on the title to the next generation. In practice, "the reason why pricing of resources might be myopic is that very few planners have the ability, or perhaps even the desire, to check consistency (in their plans) for several decades" (Nordhaus, 1973).

We conclude that the absence of forward markets could lead to a bias in either direction — toward over- or under-exploitation — but that general myopia in planning seems likely to impart a bias towards over-exploitation. (We can also think of this argument in terms of discount rates — myopic planning will make actual discount rates higher than optimal discount rates.)

Uninsurability

Resource owners face numerous risks. As we have seen, future prices are uncertain, imparting one source of risk to resource ownership. Owners may also be uncertain about future supplies and hence must bear the risks of explorations that fail, or of investing in technologies that are not proven, and so on. Also, they face the risk of losing ownership through appropriation by national governments. If risk aversion is the order of the day — if, that is, resource owners prefer to avoid risk — the resource owner will tend to discount the future heavily, preferring to secure his gains in the more accurately known immediate future. As such we would expect risk aversion to imply over-rapid rates of exploitation. On the other hand, risk aversion in exploration, as opposed to exploitation of known reserves, could work the other way, with owners being unwilling to investigate potential new sources of supply because of the risks involved. This would leave reserves available for future generations.

Future generations

Decisions about resource exploitation take place now. By definition we cannot record the votes of future generations concerning our exploitation rate. Accordingly, there may be an in-built tendency to neglect future generations and hence to produce a rate of exploitation that is "optimal" for the current generation only. As we saw in Chapter 1, there is no logical reason to exclude future generations from our concept of social welfare. The advocates of market mechanisms might point out, however, that if the current generation care about the fate of their children, and if their children can be expected to care for their children, and so on, utilities will be interdependent in such a way that the market should allocate resources correctly. That is, the existence of inter-generational concern should be sufficient to ensure that current decisions do take care of future requirements.

In reality it seems more than unlikely that such a mechanism operates. No doubt if individuals were asked to express a view, most would show concern for future generations. Others might well say that future generations can "look after themselves", although such a view would not be in the least rational once the interdependence between generations' activities is recognized. But people's *behaviour* does not in general reveal this inter-generational concern: there is an asymmetry between saying what is desirable when thinking in "social" terms and what is implied by actual behaviour. Accordingly, the view that decisions that reflect current market activity will allow for future generations' welfare is untenable. What is likely is that discount rates will reflect myopic views of the future and we shall again have the divergence between private and social rates noted earlier.

Now, if these rates do diverge, they complicate the issue as far as future generations are concerned. It is arguable that if the discount rate is too high it should be lowered for *all* investment. Holding resources *in situ* is, after all, merely one form of investment so that if high rates exist in resource ownership we would expect capital to be transferred from other economic investment to resource exploitation. But if the rate of discount is lowered across the board, while the rate of resource exploitation is reduced, the rate of capital investment in other activities will be *increased*. Unless dual rates can be justified — there being one rate for resource exploitation and one for other capital investment — the effect of lowering the discount rate must be to increase economic growth rates. This may well increase the demands on the environment through added pollution, although on the "materials balance" view, a lower rate of resource exploitation should be associated with a lower rate of residuals disposal. This raises the issue of how far we can decide on "optimal" rates of resource exploitation without considering pollution.

Pollution

On the materials balance view, faster rates of resource exploitation are associated with faster rates of residuals disposal, and hence higher rates of potential pollution. Accordingly, we might justifiably argue that, since the social costs of pollution are not included in resource prices, market prices are below their true social value. As such, the absolute level of exploitation must be higher than is optimal. If, in addition, we consider the argument in Chapter 4, that the ecological effects of some pollutants are related to their accumulated *stock* level, then resource exploitation which adds to this stock of pollutants is equivalent to shifting forward in time the real social costs associated with that exploitation. In this respect market behaviour will be biased in favour of the present and against the future.

Figure 7.8 summarizes the direction of the biases in light of this discussion.

It will be seen from the figure that, far from the biases all being in one

Fig. 7.8

| | Direction of deviation from optimum | |
Type of distortion	Under-exploitation	Over-exploitation
(1) Monopoly	✕	
(2) Discount rate		✕
(3) Absence of forward markets	✕	✕
(4) Uninsurability (a) exploitation		✕
(b) exploration	✕	
(5) Future generations		✕
(6) Pollution		✕

direction, they vary according to the type of distortion. If we accept Pareto optimality as the criterion by which resources should be allocated, it is clear that we shall not be able to say anything decisive about the relationship between actual and optimal rates of depletion unless we quantify the various distortions. This, as can be imagined, would be a highly complex task which, to date, has not been attempted. In the absence of such a detailed econometric model of an economy, only qualitative conclusions can be stated. For what it is worth, a personal view is that over-exploitation is very likely to prevail, particularly when ecological effects are considered.

7.4 Resource availability

Much of the argument about natural resource depletion centres on what resources actually are available and what the demand for them is likely to be. Again, this turns out to be a highly complex problem, partly because of limited knowledge about what resources are available, partly because what can be exploited depends on the state of technology and on the level of prices, and partly because demand projections are themselves uncertain. Also, the whole process of projecting supply and demand, apart from being subject to enormous margins of error, requires us, once again, to decide on a time-horizon. If we select an infinite time-horizon, or a time-horizon set, say, by the dying of the sun, we should be too surprised to learn that we shall exhaust known and readily imaginable resources before that time-horizon occurs. If we select a finite time-horizon of, say, 100 years, we can only derive comfort from any figures showing demand will be less than supply if we are indifferent to what happens after 100 years is up. Nonetheless, while some people might argue that forecasting resource availability is a fruitless exercise and that faith should be placed in technology, the exercise can be instructive.

Forecasting demand is clearly a hazardous venture. If our interest centres on *world* demand, not only do we need to know the overall rate of growth of each individual economy, but we also require some knowledge of the product-mix of each economy at various points in time, and the likely technical coefficients relating outputs to inputs, also at selected points in time. Obviously, such combined macro-economic/input—output analysis is feasible for short periods of forecast, but the estimates will contain large margins of error for forecasts beyond a decade or two decades.

A perfectly functioning price mechanism would, of course, ration resources over time. As an individual resource becomes scarce, so its price will rise. This will have several effects. First, the higher prices will reduce the rate of growth of demand. Second, the higher price will make the material less attractive when it is compared to its substitutes and this will further reduce the demand. Third, the higher price will make recovery of past waste a more attractive proposition — recycling will increase and again the demand for the "virgin" material will decrease. Fourth, the increased prices may stimulate explorative efforts to find further deposits of the resource. The essential point is that forecasting demand, and supply, involves an analysis of what happens to prices and hence an analysis of what feedback effects there will be of rising prices on the forecast demand itself. But such an exercise would require complex and sophisticated economic models of at least the major nations affected, and these do not yet exist in sufficiently disaggregated form for the issue in question.

In these circumstances there is little alternative to resorting to pragmatic calculations based on available information. For some countries, such as the United States, fairly sophisticated results can be obtained, but other countries have not investigated the problem in anything like the detail available for the USA. Undoubtedly the most sophisticated demand projections for non-energy non-renewable resources are contained in the report by Fischman and Landsberg (1972) to the US Commission on Population Growth and the American Future. The model is particularly interesting because it projects as far as the year 2020, and because it will already have integrated the feedback effect of price rises into the projections.

Projections of "rest of world" demand have invariably been based on simple extrapolation of past trends. The most widely used are those of the US Bureau of Mines (1970). These rely on observations of relationships between materials consumption and economic activity, so that projections of the latter, assuming unchanged coefficients between GNP and minerals consumption, will give estimates of demand in the future. Such projections are clearly questionable since: (a) technical coefficients may change; (b) changing growth prospects for less developed countries could generate much faster increases in demand; and (c) the effects of price changes will be excluded from the influences listed as affecting demand. Nonetheless, for a preliminary investigation there appears little alternative to adopting such an approach. Cumulative world demand for selected non-energy, non-renewable materials is shown in Table 7.1.

Certain other materials need to be added to the list of "problem" materials. Thus, zinc mining yields as joint-products, cadmium, thallium, indium, and germanium. Since zinc appears as one of the most critical materials, it would be important to enquire in a full study as to the uses of these jointly produced materials since their supply is an integral part of zinc supply. Some writers have also drawn attention to fluorspar which is used in electric arc and basic oxygen processes for iron and steel manufacture and in electro-slag refining processes for alloys and high quality steel; it is the major source of fluorine, and is used to make fluorine chemicals, as well as other things. According to the Bureau of Mines it is likely to be in high and increasing demand in the future and known reserves would last until only the late 1980s.

Helium gas, which is most easily recovered from natural gas supplies, has also been the source of some debate, particularly as it is of importance to future nuclear energy programmes. Current arguments favour its dissipation into the atmosphere as a useless by-product so that future supplies can be taken from the atmosphere, even though this is currently very much more costly. This argument is economically sensible if current helium gas storage costs exceed the present value of future atmospheric extraction costs, and if the technology really is available.

The measurement of reserves is no less complex than estimating demand. Current estimates tend to be of "proved" reserves and do not take account of other deposits that are available but for which the incentive to exploit does not yet exist, or which would be available if real prices rose to a level which makes exploitation profitable. Essentially, *available* reserves depend on: (a) current technology; (b) current prices. *Potential* reserves will clearly be larger if (a) and/or (b) change but will be limited by some upper bound set by the mineral's crustal abundance or, in some cases, its crustal *plus* mantle abundance.

It cannot, however, be assumed that technology *will* be available to

Table 7.1 World supply and demand for selected materials[1]

	(a) World demand[2] 1968–2020 (total) (m. tons) Low	High	(b) World[3] reserves	(c) Excess[4] demand		(d) World[5] reserves x5	(e) Excess demand	
Iron	35,000	48,457	97,000	—	—	485,000	—	—
Chromium	5.4	10.2	775	—	—	3,875	—	—
Magnesium	360	608	2,580	—	—	12,900	—	—
Phosphorus	1,942	3,950	21,800	—	—	109,000	—	—
Potassium	2,421	3,804	110,000	—	—	550,000	—	—
Nitrogen	5,965	10,269	?	—	—	?	—	—
Vanadium	3.13	4.36	10.11	—	—	50.57	—	—
Cobalt	1.54	2.27	2.40	—	(−)	12.02	—	—
Nickel	52.6	76.0	73.5	−,	+	377.5	—	—
Sulphur	5,867	9,329	2,767	+	+	13,835	—	—
Titanium	153	386	147	+	+	735	—	—
Manganese[6]	853	1,195	797	−	+	3,985	—	—
Copper	975	2,073	808	+	+	4,400	—	—
Molybdenum	11.62	16.48	5.41	+	+	27.07	—	—
Tungsten	4.23	5.57	1.41	+	+	7.06	—	—
Lead	296	377	95	+	+	475	—	—
Aluminium	2,277	4,974	1,168	+	+	5,890	—	—
Tin	15.180	26.27	4.91	+	+	24.55	—	+
Zinc	581	774	124	+	+	520	+	+
Mercury[7] (m. flasks)	8.8	13.6	3.34	+	+	16.7	—	—

Notes to Table 7.1

1. This list is intended as a guide only, and not as an authoritative list of the "critical materials". Specific materials which appear to be in plentiful supply may not be available to individual countries, particularly if OPEC-style cartels are formed in these materials, as is already the case for some bauxite and copper supplies. Equally, the limited information available on "true" reserves means that some materials may not be in such limited supply as might at first appear.

2. Cumulative world demand 1968–2020, as from L. Fischman and H. Landsberg (1972) unless otherwise indicated. The totals are obtained by calculating US demand using the Resources for the Future Macro-econometric/input–output model. Rest of world projections are taken from US Bureau of Mines, and are added to the US projections to give an approximation of world demand. The "Low" and "High" figures relate to different assumptions about rates of economic growth.

3. US Bureau of Mines (1970). Reserves are defined as those which could be secured with *current* technology and *current* prices. This is obviously a lower limit of available reserves. Thus, US mercury reserves were held to be 140,000 flasks at $200 per flask; 379,000 at $300 and 827,000 at $500 per flask.

4. + indicates excess demand, i.e. column (*a*) exceeds column (*b*). The two symbols in column (*c*) relate to the low and high demand projections respectively. − indicates excess supply.

5. The multiple of 5 is suggested by Govett and Govett (1972) and is regarded by them as an upper limit. But it seems clear that it is more suited to some resources than to others. Thus, multiplying mercury resources by 5 is held by many authorities to be an unrealistic exaggeration of possible resources. This crude procedure is the only one available in a preliminary study for allowing for reserves which exist beyond those listed in column (*b*).

6. Virtually limitless if recovery from sea-bottom nodules becomes commercially viable.

7. Mercury and silver are unaccountably omitted from the Fischman–Landsberg paper. The approach adopted here is illustrative only. Cumulative USA mercury production 1968–2020 is taken from US Bureau of Mines (1970) giving a range of 2.6–3.4 million flasks. Rest of the world cumulative demand is not quoted but is expected to be some 3.4–4.0 times the US demand. This gives total world cumulative demand of 8.8–13.6 million flasks. World reserves are taken from Bureau of Mines. Silver statistics are not given but at current rates of growth of demand, known world reserves of 5.5×10^9 troy ounces would last only 13 years. Multiplying reserves by 5 extends this life to 42 years.

exploit the full potential of reserves. Even if it becomes available regard must be had for:

(a) any pollution which results from the adoption of new technologies;
(b) the resource and energy demand of the technologies;
(c) the lead and lag times involved in their introduction;
(d) the non-smooth nature of price changes such that technologies may not be introduced at the "right" moment.

Accordingly, arguments to the effect that "technology *will* solve the problem" or that "something will turn up" must be regarded as decidedly ascientific. Technology *may* solve problems and "new" reserves *may* appear. What matters is how countries choose to behave in face of uncertainty. Adopting the above attitudes is equivalent to selecting the most optimistic option, and there can be no justification for this.

The Bureau of Mines' estimates of reserves are shown in column (b) of Table 7.1. Column (d), showing larger figures for reserves, is derived by multiplying the initial reserves column by a factor of 5. This may be regarded as a very crude attempt to allow for "undiscovered" reserves and for those reserves known but exploitable only at higher prices and improved technologies.

Forecasting world energy demand is equally hazardous. Figure 7.9 shows projected demands based on various sources (Institute of Fuel, 1973). Table 7.2 shows ranges of estimates of energy reserves. If we ignore uranium reserves for the moment, then we can get some idea of the

Table 7.2

	Known reserves ('000) MTOE	Potential reserves
Oil	80—90	250—360
Shale oil, Tar sands	97—120	280—500
Coal	91—1,540	770—3,360
Natural gas	29.2—41.3	77.4—292.4
Uranium*	0.9 m. tons	1.3—3.2 m. tons
Total (without uranium)	297.2—1,791.3	1,377.4—4,512.4

Note: * not expressed in MTOE.
Source: Adapted from Institute of Fuel, 1973.

Fig. 7.9

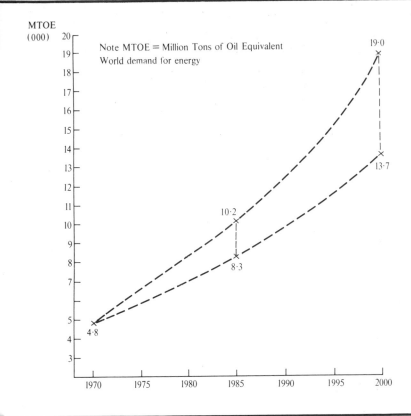

MTOE
(000)

Note MTOE = Million Tons of Oil Equivalent
World demand for energy

relative size of energy demand and supply by considering how long such
reserves would last if current consumption rates were to continue. That is,
if we take the 1970 consumption figure of 4.8 billion tons of oil equivalent, and divide it into the reserves figures we shall have an estimate of the
"life" of reserves. This procedure yields a life of between 62 and 370 years
for known reserves. If we take *potential* reserves, the respective range is
287 to 940 years. But such calculations ignore uranium. The problem here
is that the "life" of uranium depends very much on the state of technology: if breeder and fusion reactors become commercial realities,
uranium will clearly supply energy demand for much longer periods. Still
ignoring uranium, it is also the case that dividing by *present* consumption
rates will overstate the life of the reserves if future consumption is to be
higher as is suggested in Fig. 7.9. In short, if we take the reserves of

uranium as meeting the increased demand and this is being generous to an optimistic view, the "lives" quoted above might be a reasonable guide. This implies a range of between 60 and 1,000 years. We can observe that this range is extremely wide and in this respect it offers little guidance to planners. But its other feature is that even the upper limit will strike many people as being remarkably near when we consider that, until recently, and nuclear holocaust apart, the future of mankind was seen as stretching into the very distant future.

Even if we accept that forecasts of demand and supply are subject to enormous errors — perhaps uranium can be recovered from seawater (in which case reserves could go from a few million tons to a staggering 4 *billion* tons), perhaps coal reserves are understated (some estimates make them 7,600 billion tons), and so on — there remains the issue of how to plan in face of uncertain technology and reserves. We argued earlier that a cautious approach would be the sanest course of action.

Appendix. Efficient resource allocation through time: role of prices

Let $P(t)$ = price of finished product

t = time

$C(t) = C_0$ = marginal cost of extraction

r = rate of discount

Then, a profit maximizing resource owner will seek to maximize the *present value* of profits, i.e. he aims to maximize, for any time period.

$$V = [P(t) - C_0]e^{-rt} \qquad [1]$$

The first order condition is

$$\frac{\partial v}{\partial t} = [P(t) - C_0] - r \cdot e^{-rt} + e^{-rt} \frac{\partial P}{\partial t} = 0$$

or

$$e^{-rt}[-r(Pt) - C_0) + \dot{P}] = 0 \qquad [2]$$

where

$$\dot{P} = \frac{\partial P}{\partial t}$$

if we let $R(t) = P(t) - C_0$

we have the requirement, from [2], that

$$r \cdot R(t) = \dot{P} \qquad [3]$$

Dividing both sides of [3] by P gives

$$\frac{r \cdot R(t)}{P} = \frac{\dot{P}}{P} \qquad [4]$$

That is, prices must grow at the same rate as the rate of interest multiplied by the ratio of royalty (R) to price. Since $R(t)/P$ is less than unity, the rate of price increase must always be *less* than the rate of interest. But if, as assumed above, the cost of extraction stays constant ($C(t) = C_0$) then $P(t) - C_0$ must converge to P as t gets larger. Hence [4] would become

$$r = \frac{\dot{P}}{P} \qquad [5]$$

In this case the rate of price change must equal the rate of interest.

Reworking the previous analysis for the situation in which marginal extraction costs are not constant, gives

$$r \cdot R = \dot{P} - \dot{C}$$

or

$$r = \frac{\dot{R}}{R} \qquad [6]$$

i.e. the *royalty*, not price, now rises at the same rate as the rate of interest.

Notes

1. In Fig. 7.5 OR = OR$'$ since there is a fixed stock of the resource. Hence $R_{t+1}R' = OR_t$, so that consumption in period t plus consumption in period t + 1 exhausts the complete stock OR.

2. T is the "finite time horizon" or "terminal point". Since we are interested in exhaustible resources, making T finite is obviously sensible. Theorists do frequently work with infinite time horizons, so that T would be set equal to infinity. But such an assumption has no function if the world really does consist of finite resources. Nuclear fusion power, if it ever becomes reality, might perhaps be considered as a resource best treated in the infinite horizon context. Making T finite also raises serious problems, however, because the point at which the resource is exhausted obviously depends on the use rate. Hence there is a prior problem of deciding what the value of T should be. And once decided upon, what is the relevant plan for the period *after* T? While selecting values of T is clearly going to raise awkward problems, it is equally true that plans have to be made with respect to *some* time horizon.

3.   Formally demonstrating this result is not as obvious as it appears here. It is also possible to have monopoly facing demand curves with particular elasticities such that over-use, not under-use, results. See Kay and Mirrlees (1975).

8

Resource conservation

Chapter 7 looked at the various problems involved in analysing the supply and demand problems of natural resources and tried to indicate how we might decide whether resources were being depleted too fast or too slowly. It concluded that there is evidence enough to suggest that resource exploitation takes place at too high a level. This chapter looks at the policy options in light of this conclusion. What can be done to conserve resources? One obvious instrument of control is to lower the rate of global economic growth. This indeed is the solution advanced by many advocates of environmental improvement. Rather than discuss this issue here, we postpone it to Chapter 10 in which some of the so-called "doomsday" literature is surveyed.

8.1 Materials substitution
As an individual resource becomes scarce relative to its demand, we would expect the market mechanism to operate along the following lines. First, the price of the resource would rise, thus cutting back the demand for it. Either the previous demand (at the old price) will go unsatisfied, or suppliers will meet that demand from some other resource that can be substituted for the scarce resource. Second, the price rise will perhaps encourage more exploration for the scarce resource, and/or more exploitation of known reserves. Indeed, we would expect more extraction to become profitable since, at the old price, there must have existed deposits which were previous uneconomic to exploit. Third, we can expect the price of scrap materials to become relatively favourable, so that a larger amount of recycling will take place.

The possibilities of substitution between materials are undeniably extensive, but the issue is complicated by the fact that many materials have joint uses. Thus sheet copper can be substituted by aluminium which at the same time would reduce demand for soldering agents made from tin and lead. Regard must also be had for future technologies in the production of final demand goods. High-speed transportation, for example, generally requires use of the "hard" metals compared to the "soft" metals currently used in petrol and diesel engine construction, and the hard metals are particularly scarce. Given potential transport system changes in the light of the so-called "energy crisis", this supply restriction could be extremely important. Aluminium is being extensively substituted for tin, particularly in the production of metal cans and containers. Plastics are being used for insulation and anti-corrosive purposes where lead and zinc respectively were previously used. The list is endless. The essential points in any discussion on substitution, however, are:

1. That there is no evidence of a neat "phasing" of scarcity such that as one resource runs out another becomes available, and so on. There is a distinct possibility that complete *sets* of raw materials, substitutable amongst themselves, will be depleted at approximately the same time.
2. That substitution when it does take place may occur with time lags sufficient to cause disruption to an economy.
3. That substitute materials can have other unfortunate side effects: e.g. aluminium smelters may involve more pollution than their counterpart for tin.
4. That substitute materials may well require higher energy inputs, as is the case with low-grade copper exploitation.

Thus, while an overview of substitution possibilities would suggest that substitution is certainly technically feasible on the materials side, the issue does reduce to a problem of energy supplies, of acceptable pollution impacts, and of the ability to manage the substitution process so as to minimize the problems that will arise. The fact that energy supplies, for example, are themselves in question makes it all the more important to assess the substitution philosophy in a rigorous framework to establish what methods exist for reducing the energy demands for exploiting the plentiful materials.

8.2 Product life extension

One frequently encountered solution to materials shortages is to extend the durability of products by deliberate design. It is a commonplace that many modern goods are designed for early disposal (*a*) to reflect consumers' apparent desires for fairly rapid changes in their ownership of goods, and (*b*) because industry has an interest in boosting sales and profits by encouraging consumers to replace their goods more rapidly.

The effect of extending product life can be shown with the aid of some simple examples. If we consider a demand for "new" products of, say, 10 units per annum, and a replacement demand based on the fact that each product has a "life" of 2 years, the pattern of demand over time will be:

Year:	1	2	3	4	5	6	7
Demand	+10	+10	+10	+10	+10	+10	+10
Replacement demands		+10	+10	+10	+10	+10	
			+10	+10	+10		
					+10		
Total sequence	+10	+10	+20	+20	+30	+30	+40

If we now extend the product life to 4 years we obtain:

Total sequence	+10	+10	+10	+10	+20	+20	+20

Thus, over an arbitrary period of 7 years, the initial sequence sums to 160, while the new sequence sums to 100. There is a "saving" of some 37 per cent.

For exponentially growing demand we secure the same percentage gain. Thus, suppose the initial demand sequence is

Year:	1	2	3	4	5	6	7
Demand.	10	11	12.1	13.31	14.64	15.90	17.49

We have:

			10.0	11.0	12.10	13.31	14.64
Replacement demand					10.0	11.0	12.1
							10.0
	10 +	11 +	22.1 +	13.31 +	24.64 +	26.90 +	29.59

If we now extend the product life to 4 years we obtain:

Year:	1	2	3	4	5	6	7
	10	11	12.1	13.31	14.64	15.90	17.49
					10.00	11.00	12.10
	10	11	12.1	13.31	24.64	26.90	29.59

That is, over 7 years, the initial sequence sums to 198.89 and the revised sequence sums to 127.54, a saving of some 37 per cent.

Of course extending product life has some disadvantages. If product life extension requires consumers to hold on to goods for longer periods *without* an increase in durability, this may render the product less suitable for recycling due to the reduced quality of the disposed-of product. Product life extension may also require the use of anti-corrosives which themselves are potential pollutants (zinc, cadmium) so that there are social costs attached to increased durability.

Overall, however, it seems clear that product life extension has a substantial *potential* role to play. The real difficulties lie in persuading consumers and producers to forego in-built obsolescence, particularly as it is not at all clear how the normal economic instruments — e.g. taxes and subsidies — would achieve the desired result.

8.3 Recycling

Recycling is perhaps the most widely entertained mechanism for extending the life of a resource. Obviously, recycling — in the sense of the re-use of a given input or output — is applicable only to non-energy resources since the use of a material as an energy resource results in its useless dissipation into the atmosphere. However, recycling turns out to be a complex issue. As such, policies designed to increase the recycle fraction or to establish recycling industries cannot be recommended without careful study of the individual material in question.

In general, profit-seeking companies will not seek to recycle a product unless: (a) its cost is lower than use of the "virgin" material; and (b) this differential is likely to remain over time without exhibiting cyclical characteristics that make recycling profitable at one moment but not at the next. The former can be shown to apply for a number of the "scarce" metals and for waste paper of certain kinds, but it is interesting to note that the private market mechanism does not respond in any systematic way. The recycle fraction for copper in the United States, for example, bears no correlation to the real price of copper. As far as price instability is concerned, fluctuations in scrap prices are often cited as reasons why many municipal authorities have not invested in equipment to collect waste paper even though there are specialized salvage markets to which the paper can be sold.

But private decisions to recycle are not adequate guides to the social desirability of recycling. The benefits of recycling must be extended to make some allowance for: (a) the present value of the extended resource life brought about by recycling; (b) any reduction in pollution due to the reduction in residuals disposed of directly to the environment; and (c) the reduced demand for land for disposal purposes, releasing it for alternative social uses. On the cost side there will be, for some recycling processes, the added pollution generated by the recycling, particularly where this involves chemical additives to return the product to an acceptable quality standard for re-use. Assessing these costs and benefits is itself a complex issue.

Any practical discussion of recycling is complicated by the non-standard use of terminology in the literature and in the salvage and reprocessing industries. However, we may attempt a basic distinction between "old" and "new" scrap. "Old" scrap refers to those materials which have been consumed as *final* products and which are then discarded either direct to the salvage market or secondhand market, or to the rubbish dump. "New" scrap tends not to have been consumed as final product but appears as a waste product of the intermediate stages of production. It is either re-processed straight away within the industry, or between industries or is held in industrial scrap yards. Clearly, the distinction does not relate directly to what we might think of as the *stock* of waste products (i.e. those discarded to the environment from past production and consumption) and the *flow* of waste products (currently generated waste), but the distinction is widely used in the literature.

Recycling fractions as quoted by industry tend to express per cent of current consumption met by materials from both "old" and "new" scrap, so that observations of trends are difficult. In the United States, one study has given the following results for selected metals; expressed as ratio of total scraps ("old" plus "new") to current supply of consumption (Smith, 1972).

Table 8.1 USA recycling ratios (%)

	Aluminium	Copper	Lead	Tin	Ferrous metals	Paper	Rubber
1954—58 annual average	15.5	36.4	37.3	34.0	21.9	24.8	19.0
1968	17.5	39.8	40.8	28.3	21.3	18.7	9.3

It will be seen that the recycle fraction has improved for aluminium, copper and lead only, and has *fallen* for tin, paper and rubber, although how far this reflects exports of scrap material is difficult to say.

Table 8.2 (Pearce, 1976) shows some figures for selected Western nations.

Table 8.2   Western-world recycling ratios

	Aluminium		Zinc		Lead		Copper	
	1963	1973	1963	1973	1963	1973	1963	1973
France	20.7	20.0	35.7	27.0	19.8	23.0	34.8	26.9
W. Germany	26.6	25.6	8.8	12.8	14.2	18.0	37.9	27.0
Italy	6.4	24.0	35.7	29.1	3.9	19.7	28.5	29.4
Japan	24.9	28.0	24.5	12.1	32.2	22.1	42.0	35.5
UK	32.4	28.5	24.7	25.0	52.1	61.6	36.3	37.9
USA	22.2	23.8	24.9	23.4	41.3	48.1	43.3	44.7

It can be seen that: (a) recycling ratios are already significant in all countries (the German figures for zinc and lead are not comparable since some scrap use is excluded); (b) that, contrary to what one would expect, recycling ratios have been *falling* in most countries for zinc (only UK shows a slight rise), and for copper have been falling or roughly constant. These results must be treated with caution, however, since the statistics are frequently unreliable.

It is pertinent then to ask what potential for further recycling there is. Smith (1972) and Fischman and Landsberg (1972) regard the re-use of scrap from intermediate sources ("new" scrap) as being an unlikely contributor to further supplies. Hence the burden is placed on scrap from final uses ("old" scrap).

The problem here is that this scrap is not all suitable for recycling since it is more "contaminated" than "new" scrap. Thus, the costs of collecting, sorting and separating may be high for final product waste. Paper products have to be decontaminated to remove waxes, resins, bitumen and latex so as to be suitable for reprocessing. Similarly, increasing dissipation in use in final products makes it more and more costly to reprocess the material: if tin plate is applied in thinner and thinner layers to products over time, more products have to be collected, sorted and separated to reclaim a given amount of tin. Lastly, if only past final production is to be relied upon to provide recycling supplies, exponential growth rates in demand will mean that they will contribute very little.

Fischman and Landsberg (1972) have calculated the potential contribution of improvements in recycling to US resource use for some selected materials. Their conclusions are not encouraging for some products, but are for others. By analysing the likely lifetime of products in use to the year 2000, and assessing the likely upper limits to recycling fractions they suggest that for the USA, proportions of current consumption met from recycled materials would appear as in Table 8.3. These fractions assume an "active" recycling policy on the part of government or industry.

Table 8.3   USA current and possible recycle fractions (%)

	Iron	Alu-minium	Copper	Lead	Zinc
Current recycle fraction	47.3	17.3	44.0	43.9	16.5
Possible fraction	48.9	42.6	54.4	47.2	34.6

It can be seen that there is considerable scope for improvement in aluminium and zinc, with significant scope for copper, less for lead, and very little for iron.

One technological limit is that the recycled product may be a lower quality and hence may not always be re-usable for the same manufacture. In addition, energy expenditure on reclamation can be high, and hence recycling costs may be high, if extensive collecting, sorting and separating has to take place. It is also difficult to recycle resources that are used in an increasingly dissipative way — the thinner and thinner tin-plating becomes, the less and less likely it is to become reclaimable unless resource prices reach very high levels. And, in the limit, some resources, such as lead used as a petrol additive will not be recyclable at all.

Further, as has been indicated before, the recycling process may itself be the generator of pollution. In paper re-use bleaches are added to bring the paper back to something like its original "quality", as seen by the consumer. Depending on the nature of the bleaching plant, this may add particularly noxious chemicals to the environment. In many cases the issue here may be one of persuading the public to accept lower quality products. Consumers may be very willing to trade lower quality for price reductions or slower price increases.

Despite these cautions, it is clear that the scope for recycling may be large in some industries, and that the limits apparently reached in other industries may not be insuperable. Glassey and Gupta (1971) have estimated that the USA consumption of virgin wood pulp in 1970 could have been reduced from 45 million tons to 28 million tons had the most efficient use of waste been made. On the other hand, Frank (1973) has calculated that raising the UK recycle rate for copper from 40 to 50 per cent with an average product life of 25 years and an annual growth rate in consumption of 4.6 per cent, would reduce the consumption of virgin copper from 60 per cent to 50 per cent, thus adding only 4 years to the "life" of the resource (since consumption would still be growing at the same rate).

8.4 The optimal amount of recycling

Since recycling is not a costless exercise, there must be a point at which the extra costs of recycling outweigh the extra benefits. This is the point at which the economist would say the optimal level of recycling takes place. Of course, if the social value of avoided waste is held to be so high as to outweigh the resource costs of recycling then it will be socially desirable to recycle up to the technological limit. The argument that waste disposed of to the environment has extremely high costs could be sustained for many pollutants – the examples discussed in Chapter 4 – the toxic metals PCB's and some pesticides are all relevant – and, if recycling is relevant (it is for the metals, but not for the pesticides) then society should seek the maximum amount of recycling that technology permits. For many wastes, however, the "optimal" recycling level is likely not to coincide with this technological limit. Consequently, it is important to investigate the costs and benefits associated with recycling.

The private decision to recycle will depend upon the difference between the cost to the firm of using virgin materials and the cost to the firm of using recycled materials. In addition, the price differential must be sustained if the firm is to opt for recycled inputs: if, for example, there is a risk that the differential will be reversed in favour of virgin materials, the firm may nonetheless use virgin materials even if their price is initially above that of recycled materials. This requirement that the differential be a sustained one arises, of course, from the fact that firms would have to invest in recycling equipment in order to re-use products. This factor holds whether the original producing firm does the recycling or some specialist agency does it.

What the private decision ignores, of course, are the social costs and benefits associated with recycling. The benefits are: (a) the extension in resource life that recycling brings about; (b) the reduced pollution impact; and (c) the reduced demand for land for dumping and infilling. The difficulty with (a) – the extension of resource life – is that, in terms of *current* benefits, it tends to be small unless there is strategic or other importance value attached to the savings such that the shadow price is high. Its small value arises from the fact that we tend to calculate the present value of the gain in resource life and the use of a discount factor may make this small. On the other hand, if nations attach significance to reducing imports, especially if those imports are from "unstable" nations or nations likely to impose OPEC-style bargains, these gains have to be valued highly. The reduced demand for land for dumping will appear as a direct benefit from recycling. Where the reduced demand shows up in terms of lower requirements for land for sanitary infill, the gain may be less obvious since infilled land is frequently used for subsequent cultivation or recreational purposes. It can be argued that these benefits would not accrue without the infill. On balance, however, reduced sanitary infill appears to be a benefit. In each case, of course, disposal costs are saved.

The external costs of recycling are not always acknowledged. It is the case, however, that many recycling processes require external inputs which themselves become unrecyclable wastes. Hence we may count this waste problem as a debit item for recycling.

From the *private* point of view, then, the firm's problem is to minimize the total cost of resource use − i.e. to minimize

$$C = TC_V(X) + TC_R(X)$$

where TC_V and TC_R are the total costs of virgin and recycled resources respectively, each shown as a function of output, X. This is achieved when the two *marginal* costs are equalised.

From the *social* point of view, the objective is to minimize

$$S = TC_V(X) + TC_R(X) + TEC_{P,E}(X) + TEC_{P,V}(X) + TEC_{P,R}(X)$$
$$- B_{ERL}(X) - L(X)$$

where $TEC_{P,E}$ is the total external cost associated with extractive industry (these costs will possibly fall as the demand for virgin materials falls); $TEC_{P,V}$ is the total external cost of pollution from the use of virgin materials; $TEC_{P,R}$ is the total external cost of pollution from the recycling process; and B_{ERL} and L are the present values of gains in the resource life and in land respectively. We take disposal costs to be included in TC_V and TC_R.

If, for simplicity, we assume that $TEC_{P,E}$, B_{ERL} and L are insignificant the problem reduces to one of minimizing:

$$SC = TC_V(X) + TC_R(X) + TEC_{P,V}(X) + TEC_{P,R}(X)$$

Figure 8.1 shows the analysis in diagrammatic terms. The horizontal axis shows the recycling ratio, such that when r = 1 full recycling is taking place, and when r = 0 production is being met from virgin materials only. TC_R will rise as r approaches 1. TC_V, on the other hand, must be zero when r = 1 and positive when r = 0. Hence it declines as r approaches 1. Similarly, $TEC_{P,V}$ will fall as recycling increases and $TEC_{P,R}$ will rise. The policy objective of minimizing total social costs is equivalent to maximizing net social benefits. In Fig. 8.1 gross benefits are shown as a

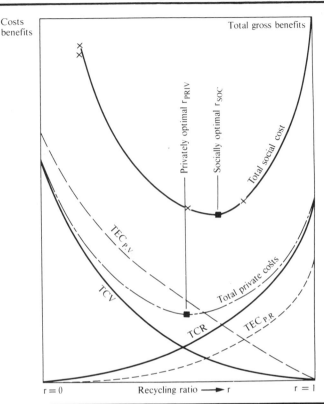

straight line because they are invariant with the recycling ratio. Net social benefits are then the distance between the total social cost curve (= $TC_V + TC_R + TEC_V + TEC_R$). It will be seen that the private optimum, r_{PRIV}, lies to the left of the social optimum r_{SOC}, implying that more recycling is socially desirable than private industry is willing to provide. This, of course, is the rationale for fiscal intervention through the use of a tax which will secure the social optimum.

We should note, however, that r_{SOC} lies to the right of r_{PRIV} in Fig. 8.1 only because of the way the diagram has been drawn. It is perfectly easy to construct a case in which the socially desirable level of recycling will lie to the *left* of r_{PRIV}, implying that recycling should be reduced, not increased. This will arise if recycling technologies are themselves more polluting than the disposal of virgin waste. No generalized conclusion is possible. Only individual case studies will show the answer for each problem.

8.5 Pollution taxes and recycling

Figure 8.1 showed an analysis of recycling in terms of ratios for a *given* output. We can now attempt to integrate this analysis with a consideration of what will happen to output levels with a pollution tax. It is often argued that one effect of pollution taxes will be to encourage recycling. Figure 8.2 shows the bare essentials.

Fig. 8.2

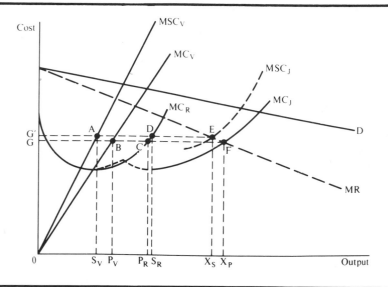

We assume an imperfectly competitive firm with demand curve D. MR is then the marginal revenue curve. MC_V shows the marginal cost of virgin materials use to the firm, and MC_R shows the marginal cost of using recycled inputs. MC_J is then the summation of MC_V and MC_R, and the firm's private objective is to set MR = MC_J since this maximizes profits.[1] This gives a private optimum of F with output X_P. Now we suppose that there are external costs associated with the use of virgin materials only: recycling is "clean". Accordingly $MSC_V - MC_V$ shows the marginal externality associated with the use of virgin inputs. The new joint MC curve is MSC_J and the socially optimal output is X_S which lies to the left of X_P. X_S can be secured by fiscal policy — i.e. the imposition of a Pigovian tax equal to the marginal external cost. The effect of such a tax is therefore to reduce output, but it also changes the recycling ratio within the firm. We can measure this ratio as the percentage of total output met from recycled inputs. For the private optimum this ratio is GC/GF in Fig. 8.2 (the amount of output from virgin inputs being $OP_V = GB$, and the amount from recycled inputs being $OP_R = GC$). With the pollution tax, however, output from recycled inputs changes to $OS_R = G'D$, and the output from virgin inputs becomes $OS_V = G'A$. The recycling ratio changes to $G'D/G'E$. Since D lies to the right of C and E to the left of F, the recycling *ratio* has risen. In other words, the firm has adjusted to the pollution tax in two ways — first by changing total output, and second by changing its combination of inputs.

8.6 Materials conservation

One of the many "lessons" of the so-called energy crisis has been that energy consumption can be reduced without significantly affecting the final quantity or quality of products. In a strict sense, energy can be "conserved". Energy conservation mainly involves improvements in thermal efficiency in converting energy resources, reductions in waste in transit, the "education" of consumers (switching off unrequired lighting, for example), and possible switches in "technology" — e.g. the substitution of public for private transport. With materials the scope is large, but less obvious than with energy. First, waste can be reduced by "educating" consumers to accept goods which are more durable, or with less materials content (small cars for large cars), or with less ostentation or less packaging. To some extent, price rises will automatically secure some of these ends — e.g. the price of petrol has led to a marked shift in preferences for smaller, lower petrol consumption cars. But whether consumers "education" can secure any significant advances is questionable. There appears little evidence that, even when faced with shortages and higher prices, consumers react by altering the *type* of goods they buy. A packaging tax is often advanced as one answer. Producers would pay a tax according to the amount of packaging their goods contain. Such proposals are so replete with difficulties that it is difficult to see how they could work. Thus, given the magnitude of consumer sales for food products, packaging becomes a means of reducing damage in transit and handling. If the damage was to occur because packaging was reduced, consumers would have to bear higher prices. Perhaps, then, the answer would be a tax which applied only to "unnecessary" packaging. But the dividing line would be immensely difficult to draw. Televisions, for example, are sold in specially designed cardboard boxes designed to fit the television and to take shaped pieces of polystyrene which protect the screen and tube of the television. Few consumers would be prepared to accept the product in anything less than this condition. Cosmetics and clothes are often presented in display packages which add nothing to the product from an instrinsic quality point of view, but arguably are vital to the producer's advertisement of his product. If so, one suspects that a packaging tax would merely lead producers to react by devoting resources to some other form of advertisement.

Note

1.   Where p is price and π is profits, the private optimum is secured from

Max $\pi = p(X) \cdot X - TC_V(X) - TC_R(X)$

The first order condition is

$$\frac{X \cdot \partial p}{\partial X} + p(X) - \frac{\partial TC_V}{\partial X} - \frac{\partial TC_R}{\partial X} = 0$$

i.e., $MR = MC_V + MC_R$

The social optimum occurs when

Max $S\pi = p(X) \cdot X - RC_V(X) - TC_R(X) - TEC_V$

i.e., when $MR = MC_V + MC_R + MEC_V$

where EC refers to external costs.

9

Population

9.1 Population growth

Not surprisingly, many people who express concern over the decline in environmental quality and resources, place the main blame on population growth. The more people there are, the more resources must be used up to feed them, clothe them and provide them with "infrastructure" (roads, houses, etc.). The more people there are, the more waste there is to dispose of, and hence the more pollution there is. Moreover, the inability of economic systems to meet the resource needs and demands of expanding populations means that many are doomed to starvation or to lives of extreme poverty and misery, albeit, in the likelihood, very short lives. Where expanding populations conglomerate to live in a few urban areas, we have the familiar problem of congestion and the stress that results with overcrowding. Unconstrained population growth thus appears as an almost unmitigated disaster.

The benefits are less easy to define. In the first place, the perfectly "rational" man and woman — familiar in textbooks — would presumably not agree to produce children if they did not regard it as a benefit. This would suggest leaving the ultimate size of any population to the micro decisions of individual families. Unfortunately, this is a facile view. We have already seen that decision-making units such as families and individuals have no real incentive to consider external effects. If population growth generates such effects, and if they are, on balance, negative, it follows that purely private decision-making cannot maximize social welfare in the sense of securing the "optimum" population. Nor do individuals consider the longer-term consequences in terms of externalities borne by future generations. The more people there are, the bigger still will be future populations unless fertility trends decline. However, a second point is relevant. It can be argued that population growth is necessary before underdeveloped nations can "take-off" economically. The issue reduces to one of attempting to weigh up the costs and benefits. Of course, if population growth really is likely to bring about ecological disaster, then, as we argued in earlier chapters, the calculation of costs and benefits would appear to be a somewhat silly exercise since, presumably, such disaster would mean that there will be no population to secure the benefits.

This chapter makes no pretence at covering all the relevant issues on population policy. Instead we look at this one issue of whether population growth can proceed so as to secure an economic "take-off" which will eventually raise the living standards of the growing population.

To put this analysis in perspective, we present some facts about world population. Table 9.1 shows the growth of world population in historical terms. Not surprisingly, even modern figures are likely to have a fair degree of error in them. Those for even 100 years ago are subject to very substantial error and those for A.D. 1 can be no more than reasoned guesses.

Table 9.1

A.D. 1	300 million	1900	1,650 million
1750	791 million	1950	2,515 million
1850	1,262 million	1970	3,607 million

Casual inspection of the table shows one remarkable feature. If we plot the figures against time, the rate of growth becomes very very fast from 1750. Thus, from 1750 to 1850 we have an increase of some 460 million; from 1850 to 1950 we have an increase of some 1,300 million, and an increase of 1,100 million in only 20 years from 1950 to 1970.

What of the future? Table 9.2 shows the projections prepared by the United Nations up to the year 2000. The table also shows the expected distribution of that population. Notice that population globally is expected to *double* by the year 2000. Note also that, if we take a developed area like North America it is, at most, expected to add another one-third to its existing population. But Asia and Oceania are expected to double their populations, Africa to more than double its population, and similarly for Latin America. Whereas some 74 per cent of the world's population now lives in Asia, Africa and Latin America, by the year 2000 this proportion will be over 80 per cent. Under the assumption of "fast fertility decline" – i.e. fairly rapid falls in forecast birth rates – many countries, such as Nigeria, Thailand, Philippines, Mexico, Pakistan,

Table 9.2 (in millions)

	Constant fertility		Medium fertility decline		Fast fertility decline	
	Number	Per cent	Number	Per cent	Number	Per cent
1970						
Asia and Oceania	2,051	56.8				
Africa	346	9.6				
Europe and USSR	704	19.5				
North America	226	6.3				
Latin America	280	7.8				
TOTAL	3,607	100				
1980						
Asia and Oceania	2,596	58.5	2,558	58.3	2,521	58.1
Africa	457	10.3	453	10.3	451	10.4
Europe and USSR	760	17.1	757	17.2	754	17.4
North America	250	5.6	249	5.7	248	5.7
Latin America	378	8.5	372	8.5	367	8.4
TOTAL	4,441	100	4,389	100	4,341	100
1990						
Asia and Oceania	3,377	60.2	3,196	59.5	3,039	59.0
Africa	619	11.0	597	11.1	578	11.2
Europe and USSR	815	14.6	809	15.1	801	15.5
North America	280	5.0	275	5.1	271	5.3
Latin America	517	9.2	491	9.2	465	9.0
TOTAL	5,608	100	5,368	100	5,154	100
2000						
Asia and Oceania	4,447	61.8	3,968	60.7	3,583	60.1
Africa	861	11.9	783	12.0	677	⁻11.4
Europe and USSR	870	12.1	854	13.1	843	14.1
North America	308	4.3	297	4.5	288	4.8
Latin America	710	9.9	635	9.7	567	9.5
TOTAL	7,196	100	6,536	100	5,958	100

Source: Finance and Development, Vol. 10, No. 4, December 1973.

Bangladesh and Indonesia, can expect their populations to increase by over 100 per cent between now and 2000. India can expect nearly an 80 per cent increase, while the "developed" nations can expect very much slower rates — 27 per cent for the USA, and 26 per cent for USSR.

9.2 The low-level equilibrium trap

The fact that rates of population increase appear to decline with a country's level of economic development would suggest that there exists a natural equilibrium solution to population and economic growth problems. Quite simply, the process of development will itself bring down the birth rate (though it reduces the death rate as well) and hence stabilize population, eventually, so that any further economic development will entail increasing *per capita* standards of living. In this way, it is argued, there will be a natural corrective mechanism and "overpopulation" cannot occur. Unfortunately, such an automatic mechanism does not operate, not least because the very growth in population can have ambivalent effects on development — it *may* stimulate it so that rising *per capita* income levels are achieved, but it may also inhibit the process, making it impossible for "take-off" ever to occur. The kinds of problems that arise are: (*a*) that the development process becomes biased toward food production in order to sustain the increasing population, instead of toward capital investment which is perhaps necessary to the growth process; and (*b*) that rapidly growing populations have a high percentage of "dependents" — people of young age — who must for some time be supported by the working population.

Several models of the development process and its relationship with population growth have been proposed. Nelson (1956) and Enke (1963) suggest that population growth will increase as real income *per capita* increases, but will then fall, in line with our observations above. The growth rate of income is assumed to increase as income per head increases, due to the fact that higher income levels permit the release of savings for investment in growth-producing equipment. The model is depicted in Fig. 9.1. We show the rate of growth in population and in income on the vertical axis $\left(\dfrac{dP}{P} \text{ and } \dfrac{dY}{Y} \right)$ and the level of real income *per capita* (Y/P) on the horizontal axis.

Now, suppose we begin at point "a". Any increase in Y/P entails a faster increase in population than in income so that the economy is driven back toward point "a". Point "a" is in fact a stable equilibrium and can be thought of as being coincident with the subsistence standard of living. The model is therefore distinctly "Malthusian": any increase in living standards above subsistence and population growth will outstrip income growth. If,

Fig. 9.1

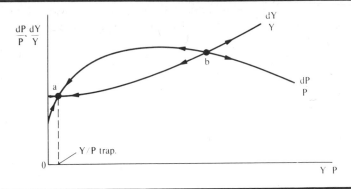

by some mechanism, point "b" could be reached, income growth would outstrip population growth and "take-off" can occur. But the very process of development is what prevents point "b" ever being achieved. Hence point "a", the stable equilibrium, is called the *low-level equilibrium trap*.

Is there an escape from the trap? One obvious escape is to lower the rate of population growth. Figure 9.2 shows the effect. If the rate of growth is lowered enough, the take-off point "b" can be brought within reach and standards of living can perhaps rise. Alternatively, the rate of growth of income could be increased: this will also bring point "b" back towards point "a" and facilitate an escape.

Fig. 9.2

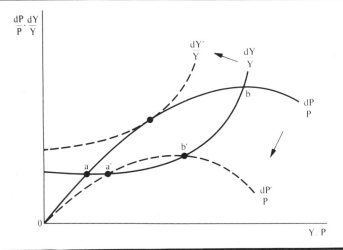

Obviously, then, the question must become an empirical one. All we have at the moment is an hypothetical model. We need some evidence to establish whether actual situations correspond to the model. The preliminary work of Moreland and Hazledine (1974) suggests that it does, although with some modifications. The significant difference that seems to result from their work is that the dY/Y curve does not slope upwards for many world regions — it has a steady downward slope. An example is shown in Fig. 9.3.

Fig. 9.3

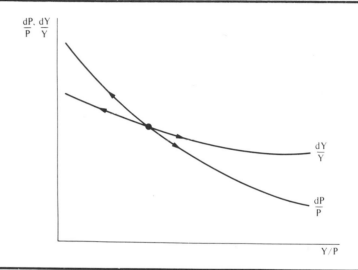

This suggests that the low-level equilibrium trap is still very much in evidence and that the chances of an escape by either of the two mechanisms available are remote because of the large absolute magnitude of the changes that would have to be made to shift the equilibrium trap to the right in any significant degree. This picture appears to fit the data for Asia as a whole. No conclusions relating to individual countries can be derived from this, however.

In other instances, Latin America is an example, Moreland and Hazledine's findings suggest that, while the low level trap still exists, escape is easier because of the narrower gap between the dY/Y and dP/P curves. The picture for the developed countries indicates that no equilibrium trap exists, but that the dY/Y curve slopes downward continuously.

This is shown in Fig. 9.4.

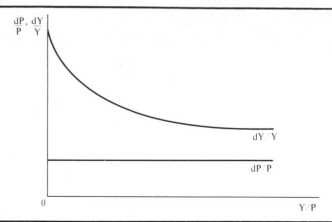

While it is early days to derive any substantive conclusions from empirical work of this kind, there can be no question that simple comparisons of rates of growth of food supply (or income) and population do not capture the various feedback mechanism that exist between the development process and population growth. The implication of studies such as that of Moreland and Hazledine is that, for some world regions, nothing less than the most massive injection of capital and widespread population control programmes will escape the low-level equilibrium trap. The existing levels of capital aid and birth control propaganda hardly begin to compare with what may well be necessary.

10

Limits to growth

10.1 General issues

Previous chapters have indicated some of the elements of the "ecological argument" which, it is suggested, have been neglected by economists in their analysis of environmental problems. For *some* pollutants, arguably the most important, we suggested that conventional externality theory is inadequate and can easily give rise to incorrect policy prescriptions (see Chapter 4). We have also indicated some of the ways in which pollution can be reduced and natural resources conserved (Chapter 8). But perhaps the most tendentious way of "solving" pollution and natural resource problems is to limit the final consumption of goods and services. Ostensibly, this policy will reduce the throughput of materials and energy in an economy and hence the disposal of residuals to the environment. Arguments of this kind have usually invoked what we might call a "blanket" policy: a total reduction in rates of growth of consumption regardless of the *type* of consumption involved. In many cases it is proposed that this reduction continue to the point where there is *zero economic growth*: i.e. a constant throughput of materials and energy over time. There are several historical antecedents of such views. John Stuart Mill, for example, spoke of the eventual necessity of a "stationary state" in which growth would be zero. But these arguments have become popular in recent times through the publication of several documents, some of which have secured widespread attention. Notable among these are Mishan's *Costs of Economic Growth* (Mishan, 1968); Daly's *Toward a Steady-State Economy* (Daly, 1972); the Club of Rome's *The Limits to Growth* (Meadows, 1972) and the Ecologist Magazine's *Blueprint for Survival* (The *Ecologist*, 1972). These documents, particularly the last two, have provoked an enormous critical literature, much of it polemical and with little intrinsic value, but some of it serious and this chapter briefly surveys some of the salient serious arguments.

10.2 "The Limits to Growth" model

Perhaps one of the reasons for the widespread attention paid to *The Limits to Growth* (LTG) document was that it purports to derive its conclusions from a computerized "global model" which incorporates the essential interconnections between resource use, economic magnitudes, population change and pollution. The use of a computer model for this exercise has meant that few people have been able to assess the actual mechanics of the model. Those that have appear generally, although not universally, critical, arguing that the computer was not necessary to produce the results of the model, results which, in any event, are open to serious doubt. It is worth noting that the LTG model makes little use of the links between economic and ecological systems: the actual mechanics by which, say, pollution can cause social collapse of one variety or another, are not spelled out. It follows that successful criticism of LTG is *not* sufficient to imply that future outcomes are satisfactory. There is a respectable ecological case for supposing the future to be a pessimistic one. It is far from clear that this case has been developed to the full, but it is clear that the elements of it have received very little attention by comparison with the major popular documents such as LTG. It is vital then to distinguish ecological arguments from the LTG model. The latter incorporates some ecological elements. It does not incorporate them all. It is one of the serious failings of the LTG literature that critics have failed to distinguish the two.

The first issue of importance is whether there are *physical* limits to the economic growth process. Almost by definition there must be. Global resources are finite unless we have 100 per cent recycling of residuals, and even with 100 per cent recycling, the throughput of the system would only be able to increase if units of throughput become more productive. Hence, if such a society ever came about, its growth rate would be determined by productivity increases through technological change. If we then consider that 100 per cent recycling is an impossibility, losses of residuals in the economic system will tend to offset productivity gains through technological change, although what the nature of this offsetting process would be is arguable. Hence there seems little point in debating the *existence* of limits to the growth process. They may occur because of resources running out, or because some pollutants seriously inhibit food production or interfere with major life-support systems (see later sections of this chapter). The only issues it seems sensible to consider are: (*a*) *when* such limits will be reached; and (*b*) what the *path* by which those limits are reached looks like. The import of LTG is that it suggests the comparative *imminence* of the limits, and that the path to collapse *or* to the global society which avoids collapse will be a painful one (and LTG does not predict collapse in the sense of saying it will irrevocably occur — it says collapse will occur *unless* drastic measures are taken).

In the LTG computer model, the variable, "quality of life", is held to depend positively on food supplies and industrial output, and negatively on population density and pollution. Then, food output, industrial output, population and pollution are inter-linked in various ways. Population growth is positively related to food output, for example, but food output is negatively related to pollution levels, which, in turn, are positively related to industrial output. These links are called *feedback mechanisms* and the feedback can be *positive* (the growth in one variable causes a change in another which causes further growth in the initial variable: the process becomes self-sustaining) or *negative* (the growth in one variable causes changes in another which reduces the growth in the initial variable). Now, if the model (which has more variables than we have listed, and more interrelationships) is run on the computer with some set of *initial* values for each *parameter* (the constants relating the value of one variable to another), the following picture (or "scenario") is obtained. This picture relates to a "do nothing" context — i.e. the assumption that things will continue as they have been continuing. Then, population growth and industrial output will grow exponentially. This will mean that we shall run out of resources. This in turn means that we shall have to use more capital to obtain what remains of resources, particularly as we have to mine low-grade ores or use energy-intensive methods to obtain previously inaccessible resources. But using the capital stock in this way reduces its use for industrial output, so that industrial output per head will fall. The growth of population will mean less and less land per head, lowering land productivity and hence food output per head. This will reduce rates of growth of population. Pollution will grow because industrial output has grown, and this will further inhibit food output and the quality of life.

Now, clearly, two general issues are relevant. First, are the initial values given to the parameters correct? Second, are the interrelationships between the variables correct?

If it is correct, the most disturbing claim in LTG is that some sort of pessimistic outcome occurs *whatever* the values of the parameters assumed. For example, if the model is re-run with expanded magnitudes for resource availability, *and* with lower resource input per unit output (which reflects improved technology), the pollution rate increases to the point that population reductions occur through the effect of pollution on population growth. After a time lag of a few decades food output declines because of low land productivity and pollution, which again reduces the proportion of capital stock devoted to industry, and the "collapse" process noted above resumes. All that happens is that the outcome is postponed for just over a decade. The same outcome occurs if we invest in massive pollution control policies, or if we have higher land productivity through agricultural technological change. Worse still, various "packages" of measures are tried, and still some sort of collapse occurs, notably with little difference in the timing. The "limits" to growth are reached in food production in 50 years, and in industrial output in 100 years or so.

Only one package of measures is deemed to work, and even then, this will result in much lower standards of living than those currently experienced. This package requires almost immediate birth-rate reduction, drastic reductions in economic throughput to preserve resources and contain pollution; shifts in the composition of economic output toward less capital-intensive output, increased durability of products, and so on. If such a package is implemented immediately, presumably by some world cooperative action, the system can become stable. If we delay, collapse of one kind or another is the only outcome. The model is "Malthusian" in the respect that it presents a gloomy picture of the future unless drastic action is taken, and in that famine, wars and disease are included in the final "adjustments" that will accompany collapse. It is of course, "neo-Malthusian" in its attempted integration of pollution with the traditional Malthusian variables.

10.3 Criticisms of "Limits to Growth"
The criticisms of LTG have been numerous. We need only look at some of the salient arguments.

First, as the most casual reflection on the materials balance approach discussed in Chapter 3 shows, zero growth will not itself prevent collapse. As we noted in the introduction to this chapter, zero growth still leaves us with a constant throughput which makes demands on resources. Depending on the success of recycling policies, resource productivity increases, and the resource demands made by recycling, zero growth still entails some "limit" to economic activity. But, if zero growth merely postpones an otherwise inevitable collapse, so does a negative growth rate of 1 per cent or 2 per cent. This would seem to suggest that *any* rate of economic activity will produce eventual collapse. Equally, however, no activity at all also entails collapse, since there will be no production to generate a positive standard of living. This dilemma in turn should lead us to ask whether it is worth worrying at all about collapse since, it would appear, it must come sooner or later. And the question then becomes one of how we decide whether to end it all now, in a few decades, in a few hundred years, or whatever. Those who are not yet born cannot have any regrets because they will never know: so one strategy might well be to have a "consumption spree" for this generation and perhaps the next. If there are physical limits, they must catch us in the end whatever we do.

How one treats this argument depends on what we consider the time scales to be, and on what moral view we take about continued existence. This is left to the reader to contemplate. Suffice it to say that, on its own terms, LTG could be held to establish a far more severe thesis than its authors perhaps anticipated, but a thesis that is arguably as permissive of rapid resource exploitation as it is of resource conservation.

Second, major criticism of LTG has centred on its assumptions about technological change. Some critics have argued that LTG has left out technological change altogether. This is of course false as inspection of the re-runs of the model with parameter changes shows. Nonetheless, the kinds of technological change considered do tend to be once-for-all shifts, and this, it is argued, is out of keeping with what we know about technological change, namely that it occurs in a continuous fashion. Boyd (1972) has re-run the model with a continuous technological change variable built-in. This generates increases in food productivity, pollution control and in resource/output ratios. The result is a far more optimistic outcome than that suggested by LTG. As we noted in Chapter 4, however, technological change is not an unequivocal benefit. First, it is not a free good: it also requires inputs and cannot therefore be treated as if it is some exogenous force in an economy. Second, some kinds of technological change can and do reduce pollution per unit of output, but other kinds do increase pollution. Indeed, as we saw, some technological changes result in increases in types of pollutant with which ecosystems are not equipped to deal. Ecosystem instability due to technological change is, according to a number of ecologists (e.g. Commoner, 1972) a very real danger. Finally, there must be serious question about arguments which support an optimistic viewpoint about technological change, arguments which in turn are designed to influence policy. For such arguments must be about change which has not yet occurred but which we reasonably expect to occur. The danger is that, if we are mistaken, our policy options may become so limited that we actually induce the kind of collapse envisaged in LTG. For example, if we use currently available fuels at a rate which reflects optimistic expectations about the development of nuclear fusion reactors, the cost of being mistaken in that expectation will be sudden and dramatic.

Third, the price mechanism scarcely figures in LTG. We might reasonably expect the price mechanism to operate as suggested in Chapter 7. As resources become scarce prices will rise and new technology will be stimulated, as will recycling and the search for substitute and "new" materials.

As pollution increases we might expect it to pass some "threshold" of perception in the population such that they begin to attach high shadow prices to pollution. This in turn should stimulate social action to correct the situation (so-called "social feedback"). Unfortunately, such arguments, while technically correct, may still not invalidate the LTG thesis, for one of the essential attributes of growth is that, being exponential, it tends to have increasingly dramatic effects over time. One might reasonably say that what LTG argues is that this exponentially increasing impact swamps any of the adaptive behaviour we might expect from the market system. That is, the adaptive mechanisms exist, but cannot cope with social and physical change which, while continuous, has an exponential character. An argument along these lines, with respect to natural resources, is contained in Common and Pearce (1973).

Fourth, many critics have taken LTG to task for using arbitrary numbers. They argue that it makes little sense to test for the sensitivity of the model to changes in parameter values if the *initial* parameter value is arbitrarily chosen. We do not, for example, know the relationship between pollution and mortality. To vary an arbitrary initial value by an equally arbitrary multiplicand to test for "sensitivity" is, virtually, by definition, to engage in an arbitrary exercise with meaningless results. Many critics have pointed to the dubious nature of the resource estimates in LTG — estimates which are taken from the US Bureau of Mines' figures for proved reserves. These estimates are concocted on various bases and are scarcely a guide to what is available even with current technology, let alone future technology and future prices. If bauxite aluminium is exhausted as a resource we know we have alumina clays to draw on, provided we perfect extraction technologies currently being researched. There can be no question that using dubious estimates of reserves as if they reflect available resources is a serious error in LTG. Again, however, it is not clear how the critics of LTG derive optimistic conclusions from such an observation. Resources are clearly greater than reserves as estimated, but we do not know how much greater in many cases. Nor is it very comforting to find some critics engaging in remarkable statements to the effect that the earth's crust contains resources "(almost) infinitely greater than what is in fact assumed" (Page, 1973) as if they support an optimistic standpoint without in turn recognizing that resource extraction is itself a resource-using activity, and one that may well exhibit increasing costs.

Is LTG a spurious exercise, designed, as many of its most vehement critics have suggested, in such a way that its conclusion was the only one that could have resulted? Whatever the motives of its authors, it must surely be a naive person who would base an entirely opposite view to that expressed in LTG on statements to the effect that the model can be redesigned to produce less pessimistic outcomes. That is, if the model can be manipulated in such a way as to produce almost *any* result, we have no more reason for being optimistic than we have for being pessimistic. Either the model is conceptually a sensible construction which requires detailed improvement (as the authors of LTG suggest) or it is conceptually meaningless and the entire exercise of "global modelling" should be abandoned (as some critics suggest). Has LTG served any useful purpose? While some critics have suggested that it can lead to a "hiding" mentality, whereby people engage in activities which prevent them from thinking about such gloomy forecasts, it would appear that it has had the opposite effect of stimulating activity in respect of social activity to influence some of the model variables. What is not clear is whether this activity is likely to be sustained, since societies appear incapable of shifting their collective attentions to issues which do not centre on at least maintaining material standards of living based on having goods and services.

Bibliography

Chapter 1 Welfare economics

A. Dasgupta and D. W. Pearce (1972), *Cost—Benefit Analysis: Theory and Practice*, Macmillan, London.

C. D. Foster and H. Neuberger (1974), "The ambiguity of the consumer's surplus measure of welfare change", *Oxford Economic Papers*.

J. R. Hicks (1939), "The foundations of welfare economics", *Economic Journal*, December.

J. R. Hicks (1943), "The four consumers' surpluses", *Review of Economic Studies*.

N. Kaldor (1939), "Welfare propositions of economics and interpersonal comparisons of utility", *Economic Journal*, September.

R. G. Lipsey and K. Lancaster (1956), "The general theory of second-best", *Review of Economic Studies*.

C. A. Nash (1973), "Future generations and the social rate of discount", *Environment and Planning*.

C. A. Nash, D. W. Pearce, J. Stanley (1975), "Evaluation of project evaluation criteria", *Journal of the American Institute of Planners*.

D. W. Pearce (1971), *Cost—Benefit Analysis*, Macmillan, London.

D. W. Pearce and J. Wise (1972), "Equity in cost—benefit analysis: a comment", *Journal of Transport Economics and Policy*, September.

P. A. Samuelson (1954), "The pure theory of public expenditure", *Review of Economics and Statistics*, November.

T. Scitovsky (1941), "A note on welfare propositions in economics", *Review of Economic Studies*. Reprinted in K. Arrow and T. Scitovsky (eds), *Readings in Welfare Economics*, Allen and Unwin, London, 1969.

D. M. Winch (1971), *Analytical Welfare Economics*, Penguin, London.

Chapter 2 Some ecology

W. Beckerman (1972), "Economists, scientists and environmental catastrophe", *Oxford Economic Papers*, November.

F. Borman and H. Likens (1970), "The nutrient cycles of an ecosystem", *Scientific American*, **223**, No. 4.

F. E. Clements (1916), *Succession*.

A. Coddington (1970). "The economics of ecology", *New Society*, April.

P. A. Colinvaux (1973), *An Introduction to Ecology*, Wiley, New York.

H. Daly (1972), *Toward a Steady State Economy*, W. H. Freeman, San Francisco.

A. Downs (1973), "The political economy of improving our environment", in J. Bain, *Environmental Decay*, Little Brown, Boston.

R. Dubos (1969), "A social design for science", *Science*, **166**.

Ecologist magazine (1972), "Blueprint for survival", *The Ecologist*, February.

K. Kapp (1972), "Environmental disruption and social costs: a challenge to economics", in *Political Economy of Environment: Problems of Method*, Mouton, The Hague.

J. A. Krebs (1972), *Ecology*, Harper and Row, New York.

I. McHarg (1969), *Design with Nature*, Natural History Press, New York.

E. P. Odum (1971), *Ecology*, Holt, Rinehart, Winston, London.

G. Rattray Taylor (1970), *The Doomsday Book*, Panther, London.

G. M. Woodwell (1970), "Effects of pollution on the structure and physiology of ecosystems", *Science*, April, 24.

V. C. Wynne-Edwards (1962), *Animal Dispersion in Relation to Social Behaviour*, Oliver and Boyd, Edinburgh.

Chapter 3   Materials balance and input—output analysis

R. V. Ayres and A. Kneese (1969), "Production, consumption and externality", *American Economic Review*.

K. Boulding (1966), "The economics of the coming spaceship earth", in H. Jarrett (ed.), *Environmental Quality in a Growing Economy* (Resources for the Future), Johns Hopkins Press, Baltimore.

CONSAD (1971), "The economic model system for the assessment of effects of air pollution abatement", US Environment Protection Agency.

J. H. Cumberland (1966), "A regional inter-industry model for analysis of development objectives", *Regional Science Association Papers,* **17**.

H. E. Daly (1968), "On economics as a life science", *Journal of Political Economy*, May.

A. G. Fazio and M. Lo Cascio (1972), "Evaluation of the economic effects of anti-pollution public policy: proposals for an econometric analysis model", in OECD, *Problems of Environmental Economics*, OECD, Paris.

A. Kneese, R. V. Ayres, R. D'Arge (1970), *Economics and the Environment* (Resources for the Future), John Hopkins Press, Baltimore.

T. R. Lakshmanan and Fu-Chen Lo (1972), "A regional economic model for the assessment of effects of air pollution abatement", *Environment and Planning*, **4**.

W. Leontief (1970), "Environmental repercussions and the economic structure: an input—output approach", *Review of Economics and Statistics*, August.

P. Victor (1972), *Pollution: Economy and Environment*, Allen and Unwin, London.

Chapter 4   The nature of pollution: economics and ecology

B. Commoner (1971), *The Closing Circle*, Cape, London.

M. Edel (1973), *Economies and the Environment*, Prentice-Hall, New Jersey.

C. L. Nobbs and D. W. Pearce (1976), "The economics of stock pollutants: the example of cadmium", *International Journal of Environmental Studies*.

D. W. Pearce (1973), "An incompatibility in planning for a steady state and planning for maximum economic welfare", *Environment and Planning*, **5**.

D. W. Pearce (1974a), "Economic and ecological approaches to the optimal level of pollution", *International Journal of Social Economics*, Spring.

D. W. Pearce (1974b), "Economics and ecology", *Surrey Papers in Economics*, July, No. 10.

Chapter 5 Methods of securing the optimal amount of pollution

W. Baumol (1972), "On taxation and the control of externalities", *American Economic Review*, June.

W. Baumol and D. Bradford (1972), "Detrimental externalities and non-convexity of the production set", *Economica*, May.

W. Baumol and W. Oates (1971), "The use of standards and prices for protection of the environment", *Swedish Journal of Economics*, March.

W. Beckerman (1972), "Environmental policy issues: real and fictitious", in OECD, *Problems of Environmental Economies*, Paris, 1972.

J. Buchanan (1969), "External diseconomies, corrective taxes and market structure", *American Economic Review*, March.

P. Burrows (1970), "On external costs and the visible arm of the law", *Oxford Economic Papers*, March.

P. Burrows (1974), "Pricing versus regulation for environmental protection", in A. Culyer (ed.), *York Economic Essays in Social Policy*, Martin Robertson, London.

R. Coase (1960), "The problem of social cost", *Journal of Law and Economics*.

J. H. Dales (1968a), "Land, water and ownership", *Canadian Journal of Economics*, November.

J. H. Dales (1968b), *Pollution, Property and Prices*, University of Toronto Press, Toronto.

A. M. Freeman (1972), "The distribution of environmental quality", in A. Kneese and B. Bower (eds), *Environmental Quality Analysis*, Johns Hopkins Press, Baltimore.

A. Kneese and B. Bower (1968), *Managing Water Quality*, Johns Hopkins Press, Baltimore.

J. C. Lambelet (1972), "Recent controversies over environmental policies", University of Pennsylvania, Wharton School of Finance, *Discussion Paper*, 237, May.

E. Mishan (1971), "The postwar literature on externalities: an interpretative essay", *Journal of Economic Literature*, March.

G. A. Mumey (1971), "The 'Coase Theorem': a reexamination", *Quarterly Journal of Economics*.

D. W. Pearce (1974), "Fiscal incentives and the economics of waste recycling: problems and limitations", plus Appendix on "The incompatibility of polluter pays and social efficiency", in *Fiscal Policy and the Environment*, Institute of Fiscal Studies, London, 1974.

A. C. Pigou (1932), *The Economics of Welfare* (4th edn), Macmillan, London.

R. Portes (1972), "The search for efficiency in the presence of externalities", in P. Streeten (ed.), *Unfashionable Economics: Essays in Honour of Lord Balogh*, Weidenfeld and Nicolson, London.

D. Starrett (1972), "Fundamental nonconvexities in the theory of externalities", *Journal of Economic Theory*, April.

J. L. Stein (1971), "The 1971 report of the president's council of economic advisers: microeconomic aspects of public policy", *American Economic Review*, September.

R. Turvey (1963), "On divergencies between social cost and private cost", *Economica*, August.

UK Royal Commission on Environmental Pollution (1972), *Third Report*, Minority Report by Lord Zuckerman and W. Beckerman, Cmnd 5054, HMSO, London.

Chapter 6 Cost—benefit analysis of pollution: the practice

J. Ph. Barde (1973), "The cost of clean growth: an international comparison", Paper read to American Association for the Advancement of Science, Mexico.

Board of Trade (1970), *The Costs and Benefits of Making Aircraft Less Noisy*, Interdepartmental Working Group on Aircraft Noise.

D. C. Colony (1967), *Expressway Traffic Noise and Residential Properties*, US Department of Transportation, Bureau of Public Roads.

Commission on the Third London Airport (CTLA) (1970), *Papers and Proceedings*, Volume VII, Chapters 18—20, HMSO, London.

Commission on the Third London Airport (CTLA): Further Research Team Work (1970), "Consumer Surplus in Housing: Report of Survey Work".

Commission on the Third London Airport (CTLA) (1971), *Report*, Chapter 7, and Appendices 22 and 23.

J. P. Crecine, O. A. Davis, J. E. Jackson (1967), "Urban property markets: some empirical results and their implications for municipal zoning", *Journal of Law and Economics*.

J. H. Cumberland (1972), "The role of uniform standards in international environmental management", in OECD, *Problems of Environmental Economics*, OECD, Paris, 1972.

A. K. Dasgupta and D. W. Pearce (1972), *Cost—Benefit Analysis: Theory and Practice*, Macmillan, London, 1972.

J. Diffey (1971), "An investigation into the effect of high traffic noise on house prices in a homogeneous sub-market", Paper presented to Centre for Environmental Studies Seminar on House Prices and the Microeconomics of Housing, London.

A. D. J. Flowerdew (1972), "The cost of airport noise", *The Statistician*, 21, 1.

I. D. Griffiths and F. J. Langdon (1968), "Subjective response to road traffic noise", *Journal of Sound and Vibration*, 8, 1.

P. E. Hart (1973), "Population densities and optimal aircraft flight paths", *Regional Studies*, 7, 1973.

B. Hedges (1972), "Attaching money values to environmental disturbance", *Paper No. 230*, Social and Community Planning Research, London.

I. Heggie (1972), *Transport Engineering Economics*, McGraw-Hill, Maidenhead, pp. 101—8.

A. Kneese and B. T. Bower (1968), *Managing Water Quality: Economics, Technology, Institutions*, Johns Hopkins Press, Baltimore.

E. J. Mishan (1970), "What is wrong with Roskill?", *Journal of Transport Economics and Policy*.

M. E. Paul (1971), "Can aircraft noise nuisance be measured in money?", *Oxford Economic Papers*, November.

D. W. Pearce (1972), "The economic evaluation of noise-generating and noise abatement projects", in OECD, *Problems of Environmental Economics*, Paris.

D. W. Pearce and C. A. Nash (1973), "The evaluation of urban motorway schemes: a case study — Southampton", *Urban Studies*, June.

D. Starkie (1971), *The Valuation of Disamenity*, Centre for Environmental Studies.

D. Starkie and D. Johnson (1973*a*), "Exclusion facilities and the valuation of environmental goods", in Centre for Environmental Studies, *Papers from the 1973 Urban Economics Conference*, Volume 1, London.

D. Starkie and D. Johnson (1973*b*), "Losses of residential amenity: an extended cost model", *Journal of Regional Studies*, 7, 2.

D. Starkie and D. Johnson (1973*c*), "The valuation of disamenity: an analysis of sound attenuation expenditures by households" (unpublished), University of Reading.

D. Starkie and D. Johnson (1975), *The Economic Value of Peace and Quiet*, D. C. Heath, London.

R. Towne (1968), "An investigation of the effect of freeway noise on apartment rents", R. Towne and Associates, Seattle.

A. Walters (1975), *Noise and Prices*, Oxford University Press, London.

M. Whitbread and H. Bird (1973), "Rent, surplus and the evaluation of residential environments", *Regional Studies*, June.

Wilson (1963), Committee on the Problem of Noise, *Noise-Final Report*, HMSO, London.

Chapter 7   The depletion of non-renewable resources

K. Anderson (1972), "Optimal growth when the stock of resources is finite and depletable", *Journal of Economic Theory*, April.

Bureau of Mines (USA) (1970), *Mineral Facts and Problems*, Washington.

M. Common and D. W. Pearce (1973), "Adaptive mechanisms, growth and the environment: the case of natural resources", *Canadian Journal of Economics*, August.

L. Fischman and H. Landsberg (1972), "Adequacy of non-fuel minerals and forest reserves", Ch. 4, of *US Commission on Population Growth and the American Future, Research Reports*, Volume III, US G.P.O., Washington.

G. Govett and M. Govett (1972), "Mineral resource, supplies and the limits of economic growth", *Earth Science Reviews*, 8, November.

G. Heal (1975), "Economic aspects of natural resource depletion", in D. W. Pearce (ed.), *The Economics of Natural Resource Depletion*, Macmillan, London.

Institute of Fuel (1973), *Energy for the Future*, Institute of Fuel, London.

J. Kay and J. Mirrlees (1975), "The desirability of natural resource depletion", in D. W. Pearce (ed.), *The Economics of Natural Resource Depletion*, Macmillan, London.

T. C. Koopmans (1973), "Some observations on 'optimal' economic growth and exhaustible resources", in H. C. Bos (ed.), *Economic Structure and Development*, North Holland.

W. Nordhaus (1973), "The allocation of energy resources", *Brookings Papers on Economic Activity*, 3.

N. Vousden (1973), "Basic theoretical issues of resource depletion", *Journal of Economic Theory*, April.

Chapter 8 Resource conservation

L. Fischman and H. Landsberg (1972), "Adequacy of non-fuel minerals and forest reserves", in *US Commission on Population Growth and the American Future: Research Reports*, Vol. III, Washington D.C.

M. T. Frank (1973), "The economics of scrap metal recovery", M.Sc. thesis, Imperial College, University of London (unpublished).

C. R. Glassey and V. Gupta (1971), "A linear programming analysis of paper recycling", O. R. Centre, University of California.

D. W. Pearce (1976), "Environmental protection, recycling and the international materials economy", in I. Walter (ed.), *International Economic Dimensions of Environmental Management*, Wiley, New York.

F. A. Smith (1972), "Waste material recovery and re-use", in *US Commission on Population Growth and the American Future: Research Reports*, Vol. III, Washington D.C.

Chapter 9 Population

S. Enke (1963), "Population and development: a general model", *Quarterly Journal of Economics*, February.

R. S. Moreland and A. Hazledine (1974), "Population, energy and growth: a world cross section study", Paper to European Econometric Society Meeting, Grenoble.

R. Nelson (1956), "A theory of the low-level equilibrium trap", *American Economic Review*, December.

Chapter 10 Limits to growth?

R. Boyd (1972), "World dynamics: a note", *Science*, August, 11.

M. Common and D. W. Pearce (1973), "Adaptive mechanisms, growth and the environment: the case of natural resources", *Canadian Journal of Economics*, August.

B. Commoner (1972), *The Closing Circle*, Cape, London.

H. Daly (1972), *Toward a Steady-State Economy*, W. H. Freeman, San Francisco.

Ecologist (1972), "Blueprint for survival", *The Ecologist*, February.

D. Meadows *et al.* (1972), *The Limits to Growth*, Earth Island, London.

E. Mishan (1968), *The Costs of Economic Growth*, Penguin, London.

W. Page (1973), "Non-renewable resources sub-system", Ch. 3 of H. S. D. Cole *et al.*, *Thinking About the Future: A Critique of "The Limits to Growth"*, Chatto and Windus, London.

Index

Modern Economics

Modern Economics Series

Editor: David W. Pearce

The aim of this series of texts is to meet the demand for rigorous up-to-date texts in the various subject areas of economic theory and applied economics.

This book is a text on the economics of environmental problems, taken in this context to mean problems of pollution (including noise) and natural resource depletion. The environment remains a highly topical and vitally important issue in modern politics with pressures to conserve natural resources and to avoid the ravages of unconstrained economic growth. This book places these issues against the background of the application of economic analysis to environment. It shows how this analysis can be used in practice and emphasises many of the limitations faced by the practical investigator. The outstanding feature of the book is that it further develops the fundamentals of an 'ecological' approach to some pollution problems and shows how ecology and economics may be synthesised in this field. The book concludes with an overview of the world population, the energy problem and recent 'world models' of environmental catastrophe.

David Pearce, B.A., M.A.(Oxon) is currently Professor of Political Economy, University of Aberdeen. He is a consultant to OECD Environment Directorate (Paris) and to UNCTAD (Geneva) and serves on several government committees concerned with waste disposal and recycling. He has written numerous articles on cost-benefit analysis and environmental economics and has contributed papers to several international symposia on environmental issues. He is editor of the *Modern Economics Series* in which this book appears.

ISBN 0 582 44623 6